THE ROYAL MUMMIES

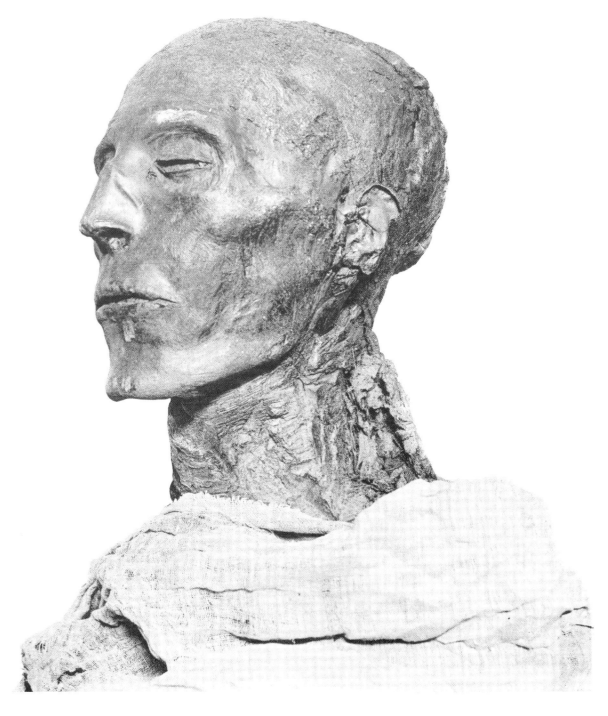

Seti I.

SERVICE DES ANTIQUITÉS DE L'ÉGYPTE

CATALOGUE GÉNÉRAL

DES

ANTIQUITÉS ÉGYPTIENNES

DU MUSÉE DU CAIRE

Nᵒˢ 61051-61100

THE ROYAL MUMMIES

BY G. ELLIOT SMITH, F. R. S.

Duckworth

First published in 1912 by
Imprimerie de l'Institut Français d'Archéologie Orientale

Reprinted in 2000 by
Gerald Duckworth & Co. Ltd.
61 Frith Street, London W1V 5TA
Tel: 0207 434 4242
Fax: 0207 434 4420
Email: enquiries@duckworth-publishers.co.uk
www.ducknet.co.uk

Foreword © 2000 by Nicholas Reeves

A catalogue record for this book is available
from the British Library

ISBN 0 7156 2959 X

Printed in Great Britain by Bath Press, Bath

FOREWORD

' "Soon we came upon cases of porcelain funerary offerings, metal and alabaster vessels, draperies and trinkets, until, reaching the turn in the passage, a cluster of mummy-cases came into view in such number as to stagger me.

"Collecting my senses, I made the best examination of them I could by the light of my torch, and at once saw that they contained the mummies of royal personages of both sexes ...

"I took in the situation quickly, with a gasp ..." '

(Émile Brugsch, as reported by Edward L. Wilson, 'Finding Pharaoh', *The Century Magazine*, vol. XXXIV, no. 1, May 1887, pp. 6-7)

Émile Brugsch, a curator attached to the Bulaq Museum, made his first, breathless investigation of the Deir el-Bahri 'cache' in the summer of 1881. Amazingly, it was the first of two similar communal burials to be brought to light during the closing years of the nineteenth century: in 1898, Brugsch's find was matched by another, equally astounding assemblage within the sepulchre of Amenophis II in the Valley of the Kings.

News of these two Theban tombs would rock the scholarly world, for they contained no ordinary mummies. The bodies hidden within belonged to the highest in the land – more than fifty kings, queens, lesser royals and nobles, gathered together and hidden for safekeeping around 1000 BC when the Theban royal cemeteries were dismantled by the State. Included among the newly discovered dead were Egypt's most famous kings: the empire-builder Tuthmosis III, Amenophis III, 'the Dazzling Sun-Disc', and Ozymandias himself, the pharaoh Ramesses II.

In purely emotive terms, these were finds difficult to match: only in Egypt, of all ancient cultures, is it possible today to look into the face of royalty itself. But scientifically, too, the caches are beginning to prove a unique heritage: through DNA analysis of the pharaohs' miraculously preserved remains, the innermost secrets of Egypt's ruling élite promise, in time, to be revealed in full.

Much has been written on the Deir el-Bahri and Amenophis II mummies and their archaeological context in the century since they were first discovered: for an update on the former, the reader is referred to J.E. Harris and E.F. Wente, *An X-Ray Atlas of the Royal Mummies* (Chicago, 1980); for the latter, to my own *Valley of the Kings: the decline of a royal necropolis* (London, 1990). Grafton Elliot Smith's *The Royal Mummies*, first published in 1912, nevertheless remains the basic reference. It was an astonishing publication at the time; and, as a glance at its extraordinary images will show, it is no less astonishing now.

London, January 2000   Nicholas Reeves

PREFACE.

In coming to a decision as to which of the manifold ways of transliterating Ancient Egyptian proper names I should adopt in this Catalogue I have been guided by two considerations to follow Sir Gaston Maspero. In the first place, those who wish to refer to the actual objects catalogued will naturally make use of his *Guide du Visiteur au Musée du Caire;* and it will be a convenience to those anatomists and anthropologists, who, like the writer, are ignorant of Egyptian philology, to find the same object referred to by the same name in both works of reference. In the second place I shall have to refer on almost every page of this Catalogue to M. Maspero's great monograph, *Les Momies royales de Deïr-el-Bahari* (*Mémoires publiés par les membres de la Mission archéologique française au Caire* sous la direction de M. Maspero, Membre de l'Institut, tome premier, quatrième fascicule, Paris, 1889); and I have striven to make the spelling of names in my text agree with that of the numerous quotations from M. Maspero's writings. When the mode of transliteration in *Les Momies royales* differs from that of the *Guide du Visiteur* I have followed the latter as being the more recent.

It is desirable at the outset to make an explicit statement in reference to certain matters, which in the future, as has happened in the past, are sure to cause misunderstandings.

In the first place I must explain the scope and nature of this Catalogue. When M. Maspero requested me to undertake this work the intention was to write a report upon such anatomical and pathological features as a careful examination of the mummies would reveal. In the case of many of the mummies, especially those in the best state of preservation, there was singularly little that an anatomist could do, provided of course that he refrained from damaging the body. In such mummies as those of Ramses III, for instance, the anatomist can add little to what any one can see for himself by looking at the body encased in its resinous carapace. Examination with the aid of the X-rays would, no doubt, have provided much additional information — and I hope this will be done at some future time — but I was unable to get such investigations carried out, except in the case of the mummy of Thoutmosis IV. In the course of my preliminary examinations of the Royal Mummies so much information came to light concerning the treatment of the body, in the process of embalming, that I asked M. Maspero to allow me to study the problems thus raised in the case of mummies less precious, historically, than those of the Pharaohs and their families. M. Maspero very generously gave me every assistance and placed at my disposal a large series of mummies, which provided the material for my memoir, *A Contribution to the Study of Mummification in Egypt* (*Mémoires de l'Institut égyptien*, tome V, fascicule 1, 1906), and a series of notes published in the *Bulletins de l'Institut égyptien*, the *Annales du Service des Antiquités de l'Égypte* (1904 et seq.), the *Cairo Scientific Journal*, the *Proceedings of the British Association*, and the *Proceedings of the Royal Philosophical Society* of Glasgow. Moreover certain colleagues and friends, Professor W. A. Schmidt, Mr. A. Lucas, Mr. W. M. Colles, Dr. Armand Ruffer and Professor A. R. Ferguson, came to my assistance, and investigated aspects of the problems of mummification, upon which their special knowledge enabled them to throw a great deal of light. The memoirs of Professor Schmidt, *Chemische und biologische Untersuchungen von ägyptischem Mumienmaterial, nebst Betrachtungen über das Einbalsamierungsverfahren der alten Aegypter* (Zeitschrift für allgemeine Physiologie, Bd. VII, 1907, p. 369-392) and *Über Mumienfettsäuren* (Chemiker-Zeitung, 1908, n° 65), and Mr. Lucas' *Preservative Materials used by the Ancient Egyptians in Embalming* (Survey Department Paper, n° 12, Cairo, 1911) are works of fundamental importance in this investigation, especially as much of the material upon which their researches are based was obtained from the Royal Mummies with which this Catalogue deals.

Thus a second and much more fruitful line of investigation was opened up, namely, the light these mummies throw upon the history of the evolution of the art of embalming. This question is fully discussed in the Catalogue.

The earliest mummy discussed here is that of Saqnounri, the last king of the XVIIth Dynasty. I have summarized the evidence relating to the evolution of embalming before his time in *the History of Mummification in Egypt* (*Proceedings of the Royal Philosophical Society* of Glasgow, 1910), and also in Quibell's *Excavations at Saqqara*, 1906-1907.

In discussing the technique of mummification and the customs associated with it one has to deal with subjects that may possibly give rise to offence, on the ground that it is not showing due respect to the memories of the powerful rulers of Ancient Egypt to display their naked remains, and use them as material for anthropological investigations. In fact a good deal of comment has been made in the past in reference to the so-called « sacrilege », on the part of modern archaeologists, in opening royal tombs and removing and unwrapping the mummies.

Those who make such complaints seem to be unaware that the real desecration was committed twenty nine centuries ago by the subjects of these rulers; and that modern archaeologists, in doing what they have done, have been rescuing these mummies from the destructive vandalism of the modern descendents of these ancient grave-plunderers.

Having these valuable historical « documents » in our possession it is surely our duty to read them as fully and as carefully as possible. In Egypt phallic ideas have held sway from the earliest times; and the evidence for, and against, the influence of such ideas in determining the technique of embalming has given rise to such pronounced contradictions, often based upon errors of observation, that no course was open to me but to let the naked bodies tell their own story.

I have endeavoured to make the discussions of the features of the mummies as concise as possible, because Brugsch Pasha's excellent photographs make minute descriptions unnecessary.

There is one other question that is constantly cropping up and giving rise to much misunderstanding : it is the problem of determining the age of a mummy. Apart from baldness, whitening of the hair and the extent of the wearing-down of the teeth — all of which, as every observant man knows, are of little value as evidence of the precise age of any individual — only the bones of the skeleton (in persons above the age of puberty) can give any definite information in reference to age. A large proportion of the mummies are so well-preserved that no access to the bones can be obtained. But even when some, or even all, of the bones are available for examination it is not possible for the anatomist, at any rate in the present state of knowledge, to make an exact estimate of the number of years the person had lived. In this Catalogue I have taken the specific case of the skeleton supposed to be Khouniatonou's (Akhenaten's), and have set forth in detail the nature of the evidence and the reasons for the uncertainty of its significance. But Khouniatonou's is a very much easier and simpler problem than that presented by Thoutmosis IV[th's] mummy. In the former the whole skeleton was available, whereas in the latter I had to deal with the mummy. One leg had been broken across at the knee, so that I was able to determine that his leg-bones were fully consolidated, and that he was *at least* 24 years of age.

Scraping away the resinous material from the part of the os innominatum, exposed in the embalming wound in the left flank, I found that the epiphysis of the crest of the ilium was fused to the rest of the bone in all except its posterior extremity, where a slight fissure, or rather, groove, still existed. The text-books state that this epiphysis maintains its independence until about 25 years of age; and therefore I assumed that Thoutmosis IV was about this age at the time of his death. I did not submit this estimate to the critical analysis, which was necessary in the case of Khouniatonou, for two reasons. In the latter case the anatomical and archaeological evidence seemed to clash and I was compelled to set forth all the reservations which might provide the way for agreement. In the case of Thoutmosis IV I was led to believe (in 1904) that the historical evidence assigned an early age to that Pharaoh; and as the anatomical evidence was in agreement there was no reason for making any reservation. Since then, however, I have discovered that historians are far from being agreed in regard to the youth of Thoutmosis IV. In the case of Khouniatonou the fact emerges that the evidence afforded by one bone alone, as in the case of Thoutmosis IV, must be received with caution. Moreover I have since discovered that no bone is more misleading than the innominate bone; for I have found that the sulcus which separates the posterior part of the epiphysis cristae may remain open until middle age. Had I been aware of these facts seven years ago, when I wrote my report on Thoutmosis IV, I would still have suggested 25 years as his age, as I suppose most anatomists would have done; but with my present experience of the variability of the relative dates of epiphyseal unions in ancient Egyptian bones, I would make the reservation that the anatomical evidence, when based upon the penultimate stage of consolidation of a single bone, cannot be regarded as conclusive.

I had no opportunity of seeing the proofs of the plates before they were printed and there are a number of points that call for comment. In some cases the engraver was unable to put several figures into a single plate, as had been intended; and, in the process of rearrangement, he has altered the order of the Plates or «squeezed out» some of them, which have had to be put at the end of the series. In Plate XXXIX (which should have been in the place of XXXVIII) «baqt» should read «Baqt».

In Plate XXXII, fig. 2 is upside down : and the details of the inscription are shown in their proper orientation in Plates C to CIII.

The description of fig. 2, Plate LXII, should read «Siphtah's feet — talipes of left foot»; that of Plate LXXIV, «Queen Makeri's baby — princess

Moutemhit »; and that of fig. 1, Plate XCVI, «An intrusive Mummy from the tomb of Thoutmosis III ».

In deleting the back-ground in the photograph from which Plate XXIX was made the engraver has left a large black mass, on the lower back part of the head, which looks like a mass of hair, a kind of flattened chignon. The true profile of the head is shown in another reproduction of the same photograph in *The Tomb of Thoutmôsis IV* (Theodore M. Davis' excavations, 1904).

CATALOGUE GÉNÉRAL

DES

ANTIQUITÉS ÉGYPTIENNES

DU MUSÉE DU CAIRE.

—⇒✥⇐—

THE ROYAL MUMMIES.

61051. **Mummy of the king Saqnounrî III Tiouâqen of the XVIIth Dynasty** (pl. I, II and III).

Found at Deîr el-Bahari in the year 1881 (*Les Momies royales*, p. 511-524) and brought to the Cairo Museum (then at Boulac), the mummy was unrolled by M. Maspero (*op. cit.,* p. 527) on June 9th 1886. The wrappings left upon the limbs by M. Maspero were removed by me on September 1st 1906. The evidence for the identification of the mummy is given by M. Maspero (*op. cit.,* p. 526), whose account of the unwrapping is as follows :

« Deux grands linceuls en toile grossière, mal attachés, la revêtaient des pieds à la tête, puis on rencontra quelques pièces de linge négligemment roulées et des tampons de chiffons, maintenus par des bandelettes, le tout gras au toucher et pénétré d'une odeur fétide. Ces premières enveloppes une fois levées, il nous resta entre les mains une sorte de fuseau d'étoffe long d'environ 1 m. 82 cent. et tellement mince qu'il semblait impossible qu'un corps humain pût y trouver place. Les deux dernières couches de toile étaient collées par les parfums et adhéraient à la peau : on les fendit au couteau et le corps entier parut au jour » (*Les Momies royales*, p. 527).

All that now remains of Saqnounrî Tiouâqen is a badly damaged, disarticulated skeleton enclosed in an imperfect sheet of soft, moist, flexible, dark brown skin, which has a strongly aromatic, spicy odour. The skin resembles that of mummies of the Coptic period after they have been exposed to the air and the preservative salts have deliquesced and softened the tissues. But my colleague Professor W. A. Schmidt has been unable to find in Saqnounrî's skin any greater quantity of chloride of sodium than occurs in untreated human tissues. The spicy odour of the skin is due to the fact that it has been sprinkled with powdered aromatic wood (or sawdust).

No attempt was made to put the body into the customary mummy-position; the head had not been straightened on the trunk, the legs were not fully extended, and the arms and hands were left in the agonised attitude (Plate I), into which they had been thrown in the death spasms following the murderous attack, the evidence of which is so clearly impressed on the battered face and skull. Instead of being put into an attitude of repose, as was the usual custom in embalming, the face was left as it was found at the time of death, the lips widely retracted from the teeth, so that the mouth forms a distorted oval, the upper lip being pulled up toward the right and the lower lip downward to the left (to Plate II). The whole attitude of the body is such as we might expect to find in the body of one who had suffered the violent death which the terrible wounds on Saqnounrî's head declare to have been his fate. M. Maspero has reconstituted Saqnounrî's death-scene with great skill (*op. cit.,* p. 528) and has also interpreted the state of the body, to which I have just referred, as being clear evidence that it was hurriedly mummified far away from the laboratories of the embalmers — he suggests the field of battle as the probable scene of Saqnounrî's death and embalming. Another explanation is suggested in the same volume (*op. cit., Les Momies royales,* Appendix IV, p. 776) by Dr Fouquet in these words : «La momie de ce roi est en très mauvais état de conservation : tué sur le champ de bataille, Soqnounrî fut très probablement transporté à Thèbes pour y être momifié. Le voyage dura plusieurs jours, et le cadavre était en pleine décomposition quand on le remit aux mains des embaumeurs». The evidence is all against this hypothesis and in favour of M. Maspero's explanation. The condition of the mummy is clearly not due to delay in being submitted to the embalmers, but to the manner of preserving the body — the method which, as will be shown in the succeeding pages, was in vogue at the end of the XVIIth and beginning of the XVIIIth dynasties; and in this case it was practised in a rough and hasty manner. If the embalming had been done in a leisurely manner in Thebes or in any other place, where there were facilities for the proper treatment of the body, the mummy would have certainly received the usual careful preparation for wrapping — the legs would have been fully extended, the arms placed in the positions defined by the conventions of the time, and the head, and especially the face, would have been submitted to an elaborate toilet. The absence of all these attentions clearly demonstrates the probability of M. Maspero's suggestion that the body was hastily embalmed on or near the field of battle.

By building up the skeleton I have been able to estimate the size and proportions of the body. Soqnounrî was 1 m. 702 mill. in height : although the teeth are so well-worn as to be almost all molariform, the fact that all the cranial sutures are still patent suggests that the king was not much more than thirty years of age at the time of death : but the complete ankylosis of the meta-and meso-sterna might be adduced as evidence of an age of at least forty. Experience in the examination of Egyptian hones, however, does not lead one to place much reliance upon the time of consolidation of the ensiform as an index of age.

The cranium is a very large, relatively flat, ovoid, o m. 195 mill., long, o m. 148 mill. broad and o m. 131 mill. in height (basi-bregmatic).

The jaw conforms to the Egyptian type : the bigonial breadth is o m. 095 mill., the bicondylar breadth is o m. 135 mill., the height of the symphysis is o m. 037 mill. and the vertical measurement to the sigmoid notch is o m. 046 mill. The length and breadth of the palate (Plate III) are o m. 059 mill. and o m. 038 mill. respectively. The face is so badly smashed by the fatal injuries that no accurate measurements can be made, but it seems to conform to the Egyptian type.

There is a complete set of healthy teeth almost entirely free from tartar-deposits. The third molars on both sides of both jaws are practically unworn, but all the other teeth are well worn (Plate III).

The maximum length of the left femur is o m. 460 mill. and the oblique length o m. 452 mill. : the whole leg, heel to head of femur, measures o m. 924 mill., the head of the femur to the upper articular surface of the atlas o m. 647 mill. and the basi-bregmatic height adds o m. 131 mill., to these measurements and brings the total up to 1 m. 702 mill.

The femur is a very massive bone, with strongly-marked muscular ridges : its shaft has a slightly forward curve : the articular surface of the head extends on to the antero-superior aspect of the neck — a feature which is usually associated with the practice of sitting in the squatting attitude.

The right humerus, as is usual in right-handed persons, is more massive than the left, and its coronoid fossa is not perforated as that of the left bone is. The length measurements of the two bones, however, are identical : maximum length o m. 332 mill., oblique length o m. 330 mill.

The length of the right radius is estimated at o m. 246 mill., and the distance from the radial surface of the lunar bone to the tip of the middle finger is o m. 190 mill.

The scapulae are very long and pointed below, and the acromial end of the clavicle has a curiously conical form, ending in a small articular facet. On the back of the right scapula there is an ulcer, o m. 02 cent. × o m. 01 cent., extending from the posterior lip of the glenoid fossa in its lower half : its edges are raised, but the nature of the lesion is doubtful.

The verbebral column presents the usual number of segments. On the left side of the atlas the vertebral canal is bridged over by a bar of bone but on the right side the bridge is not quite complete. All the cervical spines, except the first and last, are markedly bifid. There is a perfectly typical, solidly-built, five-pieced sacrum, o m. 086 mill. long (o m. 104 mill. around the ventral curve) and o m. 109 mill. broad.

In the process of embalming a vertical incision was made in the left flank o m. 156 mill. in length, its lower end being immediately in front of the anterior superior spine of the ilium. The opening is now elliptical and gapes to the extent of o m. 038 mill. Through it the greater part of the abdominal viscera had been removed and an opening (o m. 125 mill. in diameter) was made through the centre of the diaphragm for the purpose of removing the thoracic viscera.

No trace whatever of the thoracic organs now remains and as the thorax, unlike the abdomen, was not packed with linen, it is not possible to state what treatment the heart and lungs received, or whether or not they were originally left in situ in the

body. The fact that a definite opening was made into the thorax — even if we admit
the unlikely possibility that it was made accidentally when cutting out the liver
and stomach — favours the probability that some, at least, of the thoracic contents
were eviscerated.

The abdominal cavity and pelvis were tightly packed with linen forming a solid mass,
which is still well-preserved. It was the impressions on this mass of the flank
incision, of the walls of the body-cavity and the diaphragm (which was still adhering
to the linen cast) which gave me most of the information recorded in the preceding
paragraphs. Remains of some of the abdominal viscera were still attached to the
posterior surface of the mass of linen.

No attempt had been made to open the cranial cavity through the nostrils, such as was
the custom from the time of the XVIIIth dynasty onwards : nor had any packing
material been introduced into the cranial cavity through the extensive wounds
inflicted on the skull.

All of these details in the case of Saqnounrî assume very special importance, when it
is realised that his body is the earliest mummy in the Museum the authenticity of
which is beyond question. I have recently (*Cairo Scientific Journal*, vol. II, n° 27,
December 1908, p. 424) called attention to the fact that mummification was
certainly practised as early as the time of the Vth dynasty, but, with the single
exception of the mummy said to be that of Ranofir (found by Flinders Petrie in a
mastaba at Medum; and now in the Museum of the Royal College of Surgeons in
London), all the mummies earlier than that of Saqnounrî have been so fragile that
they could not be moved. Definitely mummified bodies of the period of the Middle
Empire have been found by Quibell at Saqqara and by Lythgoe and Mace at Lisht,
but the tissues were pulverised.

THE FATAL WOUNDS.

For the purpose of accurate description I shall assign distinctive numbers to the
wounds inflicted upon the head; but it must not be imagined that there numbers
have any reference to the order of infliction of the wounds.

The first wound (Plate II, arrow 1), was placed transversely in the frontal bone. It
extends from the middle line toward the right for a distance of o m. o63 mill.;
and from its mesial end a crack runs around the left half of the frontal bone to end
at the meeting place of the left temporal crest and the coronal suture. For a
distance of o m. o5 cent., in this wound a strip of bone, o m. oo8 mill. wide, has
been depressed and lies in the cranial cavity attached to the dura mater, which
was also damaged.

The scalp, cut by the blow which fractured the skull, was retracted from the edges
of the fissure in the skull. The appearance of the edges of this retracted scalp
indicates with tolerable certainty that the wound was inflicted during life. For a
distance of o m. o32 mill. along the crack extending from the fracture there was
a patch of bare bone. The scalp must have been stripped from this bone either by

a second blow or by some projection on the instrument with which the blow that caused the fracture was inflicted. At the junction of the fracture and the crack proceeding from it there were two triangular areas of bone, each about o m. o1 cent. in diameter, surrounded by fissured fractures. One of these became displaced and fell in to the cranium while I was examining the head.

This wound (or wounds) was probably caused by an axe with an edge o m. o5 cent. or o m. o6 cent. long.

Around the right extremity of this wound there is a large crescentic mass of hair matted in some black material — presumably blood. The mass is o m. o63 mill. (horizontal) × o m. o31 mill. (vertical).

Below this mass of matted hair and opposite the outer two thirds of the right supra-orbital margin (almost parallel to and o m. o18 cent. above it) there is a fusiform scalp-wound revealing a second fracture of the frontal bone (Plate II, arrow 2) coextensive with it, o m. o31 mill. long, gaping to the extent of almost o m. 10 cent. This wound also was probably inflicted with an axe. This part of the supraorbital margin, including the right external angular process and the whole of the right malar bone, is depressed more than o m. o10 mill. below its original level, the zygomatic arch being broken at the articulation between the temporal and malar bones and the supraciliary margin of the frontal bone near its inner end. The two extremities of the orbital margin of the right malar bone are dislocated and have made holes in the skin of the face (arrow 2′).

A blow across the bony part of the nose has fractured both nasal bones (Plate II, arrow 3) and depressed the lower fragments to the extent of o m. o07 mill. This blow probably destroyed the right eye and caused the injuries to the malar bone and supraorbital margin of the frontal just described. This blow was probably inflicted by means of some blunt instrument such as a stick or the handle of an axe, the skin wounds being caused indirectly by the projection of fragments of broken bones. A blow on the left cheek with some edged tool, such as an axe, cut through the skin (plate II, arrow 4) and severed the malar from the superior maxilla along their line of meeting. The wound stops above at the lower border of the orbit and below at the anterior margin of the coronoird process of the mandible, from which a small strip has been separated. Some pointed instrument such as a pike or spear was driven into the left side of the head immediately below the ear (Plate III) : it smashed off the left mastoid process, the left occipital condyle and part of the margin of the foramen magnum and was prevented from damaging the medulla oblongata because its point was stopped by the anterior part of the lateral mass (superior articular process) of the atlas. Of these five separate blows it is clear that the first two and the fourth were caused in all probability by an axe, although it is just possible that a sword may have been used. The fifth was probably caused by a spear; for it is unlikely that a narrow-bladed sword could have been used to inflict the injury. Although it is possible that the same instrument that was used in inflicting wounds nos. 1, 2 and 4 may have been employed in the case of n° 3 the fact that the clean cut skin incision of the former three is lacking in the case of the latter makes it most likely that another and much blunter instrument — probably a stick, possibly the handle of the spear, that inflicted the fifth wound — was used in the case of the third wound. Wounds 4 and 5 can only have been inflicted from the left side of the man attacked and from their situation and appearance it is probable that the other three wounds were also inflicted from the same side.

It is clear that Saqnounrî met his death in an attack by at least two and probably more persons armed with at least two (probably three or more) implements, one of which was probably an axe and another a spear. The absence of any injuries to the arms or to any other part of the body shows that no resistance could have been offered to the attack. It is quite possible that the wounds may have been inflicted while Saqnounrî was lying down on his right side.

It seems unlikely that a man 1 m. 702 mill. in height could have received from the front or left side two *horizontal* wounds on the top of his head, if he were standing up, without making any attempt to fend the blows.

Although there is no clear and conclusive evidence in favour of any one reconstruction of the fatal attack, I think the balance of evidence is in favour of the view that he was attacked while lying down (possibly asleep) either on the ground or on a low bed. This view would offer the most reasonable explanation of the fact that four of the five wounds are exactly horizontal.

For even if Saqnounrî had been attacked by men of his own stature or even by horsemen it is highly improbable that the wounds inflicted would be horizontal. They are much more likely to have been vertical or oblique. Whereas in the case of the victim being prone on the ground the blows would fall vertically and might thus be horizontal in the anatomical sense.

It seems not improbable that Saqnounrî was lying on his right side, probably asleep, when his assailants coming up behind him attacked him from above i. e. from his left side. Nevertheless there is always the possibility that he may have been felled by one blow — perhaps an arrow or spear-thrust through the occipito-atlantal joint — and then received the other four blows when lying prone upon the ground in an unconscious state.

61052. Mummy of an unknown woman, perhaps the princess Meritamon (pl. IV).

On page 539 of *Les Momies royales* M. Maspero states that from certain analogies which the coffin containing this mummy presents to that of the lady Raï he is led to believe that Sonou, whose name is inscribed on the coffin, was the husband or son of Raï; and that the queen, at whose court he was majordomo, could he none other than Nofritari. From the hieratic writing upon the shroud enveloping the mummy it appears that the latter is the body of the «royal daughter, royal sister Meritamon».

M. Maspero unrolled the wrappings on June 30th, 1886 and the condition of affairs thus revealed aroused in his mind grave doubts as to the identity of the woman's body which was then brought to light (vide *op. cit.*, p. 539 and 540). He is inclined to believe that the mummy of Princess Meritamon may have been destroyed and replaced by a body embalmed at some earlier period — perhaps even at the time of the Middle Empire.

« Quand on eut ouvert le linceul, on se trouva en présence d'une momie à moitié dépouillée de ses bandelettes, et d'un aspect particulier. Elle a la tête penchée sur l'épaule droite, la mâchoire pendante, la bouche béante et tirée vers la droite. La poitrine est soulevée violemment, les épaules sont contractées, les bras se jettent en avant d'un geste raide, les mains se tordent, la jambe droite s'enlace autour de la gauche, les pieds sont crispés : le corps entier est comme agité des derniers mouvements de l'agonie. Est-ce là un fait accidentel, ou bien devons-nous croire, qu'au moment où le personnage a été préparé pour la tombe, l'usage n'avait pas encore prévalu de disposer toujours les cadavres dans une attitude de repos [*vide supra* — my remarks on the mummy of Saqnounrî] : on momifiait les gens comme la mort les prenait. Les tombes du Moyen Empire que j'ai ouvertes à Gébéléïn, en 1886, nous donnent à cet égard des renseignements précieux. Les quatre cercueils intacts qu'elles nous ont rendus contenaient des momies fort semblables à la momie qui nous occupe. Elles étaient, elles aussi, dans l'attitude où l'agonie les avait laissées, la tête inclinée, la bouche béante, les mains contractées, les jambes ramenées l'une sur l'autre (*Rapport sur les fouilles et travaux exécutés en Égypte pendant l'hiver de 1885-1886 — Bulletin de l'Institut égyptien,* 1886, p. 210). Ajouter à cela d'autres indices, la légèreté du corps, la facilité avec laquelle la peau se brise ou se détache en écailles, le décharnement du crâne; la momie, qui ressemble tant aux momies de Gébéléïn, n'a presque point de ressemblance avec celles d'Ahmos Iᵉʳ, de la reine Anhapou, de Saqnounrî. Ce serait plutôt une momie de la XIIᵉ ou de la XIIIᵉ dynastie, que les gardiens auraient enlevée de son tombeau pour remplacer la momie perdue de la reine Miritamon » (*Les Momies royales,* p. 540).

The body, the appearance of which has been so graphically described by M. Maspero in the passage just quoted, is that of a small, old woman, roughly embalmed, shrunken, distorted and desiccated. The legs are partly flexed and the left foot is crossed over the right so that a direct measurement of height in not possible; but I have estimated the stature as 1 m. 470 mill.

The embalming-wound had been made in the usual position in the left flank and the body-cavity was packed with pads of linen soaked in a solution of resin in the manner customary in the times of the XVIIIᵗʰ dynasty. The pelvis is packed with a hard mass of resin and aromatic sawdust and a small quantity of similar material is smeared over the perineum, but not in sufficient quantity to hide the rima pudendi, as was the custom in the middle and later periods of the XVIIIᵗʰ dynasty. The body was enveloped in large quantities of linen soaked in a solution of resin, which is peculiarly distinctive of the XVIIIᵗʰ dynasty.

It is very difficult to determine the period at which this body was mummified and the reason why it was not placed in the customary mummy-position. For in the mummies of the Ancient and Middle Empires, found by Flinders Petrie, Quibell,

Lythgoe and Mace and other archæologists, the body was put into a position of repose, so that the condition in which this body was left cannot be used as evidence for the determination of its age. In the case of Saqnounrî we came to the conclusion that the neglect of the customary toilet was evidence of haste : perhaps also in this case there was some similar reason, of which however we have no knowledge. The condition of the skin, as described by M. Maspero, is due to desiccation rather than to the action of any preservative, although we have seen on the perineum some of the aromatic paste such as was used in preparing the mummies of Saqnounrî and Anhâpou (*vide infra*). On the whole I am inclined to refer this mummy to the same period as the two mummies just mentioned. The skull and face conform to the Egyptian type. The ears are pierced. The skull exhibits large symmetrical thinning of both parietal bones, such as is common in the remains of the Egyptian aristocracy from the time of the Ancient Empire onward. The cranium is a short, relatively broad ovoid : the face is a small oval with pointed chin. All the teeth on the left side of the upper jaw are carious excepting only the canine and the third molar; and the first and second left lower molars are reduced to mere carious stumps.

The skull is o m. 172 mill. long, o m. 136 mill. broad, the minimum frontal breadth is o m. 094 mill., the upper facial height is o m. 073 mill. and the bizygomatic breadth is o m. 128 mill. The bigonial breadth is o m. 085 mill.

The dimensions of the nose cannot be measured directly, because the soft parts are pressed down, overlapping the bony nares; but the length and breadth are approximately o m. 055 mill. and o m. 025 mill. respectively.

The left orbit is o m. 043 mill. broad and o m. 036 mill. high.

There is a scalp wound, apparently ante-mortem, on the occiput, such as might have been caused by a fall backward.

The body has been badly damaged by grave-plunderers, the body-wall broken in, the right arm pulled off and the left fore arm separated.

61053. The Mummy of Anhâpou (pl. IV, fig. 2, and V).

This mummy was found in the coffin of the lady Râï, nurse of Queen Nofritari. But the body of Râï, which was put into a coffin bearing the name of a man, Pa-her-pet, had been replaced in ancient times by that of another woman, whose name was written on the shroud across the breast in difficult cursive hieratic, which M. Maspero has transliterated «Anhâpou» (*Les Momies royales*, p. 531). In the same memoir (p. 624) M. Maspero adds : «Je n'hésite pas à identifier notre reine Anhâpou de Déir el-Baharî avec la reine Anhapi, mère de Honttomihi et femme ou concubine d'Ahmos Iᵉʳ».

From the study of the mummy itself I have obtained evidence, which makes it appear highly improbable that the embalming could have been done at a time later than the reign of Ahmôsis : in fact it is most likely that the body of Anhâpou was prepared for burial some time before that of the king.

The mummy, which had a garland of flowers upon the neck, was unwrapped in the Boulac Museum on June 20th, 1886, by M. Maspero, who described the appearance of the body, when first exposed, in these words : «Elle était entourée de linges poudreux, gras au toucher, semblables à ceux qui entouraient les restes de Tiouâqen [Saqnounri]. Des paquets de cheveux tressés étaient intercalés sous les premières bandelettes. Le corps, mis à nu, fut trouvé en bon état» (op. cit., p. 531).

The body is that of a big, strongly-built woman (see Plate IV, Fig. 2), 1 m. 685 mill. in height.

Certain features revealed by an examination of its state of preservation raise for discussion some points of crucial importance in the evolution of the methods of embalming. The mummies of Saqnounrî (n° 61051) and the woman (n° 61052) in Sonou's coffin had been treated in the same manner as the one now under consideration : but unlike the two former the body of Anhâpou was put into the conventional mummy-position at the time it was embalmed. The appearance of the two mummies already described was such as to suggest a very rough and crude process of embalming, done in a hurry by some one other than professional embalmers, and at some place (in the case of Saqnounrî M. Maspero suggests the field of battle) where the ordinary facilities for the practice of mummification were lacking. But there is nothing in Anhâpou's mummy to suggest haste or carelessness on the part of the embalmers. Her body had been put into the conventional position and had been treated with due care. Yet the mummy is in no better state of preservation than the bodies of Saqnounrî and the unknown woman «A». It seems possible, therefore, that the mummy of Anhâpou represents the stage to which the art of embalming had attained before the innovations seen in the mummies of Ahmôsis, Nofritari and Raï, were introduced. This is the chief interest in the mummy under consideration.

The body is fully extended, with the arms placed vertically at its sides and the hands fully extended at the lateral aspects of the thighs. The skin is of a dark brown colour, soft, moist and tough, like oiled leather. The appearance of the mummy recalls that of the crudely-preserved bodies of the Coptic period, especially such as have been exposed for some days to the air. The early Christian mummies were made simply by packing the body in large quantities of common salt; and on exposure to the atmosphere the deliquescence of the salt renders the skin soft and flexible. The mummy of Anhâpou is in precisely the same condition.

In the case of Saqnounrî I submitted a piece of skin to Professor W. A. Schmidt, of the Cairo School of Medicine, for chemical examination : but he was unable to find any excessive quantity of salt in it, in fact no greater quantity of sodium chloride than the normal tissues of the human body contain.

Unlike all other mummies examined by me (excepting only those of the Coptic period) the epidermis was not removed during the process of embalming. It is still present, peeled off, it is true; but adhering to the bandages wherever they came into contact with the body. This proves that the body of Anhâpou had not been put into a saline preservative bath, such as Herodotus, Diodorus, and other early writers describe, and of the employment of which the examination of the other mummies of the New Empire affords such a clear demonstration. It was embalmed by means of some procedure differing from that used in the case of Ahmôsis and his immediate successors.

The fact that the body-cavity was opened in the usual way by an incision in the left flank is sufficient to distinguish it from a Coptic mummy, in which no such incision was made, even if the circumstances under which it was found, the nature of the coffin, the wrappings and the writing on them, and the mode of treatment of the hair, had not made it abundantly clear that we were dealing with a body mummified fully two thousand years before the early Christian practice (circa 5ᵗʰ to 7ᵗʰ centuries A. D.) of dry-salt preservation was introduced. There can be no question that the mummy of Anhâpou belongs to the same epoch as those of Saqnounrî and the woman «A» and is almost certainly anterior to that of Ahmôsis.

From a detailed examination of Anhâpou's mummy and a comparison with the large series of other mummified bodies of known age I think that we can with some confidence reconstruct the process that in all probability was employed in embalming her body.

The usual incision was made in the left flank and part of the contents of the body-cavity removed. Salt was then applied, in all probability, to the surface of the skin of the whole body; and after a time the excess of salt was removed and aromatic powdered wood was sprinkled over the whole body, which was then wrapped in large quantities of linen saturated with a solution of resin.

The condition of the perineum is quite unlike that of any other mummy of the New Empire known to me and recalls in every particular that of the crudely embalmed bodies of the early Coptic period (see First Report on the Human Remains found during the Archæological Survey of Nubia, volume II, 1910, p. 219). It is well described in M. Maspero's monograph (*op. cit.,* p. 533) in these words : «Les organes génitaux sont ouverts et n'étaient remplis ni de chiffons, ni, comme c'est le cas ailleurs, d'une pâte noirâtre mêlée de natron et de résine. On distingue parfaitement les petites lèvres, le capuchon et l'emplacement du clitoris. La vulve est largement fendue (0 m. 07 cent. de la fourchette au capuchon). La paroi vaginale est en bon état, et les plis transversaux n'ont pas disparu : une déchirure (post mortem?), située un peu à droite à 0 m. 03 cent. en arrière de la fourchette, établit une communication entre le vagin et le rectum : au delà et à 0 m. 08 cent. de profondeur, le toucher révèle l'existence d'un corps de la grosseur du doigt qui semble être l'utérus».

The pelvic viscera are still *in situ,* a very exceptional state of affairs in a New Empire mummy. By the deliquescence of the salt the skin has become softened and flexible and, as Anhâpou was a very stout young woman at the time of her death, the usual shrinkage of the subcutaneous tissue has thrown the skin into numerous folds. This is especially the case in the face, which has become greatly distorted, partly for the reasons just mentioned, but also because some hard object of complicated pattern (probably a pectoral ornament) has been pressed against the swollen skin of the face.

The scalp has become separated from the cranium on all sides and especially over the left temple has been raised up into a large bladder, from the surface of which the hair has been separated.

Under these circumstances it is useless to attempt to make any measurements of the head or to form an estimate of its racial traits.

Fig. 1.

The hair was dressed in a peculiar manner (Plate V and Figure 1), which in itself is sufficient to indicate the beginning of the New Empire as the date of the mummy. The hair from an area of roughly 4 square centimetres was separated and plaited for a distance of about 0 m. 03 cent., then divided into three (or more) wisps each of which was tightly plaited in the form of an ear of wheat. The common plait and the stalks of the «ears of wheat» were then thickly smeared with a paste, apparently of a resinous material. This process was repeated until all the hair was plaited and the scalp was furnished with a mass of heavy wheat-ear-like plaits (Plate V).

61054. The Mummy of the Lady Raî (pl. VI and VIII).

On page 582 of *Les Momies royales* reference is made to «quelques cercueils de moindre importance», the first of which bears the name Pa-her-pet.

On June 26ᵗʰ, 1909, I unrolled the bandages from the mummy contained in this coffin. A large quantity of linen of moderately fine texture surrounded the mummy. The bandages had been soaked in a solution of resin in the manner distinctive of the early part of the XVIIIᵗʰ Dynasty. This fact caused me some surprise in view of the fact that Pa-her-pet's coffin was made in the XXᵗʰ Dynasty : but the finding of inscriptions upon the wrappings removed all doubt that it was an early XVIIIᵗʰ Dynasty mummy with which we were dealing. For the name that I found written in ink upon the bandages was deciphered by M. Daressy as Raî, obviously the lady whose coffin had been used for the mummy of Anhâpou (*vide supra*). The epoch in which she lived is known precisely, for she is described (*Les Momies royales*, p. 530) as having been the «nurse of Queen Nofritari», the consort of Ahmôsis I, the first king of the XVIIIᵗʰ Dynasty.

In the process of unrolling the wrappings many broad bandages were first removed : some of these had been wound in a circular manner, others spirally, around the body. Then a series of shrouds was exposed; and when these were removed the trunk was exposed, but the limbs were still invested in great quantities of narrow spirally-wound bandages. All the linen used in wrapping the body was of the same texture, for the practice of employing materials of very varied degrees of fineness, which obtained during the XIXᵗʰ to the XXIIⁿᵈ Dynasties, had not yet come into vogue.

The mummy of Raî is the most perfect example of embalming that has come down to us from the time of the early XVIIIᵗʰ Dynasty, or perhaps even of any period.

The Lady Raî was 1 m. 510 mill. in height, and, as her teeth are only slightly worn, she was probably still youthful at the time of her death. But the mummy is so perfect and undamaged that no attempt was made to examine the bones for more definite evidence upon the question of age.

She was a slim, gracefully-built woman with small or only moderately full breasts, which are now flattened against the chest by the pressure of the bandages.

She had a small oval face, graceful and well-proportioned; and so well preserved that she is the least unlovely of all the mummies of women that have been spared. The chin is small and pointed; the upper teeth somewhat prominent; the nose small, narrow and well-shaped. She has abundant masses of hair, apparently her own, elaborately arranged in a multitude of small plaits, which were then clumped together to form two large club-shaped masses, each o m. 28 cent. long and o m. o55 mill. in diameter, hanging down in front of the shoulders on to the chest (see Plates VI and VIII). The upper plaits are twice the thickness of those in the lower part of the mass, being respectively one centimetre and five millimetres in diameter. Each mass of hair was carefully wrapped in a spirally arranged bandage, which I left in situ upon the left side (Plate VI, Fig. 2), but removed upon the right.

No attempt was made to unravel the tangle of intertwined plaits and determine their arrangement; for to have done so would have damaged this unique mummy, which alone displays a characteristic mode of hair-dressing, well-known in the statuary of the New Empire.

The body and the face were covered with a thin layer of a mixture of sand and powdered resin, some of which can be seen in Plate VI, Fig. 2.

The skin is now reddish-brown in colour, but where the salt in the skin is deliquescing it is becoming blackened.

The hands are very small, delicately formed and almost childish in appearance. The fingers are fully extended and rest upon the thighs, the left hand being a little further forward than the right.

The embalming-wound upon the left side of the abdomen is fusiform in shape and vertical in direction. It is o m. 124 mill. long and o m. o35 mill. wide; its inner margin is o m. o70 mill. from the middle line : its upper end is near the costal margin and its lower close to the anterior superior spine of the ilium. The wound was stuffed with a plug of fine linen, freely sprinkled with a mixture of sand and powdered resin; and there is the impression of a fusiform plate, which was placed over the embalming-wound. This form of plate is distinctive of the XVIIIth Dynasty.

There is no resinous layer covering the perineum. The labia majora are in close apposition. The pubic hair has not been removed.

Without disturbing the large mass of hair it is impossible to obtain accurate measurement of the skull. The cranial length (together with the hair) is o m. 190 mill.; and o m. 140 mill. is a rough estimate of the cranial breadth.

The height from chin to vertex of skull is o m. 186 mill. : total facial height (chin to fronto-nasal suture) is o m. 112 mill. : upper facial height (alveolar edge to fronto-nasal sature) is o m. o61 mill. : bizygomatic breadth, o m. 127 mill.; minimum frontal breadth, o m. 100 mill. : external orbital breadth o m. 103 mill. ;

and the nose is o m. o5o mill. long and o m. o3o mill. at the alæ, which,
however, were somewhat dilated during the process of embalming.

On the right wrist there is a barrel-shaped, carnelian bead, o m. o2 1 mill. by o m.
oo6 mill.

61055. The Mummy supposed to be that of Nofritari (pl. VII).

In the gigantic coffin bearing Queen Nofritari's name there were «une momie d'assez
mauvaise apparence, et un cercueil plus petit, calé par des tampons de toile, où
gisait une momie très soignée. On trouva parmi les chiffons un lambeau d'étoffe
qui sera décrit plus tard, et sur lequel était dessiné un portrait de Ramsès III. Nous
crûmes tous que la momie sans caisse avait été introduite dans le cercueil quand
on transporta les corps à la cachette, et que l'autre momie représentait la reine
Nofritari. La première momie fut donc reléguée dans les magasins, où elle acheva
de se corrompre et répandit bientôt une telle odeur qu'il devint nécessaire de s'en
débarrasser. M. Émile Brugsch-Bey l'ouvrit, au mois de septembre 1885, pendant
mon absence. On reconnut qu'elle était emmaillotée avec soin, mais le cadavre fut
à peine exposé à l'air qu'il tomba littéralement en putréfaction et se mit à suinter
un pus noirâtre d'une puanteur insupportable. C'était probablement la momie de
Nofritari» (MASPERO, *Les Momies royales*, p. 535, and 536). The body was
«enterré provisoirement, car il menaçait de tomber en putréfaction» (p. 525).
The body is 1 m. 610 mill. in height and is fully extended, with the limbs in
almost the same position as Raï's. The left forearm, however, is a little further
forward, so that the left hand (now broken off and lost, no doubt by the grave-
plunderers of the XXth Dynasty) may have partly covered the pudenda. The right
hand and part of the forearm have been broken off and lost : they were placed like
the corresponding structures in Raï's mummy.

The fragments of linen that still adhere to the mummy are of the dark yellowish and
reddish brown colours (as the result of being impregnated with a resinous solution)
usually found in bandages swathing XVIIIth Dynasty mummies. The skin is blackened
like most of the mummies of this period. As in most of the mummies of the first
half of the XVIIIth Dynasty the perineum is coated with a thick plate of solidified
resinous paste.

At the time of her death Nofritari had very little hair on her head and the vertex was
quite bald. Elaborate pains had been taken to hide this deficiency. Twenty strings,
composed of twisted human hair, were placed across the top of her head; and to
these were attached numerous tight plaits, each about o m. 3o cent. long, o m.
oo9 mill. wide and o m. oo5 mill. thick, which hung down as far as the clavicle.
Other plaits were tied to her own scanty locks. The appearance of these plaits is
not unlike that of the modern Nubian women's hair.

In appearance Nofritari was not unlike the younger woman Raï, who is supposed to
have been her nurse; and she also resembles the elder of the two women found in
the tomb of Amenothes II at Bibân el-Molouk.

The mouth is slightly open : the teeth are healthy, but well worn; and the upper teeth are even more prominent than Raï's.

The body is very emaciated and it is impossible to recognise any trace of the breasts, probably by reason of senile atrophy.

The embalming-wound (o m. 120 mill. by o m. 060 mill.) is precisely like Raï's in position and form, excepting that it gapes more. It is plugged with linen, smeared with black resinous paste, which bears the impression of the leaf-like plate that once covered it.

The cranium is of a broad sphenoid form, being as much as o m. 155 mill. broad (measuring-instrument inserted between the plaits of hair) — a figure strongly suggestive of alien extraction, even if some allowance be made for the resin-encrusted scalp.

The length of the cranium is estimated at o m. 184 mill. (with scalp).

The total facial height is o m. 112 mill.; upper facial height, o m. 069 mill.; minimal frontal breadth, o m. 101 mill.; external palpebral breadth, o m. 103 mill.; bizygomatic breadth, o m. 131 mill.; bigonial breadth, o m. 096 mill.; interorbital breadth o m. 025 mill.; left orbit, o m. 041 mill. by o m. 034 mill.; and right orbit; o m. 042 mill. by o m. 032 mill.; and the chin-vertex projection o m. 178 mill. The nasal height is o m. 053 mill. and the (alar) breadth o m. 028 mill.

It will be gathered from M. Maspero's statement, which I have quoted above, that there is an element of doubt as to the identity of this mummy. All the evidence that I have set forth here is strongly corroborative of M. Maspero's inference that it is Nofritari. If this is not Nofritari's mummy, it certainly belongs to her time.

61056. The Mummy of an unknown Woman «B» (pl. IX and X).

Fig. 2

This mummy was unwrapped by M. Maspero in the year 1886, who for reasons set forth in detail in (*Les Momies royales*, p. 551 and 552) suggested that it might be the body of Ramses I.

But when I opened the coffin in June, 1909, I found the mummy of a naked woman, embalmed in the manner distinctive of the earlier part of the XVIIIth Dynasty. The technique of mummification presents a very close resemblance to that displayed in the remains of Raï.

The mummy is that of an elderly, white-haired, partially bald woman, 1 m. 570 mill. in height.

The skin is blackened, as in Nofritari's mummy, and the face is coated with black, shining resin-like material, to which linen bandages are adhering. Fragments of a coiffure such as that worn by Raï are present; but in this case it is of the nature of a wig interplaited with the old lady's own scanty hair (Fig. 2).

She has a comparatively short, broad, ovoid head, which however cannot be measured by reason of the fragments of the wig matted against the scalp. The face is short and ovoid; and the chin is pointed but receding.

It is curious to recall that this member of the royal family, who was certainly contemporaneous with Raï and Nofritari, should also like them have projecting upper teeth. Is this an indication of relationship between these three ladies?

There are small perforations in the lobules of the ears.

The embalming-wound (o m. 116 mill. by o m. o5o mill.) resembles that of Raï and Nofritari (Plate IX).

There is no perineal coating of resin, as there was in the case of Nofritari. In this respect, as well as in the symmetrical apposition of the labia majora to form a linear rima pudendi, this mummy resembles that of Raï.

The breasts are small and senile and are placed very low on the chest wall.

The body has suffered considerably at the hands of ancient grave-plunderers. The head is broken off the trunk at the neck (Plate IX). The right hand is missing.

The cranium and face are so encrusted with resinous material, bandages and hair that few measurements can be made.

The total facial height is o m. 123 mill.; upper facial height, o m. o66 mill.; the bizygomatic diameter is o m. o94 mill.; and the minimal frontal breadth is o m. o96 mill.

The bi-humeral diameter is o m. 337 mill.; the bi-acromial o m. 290 mill.; the bi-iliac (crests) diameter, o m. 242 mill.; and the bi-trochanteric diameter o m. 256 mill.

The length of the humerus is estimated at o m. 295 mill.; and from the line of the elbow flexure to the wrist o m. 257 mill.

61057. The Mummy of King Ahmôsis I (pl. XI and XII).

This mummy was unrolled on June 9th, 1886, by M. Maspero (op. cit., p. 534). On the neck there was a garland of flowers identified by Dr Schweinfurth as *Delphinium orientale*. The hieratic inscriptions written in ink on the bandages confirm the indications afforded by the hieroglyphic characters on the coffin that this is the mummy of Ahmôsis. The name of his son and successor, by whose order the body was embalmed, also occurs on a fragment of the original wrapping which was in contact with the skin; and the outer wrappings bear the name of the Priest-king Païnotmou of the XXIst Dynasty, in whose reign the body was rewrapped. Of this mummy's wrappings and coffin M. Maspero says : «Cercueil et maillot, Ahmos nous offre donc un type précieux de ce qu'était l'art de l'embaumement dans les premiers temps de la XVIIIe dynastie. Les étoffes employées étaient généralement grossières, jaunâtres, découpées en bandes assez larges. Le lacis des bandelettes était interrompu d'espace en espace par la présence d'une pièce de toile, étendue à plat dans le sens de la longueur. Le corps même était enseveli dans un linceul, noué au-dessous des pieds et au-dessus de la tête. Le tout forme une couche assez mince de cinq ou six centimètres d'épaisseur» (p. 534).

The body is 1 m. 635 mill. in height and the arms and fingers are fully extended at the sides of the body. Unlike the condition noticed in the mummies already described, the right hand is placed slightly further forward on the thigh than the left (Plate XI).

The mummy of Ahmôsis has suffered at the hands of ancient grave-plunderers, the head having been broken off the trunk and the nose smashed. It would, no doubt, have shown more evidence of this rough treatment if it were not for its strength and stony hardness, as the result of the application of an abundant layer of black resinous paste to the surface of the whole body.

The head, both face and scalp, are still thickly encrusted with this black material (Plate XII), which however is not abundant enough to hide the ringlets of moderately long, dark brown, wavy hair, with which the head is thickly clad.

The paste or paint on the face hides all trace of facial hair, but under the chin, in a fold of skin which was coated only with wax, traces of a beard were found, 4 millimetres long, and of the same, or perhaps a slightly lighter shade, than the hair covering the scalp.

Like all the mummies of the earlier XVIIIth Dynasty King Ahmôsis had a comparatively small face and no prominent features with the possible exception of the nose. In this respect these rulers present a marked contrast to many of their successors in the XIXth Dynasty and later.

The nose, which is now broken, was small and narrow, but not very prominent. The small face is ovoid and the chin narrow. The superciliary ridges are fairly prominent.

A feature already noticed in the three women of this Dynasty, whose mummies I have described, occurs also in Ahmôsis and Thoutmosis II, that is, the prominence of the upper teeth, which may possibly be a family trait.

With the head encrusted with a thick layer of material of stony hardness it is not possible to obtain accurate cranial measurements. The actual length of the head in its present state, i. e. including hair and wrappings, is o m. 207 mill., and the breadth o m. 171 mill.; but by boring holes through the lateral aspects of the carapace the actual breadth of o m. 156 mill. is obtained. The basi-bregmatic height is o m. 140 mill. : minimal frontal breadth is o m. 100 mill. (with hair and resin, o m. 143 mill.) : total facial height, o m. 114 mill.; upper facial height o m. 073 mill.; nasal height and breadth, o m. 055 mill. and o m. 030 mill., respectively; bizygomatic breadth, o m. 133 mill. : bigonial breadth, o m. 097 mill.; interorbital breadth o m. 022 mill.; right orbit, o m. 046 mill. by o m. 038 mill., and left orbit, o m. 045 mill. by o m. 035 mill.

The cranial form is what Sergi calls «beloid».

The cranial cavity is very tightly packed with linen, and as this procedure, through common after the time of Ahmôsis, is not known to have been practised before his time, it is a matter of crucial importance in the history of the technique of embalming to study the details of the operation in this mummy. This is all the more important because the method of packing the cranium in the mummy under consideration presents highly exceptional features, which seem to bear out the suggestion that in it we are really studying the earliest evidence of the introduction of a new practice, which was only in the experimental stage at the time of the death of Ahmôsis.

The necessity or the desirability of attempting such a curious procedure as the removal of the brain and the introduction of antiseptic packing materials into the brain-case may have first presented itself to the embalmer when he had to deal with the corpses of persons, like Saqnounrî, whose heads had been battered in the wars incidental to the expulsion of the Hyksos. Whether this be so or not, there is no evidence to show that, before the time of Ahmôsis, any attempt had ever been made to remove the brain in the process of mummification.

After the time of Ahmôsis it was the custom to extract the brain by passing an instrument through one of the nostrils and forcing a passage into the brain-case by that route, as I have described in detail elsewhere («A Contribution to the Study of Mummification in Egypt». — *Mémoires présentés à l'Institut égyptien, tome V*, fascicule I, 1906, pp. 1-54, 19 plates). In this mummy it is very doubtful if such a method was employed. There is no distortion of the nose, such as usually results from this operation, nor is the nasal septum damaged in any way or deflected. But as the nasal fossae are tightly packed with linen, which it was considered undesirable to remove, one cannot state dogmatically that the nasal route was not used. Against such a supposition is the fact that the cranial cavity is tightly packed with linen right down to the foramen magnum; and it seems incredible that this could have been accomplished through such a narrow cleft as either of the nasal fossae of this mummy, without damaging the septum.

Moreover, there is the curious and significant fact that the atlas is missing; and the upper surface of the axis and the neighbouring part of of the occipital bone are thickly coated with a mass of black, shining material (?resin), which must have been applied directly to the surfaces of the bones. This raises the possibility — and from the circumstances of the case it must not be regarded as more than a possibility — that through an incision upon the left side of the neck the atlas was excised and the brain removed through the foramen magnum, which would be exposed by such an operation. In favour of this interpretation there is the fact that the free edge of the skin on the left side of the neck (in the submaxillary region) has the appearance of having been cut; and further, although the atlas is missing, the axis and occipital bone are in situ and undamaged. On the contrary the difficult operation of excising the atlas is hardly the kind of procedure one would expect an XVIIIth Dynasty embalmer to attempt.

The set of teeth is complete and in good condition. They are only slightly worn, especially the third molars. There is nothing definite to enable one to estimate the age Ahmôsis had attained. But the state of his teeth, hair and the base of the skull suggest that he was a young man. From the examination of his mummy I should have estimated Ahmôsis' age as not more than 40 years, but there is definite historical evidence that he reigned at least 22 years, and apparently had come of age at the time of his succesion. Nevertheless the fact that his mother survived him for ten years is further corroboration of his youth.

The body, like the head, was smeared with a thick layer of black paste, which prevents an examination of the embalming wound.

The perineum was covered with a thick mass of resinous material; and the **external** genitalia were also coated with the same substance.

The thorax is only 20 centimetres wide, the narrowness being due, no doubt, in large measure to compression by the embalmer's bandages post mortem.

The oblique length of the femur is estimated at about 0 m. 440 mill. : oblique length of the tibia, 0 m. 375 mill. : oblique length of humerus, 0 m. 308 mill.; and of radius, 0 m. 264 mill.

The biacromial diameter measures 0 m. 292 mill. : bi-iliac (crests) diameter 0 m. 213 mill.; bitrochanteric diameter 0 m. 244 mill. : and the distance between the anterior superior iliac spines, 0 m. 181 mill.

The distance from the soles of the feet to the upper margin of the symphysis pubis is 0 m. 871 mill.; from the latter to the suprasternal notch, 0 m. 465 mill.; and from the pubic symphysis to the umbilicus 0 m. 155 mill.

The length of a foot is 0 m. 212 mill.

There is a curious concavity in the vertebral borders of the scapulae between the inferior angle and the spine.

61058. The mummy of Amenothes I (pl. XIII).

The wrappings of this mummy are in such perfect condition, with complete garlands in position, that M. Maspero decided to let it remain untouched. It has already been rewrapped twice — by the Priest-king Païnot'mou and his son Masaharti.

«La momie mesure 1 m. 65 cent. de longueur. Elle est revêtue d'une toile orange, maintenue par des branches de toile ordinaire. Elle porte un masque en bois et en carton peint, identique au masque du cercueil. Elle est couverte de la tête aux pieds de guirlandes de fleurs rouges, jaunes et bleues, parmi lesquelles le Dr Schweinfurth a reconnu le *Delphinium orientale*, la *Sesbania ægyptiaca*, l'*Acacia Nilotica*, le *Carmanthus tinctorius*. Une guêpe, attirée par l'odeur, était entrée dans le cercueil : enfermée par hasard, elle s'y est conservée intacte et nous a fourni un exemple probablement unique d'une momie de guêpe. Il aurait été désirable de déshabiller Amenhotpu comme les autres rois : les deux restaurations dont il a été l'objet ont dû laisser des traces dans le maillot, probablement une ou plusieurs inscriptions en hiératique, mentionnant des dates nouvelles. Toutefois l'aspect que la momie présente actuellement sous ses guirlandes est si joli que j'ai éprouvé quelque scrupule à la dérouler, tandis qu'elle est encore dans sa nouveauté» (p. 537).

61059. The mummy of the Prince Siamon.

Unrolled by M. Maspero, on June 29th, 1886, who states (*op. cit.*, p. 538) that it was the mummy of a child 0 m. 90 cent. in height, which had been plundered in ancient times and the body broken up : when it was restored, in the reign of Païnot'mou of the XXIst dynasty, no trouble was taken to replace the bones of the skeleton in their proper positions : they were simply thrown pell-mell into an oblong bundle.

61060. The mummy of the Princess Sitamon.

The mummy of a child, which has not been unrolled, but through a thin layer of bandages there can be felt a bundle of reeds surmounted by a skull, the whole being roughly 1 m. 20 cent. in length. M. Maspero states that although it would be interesting to find out whether there is any hieratic inscription on the inner wrappings, as in the case of Siamon, this false mummy is so curious and its general appearance so singular that he did not venture to disturb it (*op. cit.*, p. 538).

61061. The mummy of Honttimihou (pl. XIV).

This mummy was accidentally damaged during its transport from Luxsor to Cairo, where it was unrolled in December 1882 (MASPERO, *op. cit.*, p. 544).

«Les cheveux avaient été coupés et les tresses cachées dans l'épaisseur du maillot. Sur la poitrine, un paquet assez gros renfermait une masse de natron blanc, pulvérulent, très caustique, qui enveloppait le cœur de la princesse. La momie était noire, assez mal préparée, mais en bon état de conservation» (*op. cit.*, p. 544).

The body had been wrapped in an enormous quantity of bandages saturated with a solution of resin. These have been chopped away in great part by grave-plunderers. No attempt has been made to clear away from the mummy the remains of these wrappings.

The face is considerably damaged, the soft parts of the nose and some areas of the cheeks having disappeared. Large linen plugs still remain in the nostrils.

The body is packed with resin-saturated pads of linen.

As is usual in the early part of the XVIIIth dynasty the hands are in front of the thighs.

Honttimihou was an old woman 1 m. 520 mill. in height. She had a wide, flattened, beloid cranium; and her face was very short, broad and oval, quite unlike that of any of her contemporaries known to us. However, M. Maspero is of a different opinion, for he says «la momie est du même type que les momies des princesses déjà décrites de la XVIIIe dynastie»; and he adds the statement, which may give support to his view, that «sur la poitrine est tracé, en hiératique, le nom de la fille royale, sœur royale, épouse royale Honttimihou» (*op. cit.*, p. 543).

Her teeth are well worn : the right upper first premolar is carious, and there is an alveolar abscess at the root of the first molar tooth near it.

The cranium is o m. 181 mill. long and o m. 143 broad, but the chin-vertex projection is only o m. 170 mill. The total facial height is o m. 107 mill., the upper facial height o m. 067 mill. and the moderately prominent nose is o m. 050 mill. in height and o m. 030 mill. in breadth.

There is practically no hair on the top of the head and only scanty locks at the sides and on the occiput. These are stained a brilliant reddish (? henna) colour, and are interplaited with strands of hair of a black colour, forming large plaits o m. 02 cent. wide, all attached at the back of the head.

3.

61062. The mummy of Hent-m-pet (pl. XV, XVI and XVII).

I removed the wrappings from this mummy in June, 1909.

The condition of the wrapped body when found is shown in plate XV. A large hole seen in the front of the chest is the work of a robber, either ancient or modern, who was searching for jewellry on the neck and chest of the mummy.

After removing the fragmentary remains of the shroud and the five encircling bandages (pl. XV); the mummy was found to be invested with a series of loosely-applied, circularly- and spirally-wound bandages; and under them a number of longitudinal sheets and pads.

When these were removed the body of an old woman, 1 m. 613 mill. in height, was exposed. The legs were enswathed in bandages; and these were allowed to remain. The whole of the chest was hidden by a large and elaborately-contructed wig (pls. XVI and XVII). In addition to this there were found upon the left side of the head the remains of another wig resembling the coiffure seen in Raï's mummy (pl. VI). The wigs were made of wavy, brown hair; but the old lady's own hair was freely streaked with grey.

Considerable pressure had been applied to the face, presumably by the embalmers when applying the bandages; and the nose is completely flattened, so that the plugs of linen inserted into the nostrils by the embalmers have been squeezed out on to the upper lip. The gruesomeness of this disfigurement has been increased by the fact that the usual toilet of the face had not been attended to : the skin is paper-like in consistency and has a pale yellow colour, as though it had been painted with ochre.

The face is small and elliptical and conforms to the Egyptian type. The total facial height is 0 m. 114 mill. and the upper facial height, 0 m. 062 mill. : the bizygomatic breadth is 0 m. 123 cent.; and the minimal frontal breadth is 0 m. 090 mill. The chin-vertex projection is 0 m. 198 mill. The teeth are well-worn.

The remains of hair and wig upon the head prevent any measurements of the cranium being made : but its breadth is estimated as about 0 m. 140 mill.

A space varying from 2 to 4 centimetres separates the inner wrappings from the body and suggests a shrinkage of the latter after the application of its bandages.

On the left flank there is a vertical embalming-wound 0 m. 090 mill. long and 0 m. 020 mill. wide. Its lower end is 5 centimetres above the anterior superior spine of the ilium.

There is no coating of resinous paste anywhere on the surface of the body, such as we have seen in most of the mummies of the time of Ahmôsis; and the style of mummification represents a stage either anterior to that of the Ahmôsis or very much later. There is no perineal covering; but the vagina is plugged with linen.

Both forearms have been broken off by grave-plunderers and only fragments of the right now remain : but the detached left forearm has been replaced in a position transversely across the body, below the wig (pl. XVI).

In the case of the wig which is still in situ strings pass over the top of the head very much in the way we have already noticed in the case of Nofritari's mummy.

The large wig placed upon the chest (pl. XVI) is quite complete and in an excellent state of preservation. When flattened out (pl. XVII) it measures o m. 3o cent. across and o m. 24 cent. from back to front. It consists of wisps of dark brown, wavy hair about o m. 21 cent. long, the proximal end of each of which is bound round with string (pl. XVII, Fig. 2). These proximal ends are arranged around three sides of an oblong, the posterior side 13 centimetres long and the two lateral sides, each 9 centimetres long; and are fixed by plaited strings, some of which pass across (fig. 2) from one side of the oblong to the other. Among the wisps of hair a few plaits are found (see lower left hand corner of fig. 2).

Along the fourth (anterior) side of the oblong there is a thin wisp of hair, tied at each end to the framework of the wig. To this is attached a series of small corkscrew curls of lighter brown hair, which form a fringe to hang down on the forehead, when the wig is worn (fig. 1). Each curl is about 13 centimetres long.

In the right postero-lateral corner of the wig a similar fringe is tied (fig. 1) : but for what purpose it is difficult to surmise.

61063. The mummy of Sitkamos (pl. XVIII).

In a poor coffin, made in the style of the XXth dynasty, was placed this earlier mummy of the «royal daughter, royal sister, principal royal wife Sitkamos», as the hieratic inscription on the linen covering the chest has been interpreted by M. Maspero (*op. cit.*, p. 541). After removing the garlands which were placed on the breast and removing the outer shroud M. Maspero discovered (June 19th, 1886) on an inner shroud another hieratic inscription written in ink, which made it plain that this mummy was rewrapped at the same time as those of Ahmôsis I and Siamon in the reign of Païnot'mou.

This mummy was subjected to severe damage in ancient times. Grave-plunderers had chopped through the bandages and hacked away almost the whole of the anterior wall of the body (see pl. XVIII), broken off the left arm at the shoulder and smashed off the whole of the occipital region of the skull.

In the black resinous paste, which is thickly smeared over what remains of the chest-wall (and in fact over the whole body), there are very sharply defined impressions of the pectoral ornament, «un collier ouoskhit à quatre rangs», which excited the cupidity of the robbers, who worked such terrible havoc on this mummy.

Sitkamos was a large, powerfully-built, almost masculine woman about 1 m. 620 mill. in height. The method employed in embalming is perhaps most like that seen in the mummy of Ahmôsis I; but the position of the hands, covering the pudenda, is quite exceptional if this is really as early as Ahmôsis, although I have called attention to an early approximation to this position in the mummy of Nofritari (*vide supra*), and the same position is seen in the mummy supposed to be Thoutmôsis I (*vide infra*). The whole body, including the face, is thickly smeared with a black resinous paste, in which fine bandages are embedded. [A similar state of affairs is found in the mummy of Seti I of the XIXth dynasty]. It is, perhaps, characteristic of the XVIIIth dynasty embalming to cover the perineum with a large cake of black resinous paste, as is the case in Sitkamos' mummy. This practice began with Ahmôsis I, but is seen in its most characteristic form in the mummies of Amenothes II and the women left in his tomb in the Bibân-el-Molouk.

The whole back of the skull was smashed away, revealing the brain and its membranes, which are well-preserved. The fact that no attempt seems to have been made to clear out the cranial cavity is futher evidence of an early date.

The nostrils were plugged with linen. The whole body cavity was tightly packed with linen, some of it soaked in a solution of resin. Scanty, black, wavy hair o m. 23 cent. long, not plaited or dressed in any way, hangs down from the head.

The cranium is o m. 152 mill. broad : the face is much bigger and more vigorous than that of most of the women of this period, with the exception of Anhâpou (*vide supra*), to whom Sitkamos presents certain points of resemblance.

The total facial height is o m. 120 mill., the upper facial height is o m. 070 mill. and the chin-vertex projection is o m. 198 mill.

The teeth are only moderately worn, the cranial sutures are open, and the hair is not yet streaked with white. These facts are no certain index of age, but suggest that Sitkamos could not have been much more than thirty years old.

On the toes there are still visible the impressions of the string employed to fasten on the nails and epidermis.

The back of the left thigh and the right gluteal fold have been gnawed by mice.

61064. The mummy of the Royal Prince Sipaari (pl. XIX).

M. Maspero has described this prince as «a member of one of the royal families, which lived at Thebes» (*Les Momies royales,* p. 582).

With the assistance of Professor A. R. Ferguson I unrolled the wrappings of this mummy in the Cairo Museum on September 9th, 1905.

After removing the lid of the coffin (fig. 1) the mummy was found wrapped in a discoloured shroud, tied around with three bandages (fig. 2), the whole being 1 m. 09 cent. long. The mummy itself, without wrappings, is o m. 93 cent. in length.

The following notes concerning the wrappings were made during the process of unrolling them.

1. The upper of the three bandages tied around the shroud is really a sheet of linen 18 cent. wide, rolled up to form a bandage. One end is ragged, the other has a string fringe, 8 cent. long. It consists of linen of very close and regular texture, with 28 + 20 threads to the square centimetre (warp and woof respectively). It was tied a simple knot on the left side.

2. Second bandage, 7.5 centimetres wide, folded three times : torn ends : tied behind knees. Linen of regular open mesh : 20 + 11 threads per centimetre.

3. Material and arrangement like (2); tied behind ankles.

4. Shroud 1 m. 40 cent. by 1 m. 30 cent., wrapped around body : very close mesh (25 + 23), selvedged borders.

5. A soft ragged shawl of oblong form, now very much torn, but originally 1 m. 50 cent. × 0 m. 56 cent., laid on front of body. mesh 11 + 20.

6. A bandage 2 m. × 0 m. 20 cent. (mesh 22 + 17) wound spirally (clockwise) around feet and ankles. Its end, rolled into a point, is fixed by being inserted in a hole torn for it in an underlying bandage.

7. Bandage 3 m. × 0 m. 30 cent. (very irregular mesh, 30 + 15) begins behind hips, where the end is tucked under a preceding coil of same bandage, and proceeds spirally around the body up to the head.

8. Broad sheet, 1 m. 75 cent. × 0 m. 60 cent. (mesh 14 + 21), folded and placed in front of the body throughout its whole length.

9. Similarly arranged sheet, 1 m. × 0 m. 60 cent., with coarse matting-like mesh, 17 + 7.

10. Two loosely crumpled rags in front of body, 2 m. × 0 m. 60 cent. (same material as (14)) and 1 m. 15 cent. × 0 m. 95 cent. (same material as (11)).

11. A very broad bandage, torn from a sheet with selvedged border, originally 3 m. × 0 m. 5 cm., wound spirally clockwise round body beginning at head and ending at ankles. Loose rough thread, 12 + 26.

12. Irregular fragment, 0 m. 09 cent. × 0 m. 05 cent. (27 + 12), folded into an oblong and placed on right side of ankles.

13. Bandage, 4 m. 06 cent. × 0 m. 17 cent. (rough irregular mesh of uneven thread, 21 + 15), passed spirally around body from ankles to head.

14. Large irregular sheet, 1 m. 30 cent. × 0 m. 95 cent., (very fine thread, 29 + 19, no selvedges), folded four times and placed in front of the body.

15. A large unselvedged sheet, 2 m. 35 cent. × 0 m. 60 cent. of coarse sacking (16 + 9), folded on itself, covers whole front of body. At the right corners, both at head and feet, there are long strips, which were originally tied to the corresponding left corners.

16. A sheet of cloth, 3 m. 20 cent. × 0 m. 50 cent. (very ragged thread, 13 + 24), folded into four layers, placed in front of upper half of the body.

17. Another folded sheet, 2 m. 01 cent. × 0 m. 50 cent. (very regular thread, 18 + 25), covered right side of upper half of body.

18. Another covering lower part of body; very worn and ragged, originally 1 m. 25 cent. × 1 m. 12 cent. (texture exceptionally irregular, 9 + 14).

19. This bandage and numbers (20), (22), (23), (24), (26) and (27) are all torn from the same sheet (20 + 13), the edges of which are on number (23). It passes spirally around the body from the head to the chest.

20. Starts where (19) ends and passes spirally down the body to the ankles.

21. A series of pieces of rag of varied texture, some with ink inscriptions.

22. Arranged like (20).

23. A bandage, 5 m. × 0 m. 27 cent. with a thickly hemmed border and fringe (0 m. 025 mill.) down one side.

24. Bandage passing spirally from middle of body up to head, in direction opposite to hands of clock.

25. A stick extending whole length of body.

26. Wound spirally around body from the head to the middle of the body.

27. A bandage, 5 m. × o m. o2 cent., with one end fringed and selvedged and the cloth thread-drawn parallel to it, wound spirally around body from the feet to the middle of the body.

28. Extending longitudinally in front of the body there was a ragged cloth not carefully wrapped up; but fixed in front of the head by a piece of rag. Hieroglyphs written in ink upon it : also designs in red.

29. Several loose pieces of rag in front of body. One piece with very ragged edges, 1 m. × o m. o6 cent. (very loose irregular thread, 18 + 21).

30. By this time what was left of the mummy presented the appearance shown in fig. 3 (pl. XIX). Three bands are tied around the body. They consist of linen of very close texture and regular fibres (19 + 13).

On removing these bandages we found in front of the mummy in its whole length (31) a thick mass of cloth, consisting of two precisely similar sheets of fine linen (very ragged mesh, 3o + 23), folded many times. Each sheet is 1 m. o6 cent. long (i. e. in the long axis of the mummy) and 4 m. wide. One short border and one long are selvedged in each sheet. The other short border of each piece has a string fringe, on an average one string to every centimetre, but not at regular intervals. Each string is o m. 115 mill. long and consists of all the longitudinal threads of its own area interplaited.

Thus the two cloths represent on original piece 3 m. o2 cent. × 4 m.

32. A series of long irregular strips of muslin tied in knots, all converging to a large reddish pear-shaped mass of discoloured cloth o m. 35 cent. long. The colour is due to some resinous solution and perhaps in part to blood-staining. A piece of palm-stick, o m. 43 cent. long, to which is adherent one of the pieces of muslin (regular mesh of exceptionally fine thread, 23 + 35).

33. A wooden stick in contact with the mummy.

34. A shroud in direct contact with the remains of the body, 4 m. o5 cent. × o m. o4 cent., folded longitudinally four times and rolled up, except where it forms a flat pad for the head. It is a muslin formed of very fine, but also very irregular and furry, threads (3o + 24) : it has a fringe of long plaited strings like (31).

Amongst the folds of this shroud there were many barley stalks.

35. A large torn sheet like (31) and folded like it.

36. Another sheet like the last with a regularly-fringed edge. o m. 3o cent. wide, folded four times.

This wrapping was done in the XXIst dynasty, but is merely a rough reclothing of a mummy that had been stripped by plunderers. The details of the method practised in the XXIst dynasty have been described by Mr. A. C. Mace and me in *The Mummy of a Priestess of Amon* (*Annales du Service*, 1906, pp. 155-182).

When I had removed all these complicated series of wrappings, from which the simulacrum of a complete and properly-wrapped mummy had been built up, only the distorted skin and a few of the bones of a boy o m. 93 cent. in height were found (fig. 4, pl. XIX).

The soft pliable skin is of a light brown colour and forms a hollow shell which has become grossly distorted by pressure. The face has become flattened on the right side to such an extent that the mouth is almost vertical.

The scalp has been torn off the right side of the skull and bent over on to the left side. The skin of the back, together with the vertebral column, most of the other bones bones of the skeleton, and all the viscera, are missing. The greater part of the right leg is wanting : the right femur (diaphysis o m. 21 cent.) but not the left is present (see fig. 4). The left tibia and fibula and foot are present. The right scapula is present, but not the left.

The skull is very flat. The hair is cut short. The boy had a full set of deciduous teeth and presumably was about five or six years of age. Appearances suggest that he had been circumcised : but if so Sipaari is an exception to the general rule, for there are reasons for supposing that during the XVIIIth dynasty and before then the operation was performed at the time of puberty (*vide infra*).

61065. The mummy supposed to be that of Thoutmosis I (pls. XX, XXI and XXII).

M. Maspero informs us (*The Struggle of the Nations*, 1896, p. 242) that « the coffin of Thoutmosis I (in these quotations I have altered the spelling of names in accordance with M. Maspero's latest transliterations in the *Guide du Visiteur*), was usurped by the priest-king Pinotmou I, son of Piânkhi (*Les Momies royales*, p. 545), and the mummy was lost». He adds further : — «I fancy that I have discovered it in mummy n° 5283 [n° 61065 of this catalogue], of which the head presents a striking resemblance to those of Thoutmosis II and III (*ibid.*, pp. 581, 582)».

In addition to the reasons given by M. Maspero in the above quotations, and at length in *Les Momies royales*, pp. 545, 570 and especially pp. 581, 582, the technique of mummification displayed in this specimen, as well as the position in which the arms are placed, indicates that the body was embalmed at a period earlier than that of Thoutmosis II and later than that of Ahmôsis I. Thus we have exceptionally strong corroborative evidence in support of M. Maspero's suggestion, which was based upon family likeness.

The nature of the resin-impregnated bandages with which the mummy is enswathed can leave us in no doubt that the body was embalmed at some time during the XVIIIth dynasty. The excellent state of preservation of the body and the firmness and durability of the skin and tissues, indicate the attainment of a perfection in the art of embalming unknown before the time of Ahmôsis I; and the fact that this result has been attained without plastering the body with a thick layer of resinous paste may he regarded as evidence that the mummification was done at a period subsequent to that of Ahmôsis. On the other hand the mummy of Raî affords positive evidence that such perfection was attainable even in the time of Ahmôsis.

In the series of mummies so far considered it will be noticed that the hands, which at the commencement of the XVIIIth dynasty were placed on the sides of the thighs, become shifted gradually further forward, until in the mummy of Sitkamos they were placed in front of the pudenda. In the mummy under consideration there can be no doubt (see pl. XX), that the hands, although broken off and removed by ancient grave-plunderers, were also placed in front of the genital area. This position is doubly significant, not only of the fact that this mummy is later than that of Ahmôsis and represents a phase in the changing customs of placing of the hands exemplified in the case of Sitkamos, but also of a greater antiquity than the mummies of Thoutmosis II and his successors. For with Thoutmosis II the custom of folding the arms was introduced (see pl. XXIII), which became the rule and remained in force until the coming of the priest-kings of the XXIst dynasty, when a reaction set in and the embalmers reverted to the custom in vogue at the commencement of the XVIIIth dynasty; and once more began to place the hands on the thighs or in front of the pudenda (see pl. LXVII et seq.).

There are some curious exceptions to this general statement. In the mummy of the young uncircumcised prince found in the tomb of Amenothes II, and certainly contemporaneous with it, both hands were in front of the pudenda (see Bulletin de l'Institut égyptien, 5e série, t. I, p. 22 b, also infra); and in one of the women found in the same tomb (Op. cit., p. 225), the right hand was placed against the thigh, while the left arm was flexed. Then again in the mummy of Touiyou (Thua), the mother of Queen Tiyi, both hands were in contact with the thighs : but in the mummy of her husband Iouiya (Yuaa), both arms are flexed in the way that was usual in his time.

What these departures from custom may signify it is impossible to say : but I must emphasize the fact that, from the time of Thoutmosis II until the end of the XXth dynasty, no mummy of an adult man is known in which the arms were not flexed.

Seeing that some scholars have urged the view that the mummy under consideration is not that of Thoutmosis I, but is the body of Pinotmou I or some other priest-king of the XXIst dynasty, it might be supposed that the placing of the arms in the position customary in the XXIst dynasty lends support to that contention. But such an opinion is wholly untenable. The technique of embalming presents quite definite characteristics in the early XVIIIth and the XXIst dynasties respectively. The mummy under consideration conforms in every respect to the former and has none of the many peculiarly distinctive features of the latter mode of embalming.

There is then abundant evidence for placing this mummy in the series between those of Ahmôsis I and Thoutmosis II : and it is particularly unfortunate that we are unable, for the reasons stated above, to add the testimony of the mummy of Amenothes I to the discussion. Perhaps M. Maspero at some future time may give his consent to the use of the X-rays, and obtain a skiagram of the mummy of Amenothes I, which would show the positions of his arms, without disturbing the wrappings and garlands that now hide them from view.

In addition to this archaeological evidence, in support of the identification of this mummy as the body of Thoutmosis I, there is the testimony of the physical characters of the mummy itself, upon which M. Maspero based his suggestion. The points of resemblance not only to Thoutmosis II, but also to the whole group of early XVIIIth dynasty royal mummies, are manifold. Amongst a group of short men — Ahmôsis I was 1 m. 635 mill. and Thoutmosis II 1 m. 684 mill. — this man was even more undersized, being only 1 m. 545 mill. in height.

The most striking point of difference is the smallness, and especially the narrowness, of the cranium.

When we come to examine the details of the mummy there are many features, trivial in themselves when considered individually, but the cumulative value of which is so great as to dispose of any further doubts as to its definite identification as Thoutmosis I or a contemporary.

The rounding of the margins of the external auditory meatus (pl. XXII) makes it certain that the ear must have been plugged in the same manner as that of Thoutmôsis II (pl. XXIV), where a ball of resinous material is still in situ. In this respect the mummy of Thoutmosis III (pl. XXVIII) resembles those of his two namesakes who came before him. By the time of Thoutmosis IV, however, this practice was given up and it became the custom to smear the ear with resinous paste, instead of putting a round plug into the aperture. In the mummy of Thoutmosis IV evidence of the custom of piercing the lobules of the ears is seen for the first time in a king of certain date, so far as I am aware, if we except the mummy of the unknown man «C», who was probably a contemporary of the person whose mummy we are discussing and the mummy supposed to be Meritamon. The absence of such perforations in the mummy under consideration, as well as in Thoutmosis II and III, is further corroboration of its identification as Thoutmosis I.

The position of the embalming wound (seen in pl. XX at the inner side of the forearm) agrees with that already described (*vide supra*) in other mummies of this period.

The genitalia have been treated in a manner strikingly different from that shown (in pl. XI), in the case of Ahmôsis I. At first sight the body has the appearance (see pl. XX) of being that of a eunuch : but on closer examination a broad leaf, o m. 067 mill. long and o m. 038 mill. wide, may be seen flattened against the perineum; and, to the left of it, there is a similar but slightly smaller mass flattened against the front and inner side of the left thigh. Whether these structures represent the whole of the pudenda or only the scrotum must remain uncertain. These facts become of special interest when the condition of the next three mummies to be described is taken into consideration.

Apart from the eye-lashes the head is absolutely devoid of hair. The scalp is quite smooth and hairless and there is no sign of any moustache or chin-beard; but short, moderately abundant, white hairs are visible on the left masseteric region.

The skin of the face still retains obvious traces of having been much wrinkled during life.

The cranium is small, narrow, and ovoid in norma verticalis. In profile (pl. XXII) it appears to be very lofty and the occiput is moderately prominent. The narrow, relatively long ellipsoid face is said, by M. Maspero, to present «refined features»,

and «the mouth still bears an expression of shrewdness and cunning» (*Op. cit.,
Struggle of the Nations*, p. 242). But the narrow, feeble jaw, with receding chin
(pl. XXI and XXII) give an aspect of weakness to the whole face.

M. Maspero states that «the king was already advanced in age at the time of his death,
being over fifty years old, to judge by his teeth, which are worn». (*Op. cit.,*
p. 242).

The cranium is o m. 180 mill. long, o m. 133 mill. broad : its minimal frontal
diameter is o m. 093 mill. and its circumference o m. 510 mill. : total facial
height, o m. 114 mill.; upper facial height o m. 070 mill.; bizygomatic breadth,
o m. 127 mill.; bigonial breadth, o m. 098 mill.; nasal height, o m. 057 mill.
and breadth o m. 033 mill. (alar measurement, which however is of little value,
as the nostrils are widely dilated — see pl. XXI); left orbit, o m. 04 cent. by o m.
03 cent. : right orbit, precisely same dimensions. The auricular height of the cranium is o m. 113 mill.; and the chin-vertex projection, o m. 195 mill.

Height of upper border of symphysis pubis (from level of heels) o m. 830 mill. :
upper border of sternum o m. 427 mill. above symphysis pubis; biacromial
breadth, o m. 310 mill., and breadth across heads of humeri, o m. 340 mill.

61066. The mummy of Thoutmosis II (pls. XXIII and XXIV).

This mummy was unwrapped by M. Maspero (*Les Momies royales,* p. 546) on July 1st,
1886.

The mummy was badly damaged by ancient tomb-robbers. [The photograph (pl. XXIII)
represents it as restored by me on September 22nd, 1906]. The left arm was broken
off at the shoulder-joint, and the forearm separated at the elbow joint. The right
arm was chopped off just above the elbow. From the manner of folding of the skin
I was able to determine the positions of the two arms and restore them, as they are
shown in pl. XXIII. Both upper arms were vertical. From the folding of the skin in
the bend of the right elbow, it was evident that the forearm passed obliquely across
the chest, so as to bring the fully extended right hand in front of the left shoulder.
The left forearm was probably lying in contact with the chest, i. e. deeper than the
right forearm; but the hand was not quite so high as the right; and only the thumb
was extended, the fingers being fully flexed.

The whole anterior abdominal wall and a considerable part of the thoracic wall had
been hacked away by means of blows from some large, sharp-edged implement
(?axe). One stroke cut across the sternal end of the right clavicle had passed obliquely
outward through the upper four ribs on the right side : another gash passed straight
through the middle line of the anterior body-wall : a third cut through the left ribs,
from the second to the eighth inclusive, along a line passing downward and slightly
outward from a point on the second rib four centimetres from the middle line.

The right leg was completely severed from the body by a blow (probably of an axe)
which cut through the right pubic bone toward the great sciatic notch.

A slight gash is found passing obliquely upward and outward on the neck from the left sterno-clavicular articulation (pl. XXIV, fig. 2); and there is another wound, much deeper than the last-mentioned, farther round on the left side of the neck.

Two small cuts are visible on the chin (fig. 2).

The posterior (lateral) margin only is left of the embalming-wound, which must have been a widely-gaping fusiform opening, 11 cent. in length.

The skin of the thorax, shoulders and arms (excluding the hands), the whole of the back, the buttocks and legs (excluding the feet) is studded with raised macules varying in size from minute points to patches a centimetre in diameter. The skin of the head is not affected. A condition precisely similar to this is also found in the mummy of Amenothes II and in a less marked form in Thoutmosis III; and the question is raised as to whether these macules are due to some cutaneous eruption or are the result of the action of the preservative bath post mortem. On the whole I am inclined to look upon them as the manifestations of some disease, the nature of which, however, is not altogether clear : but the fact that this irregularity of the skin occurs in three successive Pharaohs suggests that it may be due to some irritant amongst the ingredients of the preservative materials employed by the embalmers at this particular time.

M. Maspero makes the following statements concerning Thoutmosis II (*The Struggle of the Nations,* pp. 242, 243). «The mask on his coffin represents him with a smiling and amiable countenance, and with the fine pathetic eyes which show his descent from the Pharaohs of the XIIth dynasty. His statues bear the same expression, which indeed is that of the mummy itself. He resembles Thoutmosis I; but his features are not so marked, and are characterised by greater gentleness. He had scarcely reached the age of thirty when he fell a victim to a disease of which the process of embalming could not remove the traces. The skin is scabrous in patches and covered with scars, while the upper part of the [scalp] is bald; the body is thin and somewhat shrunken, and appears to have lacked vigour and muscular power» (see *Momies royales,* pp. 545-547).

M. Maspero's estimate of age is based upon the condition of the upper incisor teeth (see pl. XXIV), which were exposed by removing some linen and resin from the slightly open mouth. But as these teeth project beyond the lower incisors, as in so many members of the Royal Family in the XVIIIth dynasty (*vide supra*), the absence of signs of «wear» in the upper teeth does not necessarily bear the significance thus attached to it. The late Professor Rudolf Virchow makes the following statements in reference to these matters. «Thutmes II., der Urenkel von Ahmosis, ist nach einer sehr kurzen Regierung gestorben, also wahrscheinlich noch in jüngerem Alter. Seine vollen Schneidezähne sind freilich stark abgeschliffen, aber sonst von guter Beschaffenheit. Sie sind orthognath, wenngleich etwas vortretend» (*Die ägyptischen Königsmumien im Museum zu Bulaq,* Sitzungsberichte der königlich preussischen Akademie der Wissenschaften zu Berlin, 1888, XXXIV, p. 771).

On the temples there is dark brown wavy hair about 12 cent. long arranged in curls (see pl. XXIV), which Professor Virchow regards as being the result, possibly, of artifice. On the vertex there is a very scanty covering of much finer hair, not more than 2 cent. long. The whole occipital region and a patch on the right parietal region are wholly devoid of hair; but there is the possibility that this may have fallen off during or after mummification.

Although loss of hair often occurs at a much earlier age than 30 years, especially as a result of certain diseases, the baldness of Thoutmosis II, considered in conjunction with the wrinkled skin of his face, leads me seriously to question the suggestion that he was no more than 30 years of age.

Only a few scattered hairs in the masseteric region are all that can be detected of the beard.

Each external auditory meatus is occupied by a round plug of resin (pl. XXIV). The ears are small and well-formed and the lobules seem not to be perforated.

The bridge of the nose is low and fairly broad. Both nostrils are distended with plugs of linen impregnated with resinous material : but it is clear that the nose must have been moderately broad, without being squat (see pl. XXIV). Virchow describes the nose as being «an der Wurzel breit, der Rücken stark vortretend, der Index (63.6) genau derselbe wie bei Ahmosis, etwas gross» (*Op. cit.*, p. 771).

This mummy has been measured by Dr. Fouquet (M. Maspero's Report, *Les Momies royales*), by Professor Virchow (*Op. cit.*) and by Dr. Douglas Derry and me. But there are surprisingly great discrepancies in the three series of measurements. In some cases, as for instance, stature, which, according to Virchow is 1 m. 750 mill., but according to our own measurements only 1 m. 684 mill., the difference is due to the fact that we were able to measure the height after the removal of the wrappings from the feet. But other equally disconcerting contrasts appear in measurements that were made under precisely similar conditions.

The cranium is of a broad pentagonoid form. Virchow's account of the head is as follows : — «der Kopf trotz der Länge des Hinterhaupts mesocephal (Index 79.1) und wahrscheinlich orthocephal (Ohrhöhenindex 62.8). Die Stirn voll, mit schwachen Orbitalwülsten, etwas rückwärts geneigt. Das Gesicht obwohl schmal, doch chamaeprosop (Index 88.8)» (*Op. cit.*, p. 771).

The features of this, and all the other early XVIIIth dynasty mummies so far considered, are characteristically Egyptian. It is unusual, however in pure Egyptians to find such broad crania as we see in all these royal mummies, with the noteworthy exception of the small-headed individual supposed to be Thoutmosis I. Nevertheless it should not be surprising if the members of a family, who, by their own initiative, had just freed their country from foreign domination, displayed a somewhat greater breadth of cranium than the generality of their subjects.

The length of the head is 0 m. 191 mill. and the breadth is 0 m. 149 mill. : minimal frontal breadth, 0 m. 100 mill. : circumference, 0 m. 549 mill.; total facial height, 0 m. 122 mill. : upper facial height, 0 m. 070 mill. : nasal height and breadth, 0 m. 057 and 0 m. 033 mill. respectively.

Virchow (*Op. cit.*, p. 786) gives the following measurements of this mummy. [I use the terms employed elsewhere in this catalogue]. Length of head, 0 m. 191 mill.; breadth of head, 0 m. 151 mill.; auricular height, 0 m. 120 mill.; distance of

auditory meatus from root of nose, o m. 115 mill.; circumference of head, o m.
547 mill.; minimal frontal breadth, o m. 100 mill.; length of face, from hair-
margin to chin, o m. 191 mill.; total facial height, o m. 120 mill.; upper facial
height (measured to the lip and not to the alveolar margin), o m. 078 mill.; bizygomatic breadth, o m. 135 mill.; bimalar breadth, o m. 097 mill.; bigonial
breadth, o m. 098 mill. : (internal) interorbital width, o m. 032 mill.; external
orbital width, o m. 085 mill. : nasal height, o m. 055 mill.; nasal breadth, o m.
035 mill.; length of mouth, o m. 055 mill.; and length of ear, o m. 055 mill.

I found the height of the upper margin of the symphysis pubis above the heels to be
o m. 873 mill.

In his report M. Maspero states that the prepuce was present (in 1886); but I was
unable to find (September 22nd 1906) any definite remains of the external genital
organs, although appearances suggest that they had been flattened against the
perineum as in the case of the mummy last described.

There is a funnel-shaped dilatation of the rectum, o m. 055 mill. deep, the aperture
measuring o m. 04 cent. by o m. 03 cent. Remains of the pelvic viscera are still
present.

Unlike the conditions found in many of the royal mummies the finger-nails and toe-
nails of Thoutmosis II were all neatly trimmed and cleaned.

**61067. The mummy of an unknown man « C », found in the coffin of the Scribe
Nibsoni (pl. XXV, XXVI and XXVII).**

When found in 1881 this mummy had obviously been recently plundered by some of
the people of the Luxsor neighbourhood, whose depredations led to the discovery
of the Royal Mummies (see *Les Momies royales,* pp. 574-576).

In the course of his discussion of this mummy (*Op. cit.*) M. Maspero makes the statements : « J'ai supposé jusqu'à présent que le cadavre représente réellement
Nibsoni. Comme Nibsoni était le père d'Honttouï, femme du roi Pinot'mou, il est
possible que sa parenté avec la reine lui ait valu l'honneur d'être placé dans la
cachette ». In *The Struggle of the Nations* the definite statement is made that this
mummy is « the scribe Nibsoni » (p. 509, footnote 3).

But Nibsoni lived in the times of the XXIst dynasty, whereas this is an XVIIIth dynasty
mummy, obviously belonging to the group that includes the first three Pharaohs
who bore the name Thoutmosis. The mode of embalming, the treatment of the skin,
the nature of the resin-impregnated bandages, and even such small details as the
rounded appearance of the external auditory meatus (compare pl. XXVII with
pls. XXII, XXIV and XXVIII and note the contrast between these four and all the
other plates), and the treatment of the genital organs, all proclaim this mummy to
be early XVIIIth dynasty in date.

The positions of the arms indicate that this mummy is earlier than that of Thoutmosis II. I have placed it after the latter in this catalogue merely for the sake of
convenience in discussion.

Who this unknown man can be there is no evidence to show; for if the enshrouded body in the coffin of Amenothes I is really the mummy of that sovereign, there is no king missing from the early XVIIIth dynasty series.

Moreover the features of this man present no likeness to any of his possible contemporaries among the royal family; and a tall, vigorous man, 1 m. 739 mill. in height, must have seemed a very giant amongst them, and is hardly likely to have sprung from such a puny stock. The only possibility that remains is that « C » was some high official.

He has abundant, black hair, freely streaked with grey. It is about 15 cent. long. The teeth are so much worn that they have all become molariform. There can be no doubt thas this man was well advanced in years.

Without removing the bandages to a greater extent than is shown in pl. XXV I was unable to discover any trace of genital organs; and I would not have hesitated to call this man a eunuch, if it had not been for the fact that the mode of treatment of the genitalia is almost equally puzzling in the mummies of the three other members of this group (Thoutmosis I, II and III), who were certainly not eunuchs, if we accept the history of their reigns.

The skin of the body is of a reddish brown colour, but that of the face is almost black. This man had a strong face with pronounced features; a big, heavy, broad jaw of Armenoid type; prominent brow ridges and sloping forehead; broad cheeks, and a fairly prominent nose. On the whole his features conform, not to the the indigenous Egyptian type, but to that of the alien, so-called Armenoid group.

There are small perforations in the lobules of the ears.

The cranial length is 0 m. 192 mill.; cranial breadth, 0 m. 137 mill.; minimal frontal breadth, 0 m. 105 mill.; chin-vertex projection, 0 m. 217 mill.; total facial height, 0 m. 125 mill.; upper facial height, 0 m. 069 mill.; bizygomatic breadth, 0 m. 141 mill.; bigonial breadth, 0 m. 105 mill.; biauricular breadth, 0 m. 112 mill.; nasal height, 0 m. 058 mill., and breadth (alar), 0 m. 034 mill.

61068. The Mummy of Thoutmosis III (pl. XXVIII).

This mummy was unwrapped by M. Emil Brugsch (now Brugsch Pacha) in July 1881 and rebandaged. In 1886 it was reopened (*Les Momies royales,* pp. 547 and 548) and the body was then said to have been coated with « a layer of whitish natron charged with human fat, greasy to the touch, foetid and strongly caustic » (see Mathey in Bulletin de l'Institut égyptien, 1886, p. 186). The investigations of Professor W. A. Schmidt (*Über Mumienfettsäuren,* Chemiker-Zeitung, 1908, n° 65) and my own experience of what has happened in the case of other mummies suggest that the whitish material in question was an efflorescence of fatty acids. « Towards the close of the XXth Dynasty », according to M. Maspero (*The Struggle of the Nations,* p. 289), the mummy of Thoutmosis III « was torn out of the coffin by robbers, who stripped it and rifled it of the jewels with which it was covered, injuring it in their haste to carry away the spoil. It was subsequently re-interred, * * ; but before reburial some renewal of the wrappings was necessary, and as portions of the body had become loose, the restorers, in order to give the mummy the necessary firmness, compressed it between four oar-shaped slips of wood, painted white (see *Les Momies royales*, pl. VI, A.), and placed three inside the wrappings and one outside, under the bands which confined the winding sheet. Happily the face, which had been plastered over with pitch [resin] at the time of embalming, did not suffer at all from this rough treatment, and appeared intact when the protecting mask was removed ».

In his *Procès-verbal de l'ouverture des Momies de Ramsès II et Ramsès III* (Bull. l'Inst. égypt., 1886, p. 264), M. Maspero gives us further information concerning this mummy : « Les gens qui les ont dépouillés respectaient si peu la majesté royale, qu'ils ont arraché le lobe de l'oreille avec la boucle; ou détaché à coups de hache ou de couteau les bracelets qui adhéraient trop étroitement à la peau. La momie de Thoutmosis III avait été cassée en trois morceaux ».

The head is broken off the body and all four limbs have been detached, the feet broken off, and each arm has been broken at the elbow into two fragments. By restoring the pieces to their original situations it was seen that the left forearm had been bent upward across the chest and the sharply flexed hand (thumb extended) was near the right shoulder. The right forearm was placed in front of the left and the fully extended hand was in front of the left shoulder. The precise identity of the arrangement of the hands and forearms in the cases of Thoutmosis II and Thoutmosis III shows that such posing must have some definite significance.

The right hand and forearm were tied to a piece of wood by means of a great mass of very fine linen (probably XXIst Dynasty). Probably the wrist was broken by the plunderers. The left hand is flexed in a position which suggests that it may have been grasping a cylindrical object 23 millimetres in diameter, such as the ceremonial whip, which the king is often represented as carrying in his left hand.

With Thoutmosis III the embalmers began a new custom in the selection of the site for the embalming-wound. Instead of a vertical incision extending upward from near the anterior superior spine of the ilium towards the ribs, as we have seen in all the mummies so far considered, an oblique cut was made (in the mummies of Thoutmosis III, Amenothes II and his family, Thoutmosis IV, Yuaa and Thuaa, and Amenothes III) from near the anterior superior spine obliquely downward and inward towards the pubes, following a course parallel to Poupart's ligament (see Diagram 3, p. 34).

In the XIXth and XXth Dynasties they kept to the same convention, although the wound was often enlarged upward so as to occupy part of the area which it involved before the time of Thoutmosis III (see Plates XLII and LV); but in the XXIst Dynasty a reaction occurred in respect of this, as also in so many other matters, and the embalmers returned to the infracostal region as the site of election for the embalming wound, as their early XVIIIth Dynasty forerunners were in the habit of doing.

In the case of Thoutmosis III the embalming wound extends obliquely across the abdomen roughly parallel to the left Poupart's ligament. Its anterior extremity is o m. o65 mill. from the symphysis pubis and its lateral extremity o m. o56 mill. vertically above the anterior superior spine of the left ilium. The incision is 11 centimetres long and it gapes 'to the extent of only one centimetre. Through it the cavity of the abdomen can be seen to be packed with a quantity of cloth impregnated with resinous material.

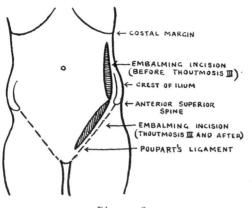

Diagram 3.

As in the case of several mummies of this particular period the pudenda seem to have been completely removed.

The skin of the whole mummy is blackened. Around the lower part of the abdomen and perineum and also around the shoulders it is studded with small projections, analogous to those seen in the cases of Thoutmosis II and Amenothes II.

The mummy of Thoutmosis III is 1 m. 615 mill. in height.

The cranium is of large capacity and of pentagonoid form. According to my measurements it is o m. 196 mill. long. and o m. 150 mill. broad; but Virchow gives o m. 193 mill. and o m. 151 mill. as the dimensions, and gives the auricular height as o m. 108 mill. to my o m. 106 mill. I quote his remarks concerning this mummy. «Thutmes III, der jüngere Bruder des vorigen [Thoutmosis II]. Obwohl derselbe erst nach einen langen Regierung sein Leben beschloss, so macht seine Mummie doch einen fast jugendlichen Eindruck. Auch sein Schädel ist mesocephal (Index 78.2) und mehr, als der seines Bruders, flach (Ohrhöhenindex 55.9). Alles an ihm hat ein mehr zartes Aussehen : die Ohren klein, die Lippen niedrig, die oberen zähne übergreifend, die unteren sehr hoch hinauftretend. Kinn gerundet und etwas zurücktretend, von sanftem Aussehen. Das Gesicht hoch und schmal, leptoprosop (Index 93.1), die Nase ungleich schmaler als die von Bruder und Urgrossvater (Index 60.0)», op. cit., p. 772.

The face is small, narrow and elliptical. The marked projection of the upper incisor teeth, which we have noted as a constant feature in this dynasty from the time of Ahmôsis I and his consort onwards, is associated in this mummy with a raising of the unworn edges of the lower incisors, only the anterior surfaces of which show any signs of wear.

Both nares are stuffed with a black resinous mass.

The nose, now badly damaged, was narrow, high-bridged and prominent, but not large.

If one restores the facial features of this damaged mummy a contour strikingly like the Deîr-el-Baharî portrait and the beautiful statue (n° 42053) described by M. Legrain (Statues et Statuettes, Cat. Gén., 1906, Plate XXX) will be obtained. The mouth is slightly opened and the lower lip is drawn outwards. The forehead is very low. The

small gracefully moulded ears have preserved their form. It is not possible to say
for certain whether the lobule is pierced; but in spite
of the appearance of Fig. 1 (Plate XXVIII) I have
been unable to convince myself that any real perforation is present (Diagram 4).

No trace of hair or beard can be found anywhere on the
head, excepting the eyebrows and a few very short
white hairs just behind the left ear. Thoutmosis III
was certainly almost completely bald.

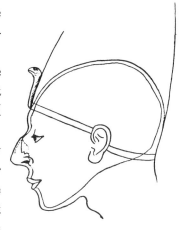

Diagram 4.

The plunderers, who did so much damage to this body
in their search for jewellry, did not complete their
work, for the remains of two strings of beads were
found on the front of each shoulder, not in direct
contact with the skin, but upon the inner most layers
of bandages. One string was composed of small cylin-
ders about one and a half millimetres in diameter with square margins : the other
of beads half the size and with rounded margins. The beads consisted of carnelian,
gold and lapis lazuli, in that order, in some places : in others of carnelian, gold
and green felspar.

OTHER MEASUREMENTS.

	VIRCHOW	DERRY and ELLIOT SMITH
Cranial circumference....	o m. 55o mill.	o m. 553 mill.
Total facial height	o 123	o 125
Upper „ „	o o86	o o8o
	(measured to lip)	(measured to maxilla)
Nasal height	o o55	o o6o
„ breadth	o o33	o o29

(The broken condition of the nose explains these discrepancies in the estimates — see Plate XXVIII.)

Bizygomatic breadth	o 132	o 13o
Bigonial breadth	o o95	o o95
Minimal frontal breadth ...	o o91	o o89
Chin to vertex (projection).	—	o 19o
Chin to hair margin......	o 183	—
Right Orbit...........		o m. o44 mill. × o m o33 mill.
Left Orbit		o m. o42 mill. × o m. o36 mill.

The left auditory pinna measures o m. o53 mill. × o m. o3o mill., and the right
o m. o54 mill. × o m. o3o mill. Virchow simply gives the length measurement
as o m. o53 mill.

Oblique length of left humerus.....................	o m. 34o mill.
Estimated length of left radius	o 255
Maximum length of hand (including carpus)	o 193

5.

Upon the lateral aspects of the cranium there are large triangular depressions due to atrophy of the outer surfaces of the parietal bones. Such depressions are of common occurrence in crania of the ancient Egyptian aristocracy. I have suggested by way of explanation that the constant wearing of heavy wigs or other headgear may be the cause (*The Causation of the Symmetrical Thinning of the Parietal Bones in Ancient Egyptians,* Journal of Anatomy and Physiology, volume XLI, 1907).

61069. The Mummy of Amenothes II (in his tomb at Bibân el Molouk).

The tomb of Amenothes II was opened by M. Loret in 1898 (*Les tombeaux de Thothmès III et d'Aménophis II,* dans le *Bulletin de l'Institut égyptien,* 3ᵉ série, nᵒ 9 (année 1898), p. 91-112, pl. I-XIV) and the mummies of that Pharaoh and four others were left in the tomb, while those of Thoutmosis IV, Amenothes III, Siphtah, Seti II, Ramses IV; Ramses V, Ramses VI and an unknown woman lodged in the lid of the coffin of Setnakhiti (and, until unwrapped, supposed to be that Pharaoh) were removed to the Cairo Museum in 1902 by M. Maspero.

In the year 1902, M. Maspero removed some of the wrappings from the mummy of Amenothes II and described the condition of the mummy at that time in a report appended to Mr. Howard Carter's account of the robbery that took place in Amenothes II's tomb in that year. (*Procès-verbal d'examen du corps du Pharaon Aménothès II,* dans les *Annales du Service des Antiquités de l'Égypte,* t. III, 1902, p. 120-121, pl. I et II).

With M. Maspero's permission, in 1907 I made a hasty examination of four of the five mummies left in the tomb. Mr. A. E. Weigall, the Chief Inspector of Antiquities for Upper Egypt, was present and helped me in the task; but as I was able to spend only one day in the Bibân el Molouk, I devoted the whole of my attention to the four complete mummies, and did not look at the damaged remains of the «Momie dans une barque» of M. Loret's account.

The general appearance of the mummy of Amenothes II is already well known from the excellent photographs made under Mr. Howard Carter's supervision to illustrate M. Maspero's procès-verbal, already quoted. The body is that of a man 1 m. 673 mill. in height. So that Amenothes II was taller than his father, Thoutmosis III (1 m. 615 mill.) and his son Thoutmosis IV (1 m. 646 mill.). He has wavy, brown hair (when straightened 0 m. 17 cent. long.) like that of his son and successor Thoutmosis IV; but, unlike the latter's, it is abundantly interspersed with white hair; and there is a large patch of baldness over the upper occipital and parietal regions. These facts, together with the evidence of the well-worn teeth, indicate that Amenothes II was a much older man than Thoutmosis IV. There are however, no data to enable us to estimate with any precision the age Amenothes II had reached; but from his general appearance he was probably somewhere between forty and fifty years old at the time of his death.

There is a most striking resemblance in face and cranial form between Amenothes II and Thoutmosis IV, in spite of the fact that the general appearance of strength and decision of character in the face of the former are in marked contrast to the effeminate weakness of the latter. The shape of the head, with its curious sloping forehead and slender but prominent nose, is identical in these two pharaohs.

On various parts of the body, and especially the legs, there are gashes produced by the axes of plunderers when chopping through the wrappings.

The well-worn teeth are in a good state of preservation. In this respect they present a marked contrast to those of his grandson, Amenothes III, which are badly affected with dental caries, leading to alveolar abscesses, which had riddled the jaws.

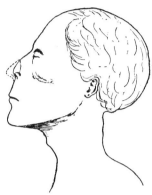

Diagram 5.

Like all other known adult Egyptian men Amenothes II was circumcised.

His arms were in the position customary in the mummies of kings of the XVIIIth (after Thoutmosis Ist) XIXth and XXth dynasties, i. e. the upper arms were placed vertically at the sides and the forearms were crossed over the chest, but in a much lower situation than usual.

The right forearm is placed in front of the left and is almost horizontal : the right hand is tightly clenched, with the thumb extended : unlike most of the royal mummies of this period Amenothes II had no staff in his right hand and in his left there was no room for anything of a larger diameter than a common lead-pencil; and there is no sign of even this space having been occupied by any object. The fingers of the left hand were not clenched so tightly as those of the right hand.

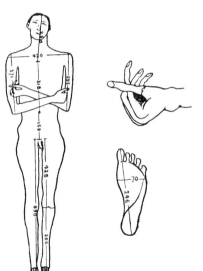

Diagram 6.

The skin over the whole body is thickly studded with small projections or tubercles varying from o m. oo2 mill. to o m. oo8 mill. in diameter. At present I am unable to determine whether they are the results of some disease or merely the effects of the embalmer's salt-bath, but they are certainly unusual.

In Mr. Howard Carter's photographs (*op. cit. supra*) several pieces of resin-soaked linen will be seen

Diagram 7.

adhering to the nose and mouth and hiding the features of the face. As these fragments served no useful purpose and interfered with a view of Amenothes' countenance I removed them on October 19th, 1907.

In the resin covering the fifth dorsal spine there is the distinct impression of a series of beads arranged in the pattern of the well-known pectoral ornament (Diagram 7).

On the back of the sacrum there was a geometrical pattern (Diagram 8) impressed on the resin. There is no trace whatsoever of the objects which produced these imprints on the surface.

The pudenda were pushed in against the perineum and embedded in a great mass of resinous paste, which was spread over the whole perineal region.

Diagram 8.

The following figures will give some idea of the proportions of the head.

Maximum length of head	191 mill.
Maximum breadth of head (with hair)	144
Minimum frontal breadth	90
Auricular height	121
Circumference	538
Bizygomatic breadth	134
Total facial height	124
Upper facial height	75
Nasal height	58
Nasal breadth	31
Space between inner canthi	31
Left orbit	47 × 39.5
Right orbit	47 × 41
Bigonial breadth	100

During my visit to Bibân el Molouk there was not time to obtain photographs of Amenothes II, but Mr Weigall and I made rough sketches; and from these and Mr Howard Carter's photographs (*Annales, op. cit. supra,* Pl. 11) I have drawn Diagrams 5, 6, 7 and 8. The nose of the mummy is now flattened. In the diagram I have indicated by dotted lines its probable contour before flattening.

61070. The Elder Woman in the Tomb of Amenothes II (pl. XCVII).

The general appearance of the three mummies found in room III by M. Loret has been very accurately and realistically shown in the excellent drawing by M. Félix Guilmant (*Les tombeaux de Thothmès III et d'Aménophis II,* dans le *Bulletin de l'Institut égyptien,* 3e série, n° 9 année 1898 pl. XI). The heads of these three mummies are represented in the photographs (pl. XII, XIII and XIV) in the same work.

The first mummy (M. Loret's memoir, *op. cit.,* p. 103; also pl. XII) is a small (1 m. 455 mill.) middle-aged woman with long (0 m. 30 cent.), brown, wavy, lustrous hair, parted in the centre and falling down on both sides of the head on to the shoulders. Its ends are converted into numerous apparently natural curls. Her teeth are well-worn but otherwise healthy. The sternum is completely ankylosed. She has no grey hair.

She has small pointed features.

The right arm is placed vertically-extended at the side and the palm of the hand is placed flat upon the right thigh. The left hand was tightly clenched, but with the thumb fully extended : it is placed in front of the manubrium sterni, the forearm being sharply flexed upon the brachium.

On the under surface of the left heel there is an elliptical ulcer (o m. 022 mill. × o m. 012 mill.) with indurated edges, and on the inner surface of the same heel a much larger ulcer (o m. 044 mill. in diameter) of the same nature. These wounds have all the appearance of ante-mortem injuries with inflammatory reaction around the edges. It is possible, however, that if they were done immediately after death the action of the salt bath on the cut edges may have given rise to the appearance presented by these ulcers. In some other mummies of women I have found the skin cut away from the heel. If these ulcers were not ante-mortem they were certainly done before the embalming-process was completed, because the linen is packed into them and is adherent to the bone.

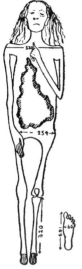

The whole of the front of the abdomen and part of the thorax is broken away, as the result of the plunderer's work.

As in the mummy of Amenothes II the perineum was thickly plast-ered with resin in the form of a large cake.

The rima pudendi is widely open and is stuffed with linen from the inside (from the pelvis). The resinous paste was applied to the surface of this linen plug and to the skin-areas surrounding it.

The cranial length is o m. 177 mill.; cranial breadth, o m. 135 mill.; minimal frontal breadth, o m. 091 mill.; auricular height, o m. 114 mill.; total facial height, o m. 107 mill.; upper facial height, o m. 062 mill.; bizygomatic breadth, o m. 121 mill.; bigonial breadth, o m. 087 mill.; nasal height and breadth (alar), o m. 050 mill. by o m. 027 mill., right orbit, o m. 042 × o m. 031 and left orbit, o m. 039 × o m. 031.

Diagram 9.

61071. The Mummy of the Boy in the Tomb of Amenothes II, probably the Royal Prince Ouabkhousenou (pl. XCVIII).

The second mummy, described by M. Loret (op. cit., p. 103) as « celui d'un enfant d'une quinzaine d'années » is a small boy (1 m. 242 mill.) whose general appear-ance is suggestive of an age of about nine or ten years : but as permanent canine teeth are present and fully grown he cannot be less than eleven years of age (see Loret, pl. XII).

Although M. Loret distinctly refers to this mummy as that of a prince certain writers have called it the body of a girl. The hair has been shaved from the greater part of this boy's scalp : but on the right side of his head (corresponding roughly to the extent of the right parietal bone) the hair has not been cut and forms a great, long, wavy, lustrous mass (o m. 275 mill. long), which from the nature of its waviness was probably plaited at some time (see Loret's pl. XIII).

It is particularly interesting to note that this boy of eleven years of age, who still wears the Horus-lock of hair, is *not* circumcised. His ears are pierced.

Both hands are placed in front of the pudenda (see Loret's pl. XI) : the left hand is flexed, but the thumb is extended; and the right hand is fully extended, with the exception of the small finger, which is flexed.

The chief damage done by the plunderers consists of a large gash in the left side of the neck and thorax, smashing away the greater part of the left clavicle, the gladiolus and half of the manubrium sterni. There is also a large oval hole (o m. 07 cent. × o m. o1 cent.) in the right side of the frontal bone.

When the embalmers were opening the cranial cavity by means of an instrument passed up through the nose the aperture was made not through the ethmoid but through the sphenoid into the sella turcica. The mass of brain and resin in the cranial cavity forms a perfect mould of the occipital fossae and the groove for the superior longitudinal sinus turning into the right lateral sinus.

The head of this boy is beloid, its length o m. 182 mill., its breadth o m. 147 mill. and its minimum frontal diameter o m. 091 mill.

The material obtained from the cranial cavity of this mummy has been analysed by Mr. A. Lucas (*Preservative Materials used by the Ancient Egyptians in Embalming*, Survey Department Paper, n° 12, 1911, p. 13).

This boy presents an extraordinary likeness to a beautiful statue of the god Khonsou, discovered at Karnak, which has been described by M. Maspero in the *Annales du Service*, t. III, p. 181. Not only does the god wear a Horus-lock like that of this prince, but the statue is characterised also by his exceptional brachycephalism.

In view of the evidence for the relationship of this boy to Amenothes II (*vide infra*), it is of interest to note that there were found in the tomb «statuettes en bois du roi et de plusieurs divinités, *Répondants* au nom d'Aménôthès II et d'un prince royal Ouabkhousenou» (*Guide du Visiteur*).

61072. The Mummy of the Younger Woman in the Tomb of Amenothes II (pl. XCIX).

The examination of this mummy yielded the most surprising results, because M. Loret had described it as a man's body, whereas it requires no great knowledge of anatomy to decide that the excellently preserved naked body (Loret's pl. XI and XIV) is a young woman's. Every later writer has followed Loret in his description of this mummy as a man. The only reason I can assign for such a curious and obvious mistake is the absence of hair on the head. All the hair had been clipped very short or shaved.

The mummy is a young woman (1 m. 580 mill. in height), less than 25 years of age. As it is not possible to examine the epiphyses without damaging the mummy, the exact age cannot be determined. [In the remote Bibân el Molouk, it is hardly feasible to examine the body with the x-rays.] Judging from the condition of the iliac bones and the fact that the third molar teeth are not erupted, the above

estimate has been made. The embalming wound is a large gaping oval opening
(o m. 145 mill. × o m. 056 mill.) placed alongside Poupart's ligament in the same
situation as those of Amenothes II, Thoutmosis IV and Amenothes III. As in these
mummies the abdomen was stuffed with balls of linen soaked in a solution of resin.
As in the other mummies left in this tomb a large mass of resin was spread over the
whole perineum. Both in this mummy and in the other woman (n° 61070) the
rima pudendi was widely open and plugged from the inside with linen, on the
surface of which the perineal mass of resin was smeared.

In this mummy (as also in another mummy said to be contemporaneous with
     Amenothes II, which Mr. Weigall permitted me to examine) the diaphragm had
     not been removed : but a small aperture had been made in it opposite each side of
     the thorax for the purpose of removing the lungs, the heart and the mediastina
     being left intact. Only the abdominal cavity was packed with linen (soaked in resi-
     nous solution), but great buttons of linen projected upwards into the thorax through
     the apertures in the diaphragm.

Two small perforations are found in the lobule of the left ear. The right ear is broken.

The tomb-robbers smashed the anterior wall of the chest, leaving a large gaping
     wound in which the upper surface of the diaphragm is seen. The heart and peri-
     cardium have shrunk into the form of a vertical septum in the chest cavity. The
     left side of the mouth and cheek, including the corresponding parts of the jaws,
     was also broken away.

An oval opening (o m. 038 × o m. 030) was made in the frontal bone just in front
     of the coronal suture. The right arm was torn off just below the
     shoulder. In my notes, hurriedly made during my short visit to the
     tomb of Amenothes II, I find no further reference to this arm : but
     these remarks occur, «hands in front of thighs», and «along with
     these three mummies there is the well-preserved right forearm of a
     woman, which had been flexed at the elbow», and «the hand was
     clasped».

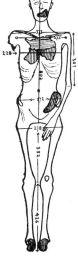

The technique of embalming displayed in this mummy and the other
     two (n°ˢ 61070 and 61071) associated with it is precisely similar
     to that of Amenothes II. There can be no doubt that these individuals
     were contemporaries of his; and as they were placed in his tomb,
     the obvious presumption is that they were royal personages and
     members of his family.

The face of the elder woman (n° 61070) presents an undoubted like-
     ness to Nofritari; and the younger woman (n° 61072) has the
     projection of the alveolar process of the upper jaw, which is such

Diagram 10.

a constant and distinctive trait of the royal family of the XVIIIth Dynasty.

The features of the boy present a considerable likeness to the beautiful portrait-statue
     (n° 42073) of Amenothes II in his youth (see M. Legrain's *Statues et statuettes de
     Rois et de Particuliers,* Catalogue général, 1906, pl. XLIII). The natural assumption
     is that this prince is the son of Amenothes II.

In the accompanying text-figure the proportions of the body are shown in a drawing made to scale : pubes to vertex, o m. 802 mill.; pubes to sole, o m. 778 mill.; thigh (from pubes to lower end of femur) being o m. 352 mill., and the rest of the leg, o m. 426 mill; bihumeral diameter, o m. 373 mill.; bicoracoid diameter, o m. 275 mill.; transverse diameter of thorax, o m. 228 mill.; bi-iliac diameter, o m. 272 mill.; bitrochanteric diameter, o m. 278 mill.; shoulder to elbow, o m. 307 mill.; suprasternal notch to vertex, o m. 275 mill.; and chin to vertex, o m. 200 mill.

The cranium is beloid in form, o m. 176 mill. in length, and o m. 141 mill. in breadth, the minimal frontal breadth is o m. 094 mill.; auricular height, o m. 112 mill.; circumference o m. 500 mill.; total facial height, o m. 119 mill.; upper facial height, o m. 073; bizygomatic diameter, o m. 122 mill.; bigonial diameter, o m. 097 mill.; and nasal height and breadth, o m. 056 mill. and o m. 025 mill.

61073. The Mummy of Thoutmosis IV (pl. XXIX and XXX).

M. Daressy's procès-verbal of the unwrapping of this mummy, is published in the *Annales du Service;* I quote in his own words.

« Le 26 mars 1903, à deux heures de l'après-midi, dans une des salles du Musée des antiquités égyptiennes au Caire, par les soins de M. Maspero, directeur général des Musées égyptiens et du Service des Fouilles, de M. É. Brugsch bey, conservateur du Musée et M. Daressy, conservateur adjoint, il a été procédé à l'ouverture de la momie du roi Thoutmôsis IV.

« La momie avait été extraite de son cercueil, peint en blanc et portant sur le devant l'inscription [hieroglyphs], découvert par M. Loret, en 1898, dans le tombeau d'Aménôthès II à Biban el Molouk, et apporté en 1900 au Musée du Caire, où il est inscrit sous le n° 34559.

« Le corps reposait sur une planche peinte en blanc des deux côtés, provenant évidemment d'un grand coffre rectangulaire et dont les angles avaient été coupés de manière à pouvoir entrer dans la cuve.

« La longueur de la momie emmaillotée était de 1 m. 71 cent., elle était entièrement recouverte d'un grand linceul en toile jaunie, pliée en deux, noué sous les pieds. Sur la poitrine le cartouche-prénom du Pharaon était tracé en grands signes hiératiques à l'encre bleue, qui se transcrivent [cartouche]. La partie supérieure du linceul était maintenue par une large bandelette qui entourait le front et passait du cou au buste en croisant sur le haut de la poitrine. Le linceul ne faisait pas corps avec le maillot et était tendu de la poitrine aux pieds, laissant un vide au-dessus des jambes.

« Ensuite on trouva un réseau de bandelettes, mélangé de petites compresses de linge froissé, représentant quatre ou cinq épaisseurs, puis on rencontra un suaire enveloppant incomplètement le corps, les bords en avant étant éloignés d'environ huit centimètres, mais relié par un cordon composé de petits morceaux de toile noués bout à bout, passant cinq fois d'une lisière à l'autre à travers des trous pratiqués irrégulièrement. Immédiatement au-dessous une serviette teinte en rose couvrait le buste, un grand linge le reste du corps, puis recommençait une série de bandelettes et de tampons d'étoffe; tout ce linge était de grosseur moyenne, jauni, taché ou brûlé par le bitume.

« La tête était maintenue par un fort lien de toile tordue, allant entourer le haut des bras. On ne rencontra ni couche de bitume, ni poudres absorbantes, ni aucun objet.

« Enfin le corps apparut, en bon état sauf les pieds qui sont désarticulés. Les bras sont croisés sur la poitrine; les mains fermées tenaient probablement des emblèmes qui ont disparu. La peau a été noircie par le bitume. Il est évident que nous n'avions pas l'emmaillotement primitif, et que l'appareil funéraire avait été refait par les prêtres chargés de la surveillance des tombes royales longtemps après l'ensevelissement et sans beaucoup de soins. La tête est belle et expressive; les dents ne sont pas visibles, mais s'il fallait en juger par l'aspect général, on serait tenté de croire que le roi avait une trentaine d'années. C'est là toutefois un critérium trop incertain pour qu'il faille s'y fier. La longueur de la momie est de 1 m. 68 cent., ce chiffre est trop fort et il ne donne pas la taille réelle du Pharaon, les jambes ayant été brisées, ainsi qu'il a été dit plus haut. L'examen médical pourra seul donner une évaluation exacte. »

The body is that of an extremely emaciated man, 1 m. 646 in height. It shows no sign of any ante-mortem injuries.

Both feet have been broken off at some time, long after the body was embalmed; and the right leg was broken off at the knee joint. A transverse abrasion on the front of the neck may have been produced at the same time as these other injuries. For surposes of embalming the abdominal wall had been removed in the whole of the left iliac and part of the hypogastric regions, leaving a large triangular opening measuring o m. 5o cent. transversely, o m. 1o cent. in the vertical direction and o m. 14 cent. along the third margin, which was parallel to and just above Poupart's ligament. The whole abdominal cavity was tightly packed with cloth saturated with resinous material, which formed a very hard solid mass.

The body was lying in a fully-extended position. The shoulders were slightly raised : the upper arms were placed vertically, and the forearms were crossed on the front of the chest, the right arm being in front of the left. The hands were flexed in such a manner that they must (at the time of embalming) have been grasping vertical rods, each about o m. 15 mill. diameter.

The skin is very dark and discoloured, so that it is not possible to form any accurate idea of its original colour.

The head has a very effeminate appearance. The face is long, narrow and oval, the chin being narrow, prominent and somewhat pointed. The forehead has a marked slope. The nose is small and straight, and narrow and aquiline in shape. The lips are thin. In norma verticalis the head presents the form called «beloides ægyptiacus» by Sergi. The ears are well-moulded, with free lobules, which are pierced.

The hair of the head is wavy, about o m. 16 cent. long, and is of a dark reddish-brown (henna-colour) tint : it has the appearance of having been parted in front slightly to the left of the middle line, but elsewhere is matted together in a hopeless tangle of thick locks. Examined microscopically, the hair was found to be dark brown, and its surface was studded with masses of dark foreign matter (embalming material).

The eye-brows were moderately thick, and met across the middle line, by means of a thinner group of hairs on the bridge of the nose.

The moustache and beard were closely shaved. It was possible to recognize the cut ends of a fairly thick moustache, which was most dense at the angles of the mouth. There was also a thick patch of hair in front of and coextensive with the auditory pinna; but over the masseteric and buccal regions the hair was very scanty. It was impossible to find any trace of hair on the polished chin or on the lower lip : nor was any hair visible on the neck. Neither on the limbs, thorax, nor on the pubic area could any hair be detected.

All parts of the surface of the body were well-preserved, including the genital organs, which appear to have been circumcised.

As the body had every appearance of being that of a young man, a careful examination of the left ilium (which was exposed in the embalming-incision) and the upper end of the tibia (exposed in the broken right leg) was made, and other parts of the body were examined by means of the Röntgen-rays. It was found that the epiphysis of the crest of the ilium was in process of union, being united in front but still free behind. This seemed to indicate that the body was that of a man of not more than 25 years, if we accept the statements current in most of the text-books of Anatomy. But certain authors put no such limit on the obliteration of the groove between the epiphysis cristae and the rest of the bone. Thus in Piersol's *Human Anatomy,* which was published three years after (in 1907) my report on this mummy was written, the following statement occurs : — «they [the secondary centres of ossification of the innominate bone] are fused at twenty, excepting perhaps, that for the crest of the ilium, the union of which may be delayed; the suture marking its presence is one of the last in the body to disappear» (p. 337).

The innominate bone of the mummy supposed to be Amenothes IV (see Diagram 11) is in precisely the same state as that of Thoutmosis IV; and all the reservations I have made in the discussion of the question of his age (*vide infra*) apply with at least as much force to the case of Thoutmosis IV.

But during the eight years that have elapsed since I examined this mummy, and, on the assumption that the data given in all the text-books of Anatomy in reference to this matter were reliable, estimated his age as 25 years, I have examined the epiphysis of the iliac crest in several thousands of Egyptian skeletons. In the course of this investigation I have discovered that in the Ancient Egyptians it was no uncommon event for the union of the posterior end of the epiphysis cristae to be delayed; and that the corresponding part of the sulcus often persisted well on into middle age. Hence at the present moment I feel much less certain of the youth of Thoutmosis IV than I did in 1903 before I had learned to distrust the data given so positively in treatises on Anatomy.

In the skiagrams of this mummy, that were taken by Dr. Khayat in 1903, the epiphysis of the vertebral border of the scapula appears to be separate. One cannot decide a question of this kind on the impression of a somewhat hazy shadow : but so far as it goes appearances support the low estimate of age, even if we accept Testut's date for the union of this epiphysis (*vide infra* in the report on Amenothes IV), and thereby extend the limit to 28 years. Judging from the texture of the bones as revealed by the *X*-rays one would be inclined to admit that Thoutmosis IV might possibly have been even older than this.

When a small quantity of resinous material was scraped away eight of the upper teeth were exposed. They are unworn, white and in excellent condition. None of the lower teeth are visible, and it is clear that the upper incisors projected beyond the lower teeth, as we have seen to be the case in almost every member of the royal family, male and female, throughout the XVIIIth Dynasty.

Thoutmosis IV presents a striking resemblance to Amenothes II, but the latter had a more virile appearance and was considerably older.

In my reconstruction of the face of the latter (Diagram 5) I may have unduly exaggerated the prominence of the nose. Perhaps his face bore an even stronger likeness to the refined outlines of Thoutmosis IV[ths] features than my crude sketch suggests.

	Metre	mill.
Height of body	1	646
Height of chin	1	452
Height of shoulders	1	410
Height of suprasternal notch	1	340
Height of umbilicus	1	040
Maximum length of head } cephalic index 77,07	0	184
Maximum breadth of head }	0	143
Maximum frontal breadth	0	095
Circumference of head	0	537
Length of nose	0	055
Breadth of nose	0	029

Vertical projections :

Vertex to root of nose	0	077
Vertex to mouth	0	145
Vertex to chin	0	185
Vertex to tragus	0	111
Chin to glabella	0	121
Upper lip to glabella	0	083.5
Biauricular breadth	0	130
Bizygomatic breadth	0	130

Diameters of face :

External orbital breadth	0	097.5
Internal orbital breadth (only roughly)	0	028.5

	Metre	mill.
Bigonial breadth...	0	102
Ear (pinna) [left better preserved] Maximum length...........*r.* 0 m. 052 mill., *l.*	0	052
Maximum breadth.........*r.* 0 m. 024 mill., *l.*	0	030
Biorbito-nasal arc..	0	113
Breadth of shoulders...	0	382
Breadth of hips..	0	270
Breadth at iliac crests	0	265
Breadth between anterior iliac spines...........................	0	200
Axial length of right tibia......................................	0	376
Length (with malleolus) of right tibia.........................	0	386
Length from prominence of great trochanter to external condyle (right femur)...	0	440

Right arm :

Length from tip of acromion to external condyle of humerus.....	0	358
Length from tip of acromion to olecranon......................	0	363.5
Length from external condyle to radial styloid.................	0	277

Length of foot 0 m. 022 mill. 2, maximum breadth 0 m. 067 mill.; first and second toes same length.

In deleting the background in the photograph from which Plate XXIX was made the engraver has left a large black mass on the postero-inferior aspect of the head, which makes it look more effeminate than is really the case, because the black area looks like a chignon of hair.

61074. The Mummy of Amenothes III (pl. XXXI, XXXII, XXXIII, XXXIV, XXXV, C, CI, CII and CIII).

This is one of the mummies discovered in 1898, by M. Loret, in the tomb of Amenothes II. It was contained in a coffin upon the lid of which the king's name was painted (pl. XXXI), as well as records of inspections of the mummy in the reigns of the priest-kings. Upon the shroud (as well as the bandages surrounding the mummy) there is a long hieratic inscription in ink written vertically. It is shown in plate XXXII, in situ on the mummy in fig. 1, and on a larger scale in fig. 2 (which has been printed upside down); and various parts of the inscription are reproduced upon a still larger scale in plates C, CI, CII and CIII. With the assistance of Dr. Maynard Pain I removed the wrappings from this mummy on September 23rd, 1905.

There were some fragments of broken garlands lying upon the mummy. Two of these can be seen in fig. 1 (pl. XXXII) lying on the left side of the neck, and another a little above the midpoint of the left side of the body.

There were six bands encircling the body and holding in position the shroud. Upon the latter, as well as on the retaining bandages, an inscription had been made in ink after the process of wrapping the mummy was completed. The inscription extends longitudinally. It is seen in situ in fig. 1, plate XXXII, and on a larger scale in fig. 2. In order to obtain the latter, sharply-focussed reproduction of the writing, I pinned on to the shroud those parts of the circular bandages that were inscribed and then cut out the whole of the inscription, and pinned the sheet of linen upon a flat board. The photograph is reproduced as fig. 2, which unfortunately is shown upside down. In plates C, CI, CII and CIII, the writing is shown upon a still larger scale.

Underneath the shroud there was a longitudinal strip of very soft bandage which extended the whole length of the body. Beneath this a small sheet was wrapped around the upper three-fourths of the body, and was tied to the last mentioned bandage behind the head.

A bandage starting on the left side of the foot was wound in a circular manner around the ankles, and then spirally up the legs, where its end was intertwined with, but not tied to, another bandage, which continued the spiral course upward as far as the pelvis. A bandage, starting at the back of the neck, passed twice around the head, and then obliquely across the chest to the right hip, across the back to the left hip and then obliquely upward in front to end on the right shoulder.

A tasseled bandage, beginning at the right hip, passed circularly around the hips and abdomen to end in front of the chest, where a similar strip began and invested the thorax and shoulders.

The next to be removed began on the right hip and passed around the pelvis and thighs, where another bandage began and passed spirally down the legs as far as the ankles.

The next began behind the left shoulder, passed once around the shoulders and then behind the neck, where its end was intertwined with the end of a bandage, which was wound spirally around the head and ended upon the right side of the face. There another bandage began and passed spirally around the head in the opposite direction to end on the back of the head, where another began and passed around the head and shoulders to end in front of the right shoulder.

The next bandage began upon the right side of the head and passed around the head, its end being intertwined, in front of the face, with another bandage wound around the head.

The next two bandages encircled the head, the deeper one being intertwined with the end of a large sheet, upon which the body had been laid and the sides of the sheet pulled up in front of the body, where however they did not meet. The ends were collected into bunches, above the head and below the feet respectively, where they were tied with strings of bandage.

Beneath this sheet there was a ragged bandage of soft muslin wound in a loose spiral around the body from the head to the hips. Then there was a loose sheet of cloth wrapped once round the middle of the body; and a sheet of linen, with squares marked upon it in red ink, was found placed in front of the legs.

Then another bandage wound around the legs spirally down to the feet and then back again beyond the knees. There were pieces of pebble in this bandage.

Then a narrow strip of bandage tied around the feet held in position a large sheet, folded many times and investing the whole body.

Under it was another sheet, folded many times, covering the front of the body, exclusive of the head and feet.

Then a number of rolls of bandage were found in front of the body, apparently left there inadvertently.

Then there were two spirally-wound bandages surrounding the body from hips to shoulders, held in position by a loosely-applied figure-of-8 bandage around the chest and shoulders. Then there was another figure-of-8 bandage around hips and shoulders, underneath some of the folds of which there were some loose cloths, pads of linen and fragments of black resinous material containing scraps of bone, no doubt parts of the mummy.

Then two bandages, wound spirally around the head, were removed; and another from the legs.

Then a large sheet spread in front of the body was exposed : and under it a folded sheet in front of the head and another covering the front of the body, held in position by a bandage around the feet and ankles.

A circular bandage passing around thorax, abdomen and hips, held in position two inscribed cloths, one a torn sheet with hieroglyphs in black ink and red lines, and another with red lines only.

A bandage wound spirally around the head and neck bore a hieratic inscription in black ink.

A sheet of cloth saturated with some gum-like material was placed in front of the face.

A large sheet placed in front of the body was held in position, below by a bandage around the ankles, above by being gummed to deeper-lying wrappings.

Linen pads on the feet were fixed in position by means of a figure-of-8 bandage around the ankles and feet.

A bandage, beginning on the front of the hips, passed spirally around the thighs and lower part of the abdomen, and then vertically up the left side over the head to the right shoulder (where it was overlapped by a turn of the bandage described next but one after this), and then described two figures-of-8 around shoulders and chest.

A bandage wound spirally around thighs and legs was then removed : and then a brittle, gum-saturated spirally-wound bandage was unwound from the head, neck and thorax.

Then was exposed a longitudinal sheet of cloth extending from the feet to the face. Its lower end was split, one half passing on each side of the feet, below which they were intertwined. The upper end of this bandage was also split, one half passing on each side of the head; and the two were tied above the head, thus fixing it in position, for it had been broken off the body by the tomb-robbers.

Another bandage spirally wound around the legs was then removed and the remains of the mummy itself were exposed. In front of the feet was a large roller bandage, which had been used as a pad to take the place of the missing toes. Part of this bandage (the roller) was wound around the ankles which served to hold the unrolled part in position.

Numerous short bandages of varied textures and loose scraps of linen were scattered in front of the body.

[In this account I have been describing the bandages as I took them off, i. e., those

that were applied last were described first, and of course I *began* the unrolling of a
bandage where the bandager *finished*.]

When the body was eventually exposed (pl. XXXIII) it was found to have been most
severely damaged by the ancient grave-robbers.

The head was broken off (pl. XXXIV and XXXV); and practically all the soft tissues of
the head were gone with the exception of the part of the scalp that lies behind the
coronal suture. Almost the whole of the front wall of the body is missing and the
back is broken across the loins.

The right leg is broken away from the trunk and the thigh is separated from the rest
of the leg. All of the right metatarsal and phalangeal bones and the distal row of
phalanges of the left foot are missing (pl. XXXIII).

The broken fragments of the body were held together by means of three bandages tied
around them. Among the lumps of resin-impregnated linen inside the body-cavity
were found the leg bone of a fowl and another bird's limb bone, a human great toe,
and a left ulnar and radius.

The bird-bones were obviously parts of mummified food-offerings such as were found
in most royal tombs of this period.

Although it was a great disappointment to find only these broken and blackened bones
to represent the body of Amenothes «the Magnificent», the study of the remains
revealed certain facts of singular interest to the student of the history of embalming.

For the attempt had been made to restore to the limbs and body of the dead Pharaoh
some semblance of the form these parts had possessed in life, but had lost during
the earlier stages of the process of mummification. This was accomplished by stuffing
under the skin of the legs, arms, neck, and perhaps other parts of the body, a
resinous mass, which was moulded into form; so that when it set, the members of
the mummy consisted of masses of stony hardness with a covering of skin.

Precisely how the packing material was inserted under the skin in the case of Amenothes III is unknown; but if we study the analogous process of packing that was
revived three dynasties later (*vide infra*) we shall obtain very precise information as
to how it was done in the times of the XXIst and XXIInd dynasties, and how it *may*
have been done in the case of Amenothes III.

A sample of the packing material taken from Amenothes' left arm was examined by
Mr. A. Lucas, Director of the Government Analytical Laboratory in Cairo. He found
it to consist of resin mixed with 14.3 o/o of inorganic matter, of which 7.5 o/o
consisted of a mixture of the carbonate, sulphate and chloride of sodium, *i. e.*, crude
Egyptian «natron».

Resinous material such as this is not known to have been employed at any other period
for packing underneath the skin. In the time of the XXIst-XXIInd dynasties; linen,
mud, sand, sawdust or cheese-like substances (mixtures of fat and soda) were the
stuffing materials employed.

In no mummy earlier than that of Amenothes III is there any evidence to indicate, or
even to suggest, that any such curious procedure was put into practice; and as I
have examined the mummies, not only of Amenothes' immediate predecessors, but

also of his wife's parents, Yuaa and Thuaa, without finding any trace of stuffing in the limbs, it is safe to conclude that this addition to the embalmers' technique was invented at or near the close of the reign of Amenothes III, when the spirit of change was rife in Thebes, and the old conventions in the Arts, as well as in worship, were being overthrown. Whether or not the bodies of the XVIIIth dynasty successors of Amenothes III were submitted to this strange process of packing it is now impossible to say, because nothing but skeletons of same of them have come down to us. But we do know that none of the Royal Mummies of the XIXth and XXth dynasties were so treated : and it was not until the close of the XXth or the beginning of the XXIst dynasties that the practice was revived, and became part of the regular routine of mummification during the XXIst and XXIInd dynasties.

It is of some historical interest to note that this striking innovation must necessarily have been put into practice during the first *days* of the reign of Amenothes IV, thereby suggesting that the spirit of reform was already operating, and that its inspiration may have been Tìyi or even Amenothes III, rather than their erratic son.

This stuffing of material under the skin must not be confused with the process of packing the cavity of the body, which always formed part of the process of embalming from the time of the Ancient Empire until Roman times.

Amenothes III was almost completely bald, having only scanty hair on the temples. The temporal parts of the coronal suture were obliterated. The teeth however were worn only to a moderate degree. On the right side, though not on the left (pl. XXXIV), the teeth of both upper and lower jaws were thickly encrusted with tartar : and there had been an extensive alveolar abscess below the right lower incisors, and a smaller one above the right upper canine. The upper incisor teeth had been lost before the death of Amenothes and the alveolar process absorbed in part : the right upper lateral incisor had been recently lost, for its alveolus and the perforation (facial) of a small alveolar abscess are still present (pl. XXXV). There is also evidence of suppuration around the anterior lateral root of the left, lower, first molar. [All of these points can be verified by examining plates XXXIV and XXXV with a hand-lens]. The cavity of the mouth is still occupied by a large mass of resin, in which is embedded the left, lower, median incisor, which must have fallen out of its socket after the body was embalmed (pl. XXXV).

During the last years of his life Amenothes III must have suffered most acutely from tooth-ache and dental abscesses.

It is not possible to form any precise estimate of the king's age from the data available. Whether he was nearer forty or fifty years must remain an open question. The skull is large and pentagonoid, with moderate superciliary ridges and a fairly prominent occiput. The face is a long, narrow, ovoid, or, when the resin stuffing of the cheeks is taken into account (see pl. XXXV), ellipsoid : the orbits are small and slightly oblique : the nasal skeleton is moderately flat, like those of the Pharaoh's ancestors. The chin is narrow and pointed; the mandible low and slightly built : its typically Egyptian form is in marked contrast to the equally definitely alien shape seen in the next skeleton to be discussed (see pl. XXXVI and XXXVII).

The cranial length is o m. 194 mill. : the cranial breadth (not including scalp),
o m. 148 mill. : circumference, o m. 550 mill.; auricular height, o m. 118 mill.;
total facial height (after allowing for slight separation of the jaws), o m. 122 mill.;
upper facial height, o m. 073 mill.; minimal frontal breadth, o m. 095 mill.;
bizygomatic breadth, o m. 133 mill.; bigonial breadth, o m. 094 mill.; nasal
height, o m. 053 mill.; nasal breadth, o m. 026 mill.; interorbital breadth,
o m. 027 mill.; left orbit, o m. 039 mill. × o m. 034 mill. : right orbit,
o m. 039 mill. 5 × o m. 034 mill. 5 : and chin-vertex projection, o m. 210 mill.
Amenothes III was 1 m. 561 mill. in height.

Small pads of cloths, saturated with some gummy material, were removed from the
nostrils; and it was then found that in forcing a passage into the cranial cavity the
nasal septum and the turbinate ridges had been completely ablated, and the whole
ethmoid broken away.

The arms were placed in positions similar to those already described in the cases of
Thoutmosis II and his successors.

61075. The bones of a skeleton supposed to be that of Amenothes IV (Khou-niatonou) (pl. XXXVI and XXXVII).

In January 1907, during the course of the excavations in the Bibân el Molouk sub-
sidized by Mr. Theodore M. Davis, a tomb was found containing a large series of
objects, some of which had obviously been part of the furniture of Queen Tìyi's
tomb, and others equally surely had come from the tomb of her son, the heretic
king, Khouniatonou or Akhenaten (also variously transliterated Ikhnaton, Khuenaton
and in many other spellings). The full account of the circumstances of the discovery
and of the nature of the objects found in the tomb has been given by Mr. Davis,
M. Maspero and others, in *The Tomb of Queen Tìyi* (Theodore M. Davis' Excavations :
Bibân el Molûk, London, 1910).

From the circumstances under which the coffin and the human remains were found,
in association with many inscribed objects bearing the name Khouniatonou, which
also appeared not only on the coffin itself but also on the gold bands encircling the
mummy, there can no longer be any doubt that the body found in this tomb was
either that of the heretic king or was believed to be his corpse by the embalmers.
Although it frequently happened (*vide supra*) that mummies of royal personages
were placed in coffins that were not made for them, it must be remembered that
this was done only during the hasty preparations (in the XXIst Dynasty) for removing
them to a hiding place at Deïr el Baharï. The mummy under consideration, however,
was not rewrapped. It had not been plundered, but was found in its original
wrappings, upon which were gold bands bearing the name of Khouniatonou. It is
hardly credible that the embalmers of the Pharaoh's mummy could have put some
other body in place of it.

Thus we have the most positive evidence that these bones are the remains of Khouniatonou.

I do not suppose that any unprejudiced scholar who studies the archaeological evidence alone would harbour any doubt of the identity of this mummy, if it were not for the fact that it is difficult from the anatomical evidence to assign an age to this skeleton sufficiently great to satisfy the demands of most historians, who want at least 30 years into which to crowd the events of Khouniatonou's eventful reign.

Under these circumstances I must set forth the anatomical evidence in greater detail than was thought desirable in *The Tomb of Queen Tiyi,* from which Mr. Davis requested me to omit all technicalities.

The ages assigned by different anatomists as the times when the epiphyses join and become consolidated present a considerable range of variation. Hence, in the present state of our knowledge, it would be rash and altogether unjustifiable to give in figures the precise age of a skeleton without making the reservation that it might be several years older or younger than the estimate.

This will appear from the following detailed summary.

Scapula completely ossified.

Poirier (*Traité d'Anatomie humaine,* par Paul Poirier et A. Charpy, tome Ier, 1899, p. 139) states that the marginal epiphyses do not join until from 25 to 28 years of age : according to Testut (*Traité d'Anatomie humaine,* p. 259) they join between 22 and 25 years : various other books mention «20 to 25 years» or before 25 years. Thus the evidence of the completely ossified scapula might be interpreted as meaning that the individual was 25 years old or perhaps more than 28 years.

The vertebral column presents the following conditions.

The first three vertebrae are completely ossified.

Thomson (*Cunningham's Text Book of Anatomy*) says the inferior epiphysis of axis joins body at 25 years : according to Piersol (*Human Anatomy*) the process is complete at 20 years : according to Testut between 20 and 25 years (p. 87), but four pages later on, in the same treatise, it is stated that the ossification of the vertebral column progresses with extreme slowness and is not complete until from the 25th to the 30th years.

Fourth cervical vertebra : inferior epiphysis of body not completely fused.

Fifth cervical vertebra : same condition.

In view of the above statements this condition may indicate an age of not more than 30 years, or than 25 or even 20 years, according to different authorities.

Sixth and seventh cervical vertebrae : completely ossified.

In the dorsal series the seventh, ninth, tenth, eleventh and twelfth vertebrae are completely ossified : but in the cases of the rest the epiphyses have fused only a short time before death : the lower epiphysis of the fourth and the upper epiphysis of the fifth dorsal vertebrae had only just begun to fuse to the bodies.

All five lumbar vertebrae are completely ossified.

Poirier (p. 343) tells us that the ossification of the 7th cervical vertebra is finished at 25 years : the epiphyses of the upper dorsal vertebrae are almost fused, and the process of fusion has begun in the lumbar and lower sacral segments. Between 25 and 30 years the union of the other epiphyses is effected.

The sacrum is four-pieced : its lateral masses are completely consolidated, but the three intercentral fissures were just closed or in process of closing.

The suture between segments 3 and 4 was just closed; that between 3 and 2 was closed laterally; and that between 2 and 1 was in process of closing laterally.

According to Thomson (*op. cit.*, p. 94) the fissure between segments 3 and 4 begins to close at 18 years, and the junction between 1 and 2 is not complete until 25 years or later, even up to 30 years, according to Poirier (p. 347). Testut states (*op. cit.*, p. 30) that the fusion of the sacral vertebrae is not complete as a rule until from 25 to 30 years.

Thus if we take into consideration the fact that half the vertebral column is fully ossified and that in the other half the process is in the penultimate stage of completion, the possibility is opened up, provided we follow Testut in preference to other authorities, that this individual may have been old enough to satisfy the demands of the historians as to Khouniatonou's age.

The coccyx was not amongst the bones sent to me in Cairo from Luxsor.

The epiphyses on the heads and tubercles of the ribs were just joining in most cases, but were separate in a few instances.

According to Thomson the fusion of these elements is completed by the 25th years : Testut gives the age as 16 to 25 years. Unless there are exceptions to these estimates the state of the ribs in this case would impose a limit of 25 years to the age.

Although the first segment of the mesosternum is separate there is just a possibility that it may have been broken off, after having been in the process of joining at the time of death.

Testut assigns 20 to 25 years as the time during which this process of joining may occur : Thomson says (*op. cit.*, p. 96, 97) : « Union between these segments occurs rather irregularly, and is liable to much variation »; and « fusion of the second with the first segment may not be complete till the 20th to 25th year ».

The sternal epiphysis of the clavicle is still separate.

Poirier (*op. cit.*, p. 129) and Testut (*op. cit.*, p. 254) give 22 to 25 years as its time of joining; Thomson, « 25 or thereabouts ».

All the limb-bones, excepting the ossa innominata and clavicles only, are fully ossified and consolidated.

Testut (*op. cit.*, 266) states that the upper epiphysis of the humerus does not join until 25 or 26 years; according to Thomson, « about 25 years ».

Thus, if we adopt these estimations, the state of the humeri neutralizes the suggestion of an age less than 25 or thereabouts, in support of which the data supplied by the clavicles and ribs might be adduced. Against this, however, is Poirier's statement that the upper epiphysis of the humerus joins the shaft at from 22 to 25 years of age in the male.

In the ossa innominata the epiphyses of the ischial tuberosities are consolidated and those of the pubo-ischial rami were in process of joining at the time of death. The epiphysis of the crests is joined to the ilium; but, in the posterior 45 millimetres of its extent on the right side (Diagram 11) and 30 millimetres on the left, a slight cleft is present along the inner edge of the epiphysis cristae.

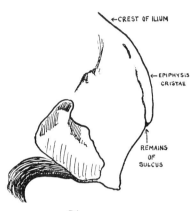

←CREST OF ILIUM

←EPIPHYSIS CRISTAE

REMAINS OF SULCUS

Diagram 11.

Testut (*op. cit.*, p. 300) says the crest of the ilium does not lose its independence until 24 or 25 years of age.

In the skull the cranial sutures show no signs of obliteration : the teeth are unworn and the right upper «wisdom-tooth» is not erupted.

If we take into consideration all the facts set forth in this statement, not only the data concerning the immaturity of certain bones, but also those of the fully ossified parts of the skeleton; and bear in mind the wide range of variation of the control figures — in some cases as much as ten years between different authorities' estimates of when particular bones cease growing — upon which any argument as to age must be based; two judgments emerge quite clearly from this mass of apparent contradictions : *a*) that, if we accept the generally admitted criteria, this skeleton is that of a man about 25 or 26 years of age; and *b*) that no anatomist would be justified in refusing to admit that this individual may have been several years younger or older than the above estimate, which after all is based upon averages.

To turn to the specific problem before us, if, with such clear archaeological evidence to indicate that these are the remains of Khouniatonou, the historian can produce irrefutable facts showing that the heretic king must have been 27, or even 30, years of age, I would be prepared to admit that the weight of the anatomical evidence in opposition to the admission of that fact is too slight to be considered absolutely prohibitive.

I do not think there can be any serious doubt that these are really the remains of Khouniatonou : but in the light of the anatomical evidence it is important that the historical evidence should be submitted to most searching and critical examination for the purpose of deciding how old the Heretic really was at the time of his death. There is information suggesting that he was a minor at the time of his father's death and that he reigned seventeen years. Surely, then, there need be no great straining of the evidence to bring the anatomical and historical facts into harmony, the one with the other.

The skull presents a number of interesting and significant features. The cranium is broad and relatively flattened, its measurements being o m. 189 mill. in length; o m. 154 mill. in breadth; o m. 136 mill. in height (basibregmatic); o m. 099 mill., minimal frontal breadth; and a circumference of o m. 545 mill.

Although o m. 154 mill. is quite an exceptional breadth for an Egyptian skull, all the other numbers are smaller than those obtained in the case of Amenothes III. Nevertheless, the form of the cranium and the fact that it is exceptionally thin in most places and relatively thick in others indicate that a condition of hydrocephalus was present during life. When in Egypt I showed this cranium to my colleague, Professor A. R. Ferguson, Professor of Pathology in the Cairo School of Medicine, and he assured me that the signs of hydrocephalus were unquestionable.

Unfortunately the facial skeleton was badly damaged (in ancient times) by the collapse of the lid of the coffin, which fell upon the face. The right side of the skull was smashed in and the face broken into fragments. To add to this misfortune, when these fragments were being packed in Luxsor for transmission to me in Cairo many of the smaller pieces of bone were overlooked or regarded as useless trifles. Hence, when I came to build up from the pieces the left side of the face (pl. XXXVI) — the right side was much too damaged and incomplete — the nasal skeleton was found to be missing.

However, sufficient of the facial skeleton has been restored to give one a fairly accurate conception of its form when it was intact.

The general form of the face presents a marked contrast to that of Amenothes III (compare pl. XXXVI with pl. XXXIV); but the configuration of the upper part of the face, including the forehead, is identical with that of Khouniatonou's maternal grandfather, Iouiya (see Quibell's *Tomb of Yuaa and Thuiu*, Catalogue général, 1908, pl. LVIII). The contrasts in the architecture of the facial skeleton in Amenothes III and his son are far more than mere individual differences, for they are racial. Amenothes III$^{rd's}$ face is cast in the Egyptian mould : but in the case of Khouniatonou, the jaw is typically Armenoid, a fact that is most clearly demonstrated in the form of its ascending ramus (pl. XXXVI). The prominence of the superciliary ridges and the sloping forehead are other signs of this alien influence. But there are some curious points of resemblance to Amenothes III and his family. The projection of the upper incisors (pl. XXXVI), to which I have frequently referred as a family trait of the Royal House in the XVIIIth Dynasty, is seen in this skull also.

In the skull of Amenothes III a curious bony ridge passes from the nasal spine to the alveolar point, leaving a well-marked depression on each side of it. In this skull the same peculiarities appear in an even more pronounced form.

There are also points of resemblance in the molar teeth.

Khouniatonou was a bigger man than his father, who was 1 m. 561 mill., though not so tall as Amenothes II (who was 1 m. 673 mill.) on the paternal side, nor Iouiya (who was 1 m. 651 mill.) on the maternal side of his ancestry.

The following figures were obtained on measuring the bones of this mummy.

Right femur, oblique length (o m. 450 mill. 5), maximum length (o m. 455 mill.). (The corresponding measurements in the case of Amenothes III are o m. 421 mill. and o m. 424 mill. 5 respectively).

Left femur, obl., o m. 453 mill., max., o m. 455 mill. 5.

Left tibia, axial length, o m. 355 mill. 5; Right tibia, axial length, o m. 354 mill.

Tarsal height (astragalus and calcaneum) o m. 066 mill.

Left humerus, oblique length, o m. 311 mill.; maximum length, o m. 319 mill.

The corresponding measurements of the right humerus are o m. 314 mill. and o m. 322 mill. respectively; and of the right humerus of Amenothes III, o m. 281 mill. 5 and o m. 285 mill. respectively.

61076. The Mummy found in Baqt's Coffin (pl. XXXIX).

This is the mummy contained in the coffin bearing the inscription «royal daughter, royal sister Mashonttimihou», concerning which M. Maspero makes the following remarks : «La momie, décorée de guirlandes, est fausse comme celle de la princesse Sitamon [*vide supra*]. Elle a été fouillée par les Arabes, et on en distingue les éléments à travers les trous pratiqués dans le maillot. Un morceau de cercueil à vernis jaune, de la XXe dynastie, accompagné d'un manche de miroir et de quelques autres menus objets, tient lieu de corps : un paquet de chiffons simule la tête, un paquet de chiffons les pieds» (p. 544).

The appearance of this mummy proved to be most deceptive. It consisted of an enormous mass of linen filling the whole coffin. Plunderers had made two deep holes into this mass, revealing the fragment of gaudy yellow coffin-lid referred to in M. Maspero's account; but nothing else could be felt through these holes. On June 27th, 1909, I unrolled the wrappings and found amongst a mass of brown friable bandages, occupying the lower part of the large bundle, most of the bones of the skeleton of a young woman about 21 years of age. She was exceedingly slenderly built.

She has a small ovoid face, a moderately prominent nose, and small horizontal elliptical orbits; but the mandible conforms to an alien (non-Egyptian) type, one however which has been common in Lower Egypt since the time of the Ancient Empire, and is fairly often seen among the remains of the Upper Egyptian aristocracy. The skull has the large, broad, flat ovoid form usually seen in association with the jaw, to which I have just referred (pl. XXXIX).

The maximum length of the skull is o m. 186 mill., maximum breadth o m. 144 mill., minimum frontal breadth o m. 095 mill., basi-bregmatic height o m. 124 mill., Bizygomatic breadth o m. 128 mill., total facial height o m. 115 mill., upper facial height o m. 069 mill. and the nasal height and breadth respectively o m. 048 mill. and o m. 024 mill. The presence of the skin on the forehead prevents the accurate measurement of the cranial base (including the skin it is o m. 100 mill.), but without it would be probably o m. 098 mill.; the facial base is o m. 093 mill. For the same reason it is not possible to measure the orbits accurately but each is about o m. 038 mill., broad and about o m. 034 mill. deep.

The maximum and oblique lengths respectively of the right femur are o m. 440 mill. and o m. 433 mill. and of the left o m. 438 mill. and o m. 435 mill. : the diameter of the right femoral head is o m. 037 mill.

The maximum and oblique lengths respectively of the right humerus are o m. 311 mill. and 304 and of the left o m. 302 mill. and o m. 299 mill. The left coronoid fossa, but not the right, is perforated.

The third molar teeth are just erupting. The epiphyses of the bodies of the vertebrae
   and of the crests of the ilia are still separate : the lower epiphyses of the ulnae and
   radii are just joined.

There is nothing to indicate with certainty whose mummy this is or when it was mummified. If the bandages found in the immediate neighbourhood of the bones formed
   part of the mummy the latter may have been of XVIIIth Dynasty date.

61077. The Mummy of Seti I (pl. XXXVIII, XL, XLI and FRONTISPIECE).

This mummy was unwrapped by M. Maspero on june 9th, 1886. The procès-verbal
   has been briefly set forth in *Les Momies royales* (p. 554, 555, and Appendix, II,
   p. 772 and 773); and with greater detail in the *American Journal of Archaeology*,
   1886, volume III, p. 331 to 333, and also in *Recueil de travaux*, t. VIII, p. 179
   to 181.

There is nothing in the mode of treatment of this mummy to distinguish it from that
   in vogue at the latter part of the XVIIIth Dynasty. The head is in a good state of
   preservation and reveals to us one of the most perfect examples of manly dignity
   displayed in a mummy that has come down from ancient Egypt. But the body has
   suffered severely at the hands of the tomb-robbers. The head is broken off the trunk
   and the anterior wall of the abdomen has been smashed.

The identification of this mummy as Seti I was based wholly upon the inscription on
   the lid of the coffin, where the name appears in hieroglyphs. Three hieratic inscriptions
   on the coffin describe the attention given to the mummy and its wanderings.
   «D'après le premier, «l'an VI, le 7 du deuxième mois de Shaît, le premier prophète d'Amon, Hrihorou, envoya restaurer l'appareil funéraire du roi Séti Ier»; le
   second déclare que, «l'an XVI, le 7 du quatrième mois de Pirit, sous le roi
   Siamou Hrihorou, on retira le roi Séti Ier de son tombeau pour le déposer dans la
   tombe de la princesse Anhapou». L'opération faite, le prêtre chargé du culte royal
   témoigna devant le Pharaon de la condition de la momie, et déclara que le corps
   n'avait souffert aucun dommage dans le transfert. Enfin «en l'an X, le 11 du
   quatrième mois de Pirit, sous le grand prêtre Pinotmou Ier, le roi Séti Ier fut transporté dans le tombeau d'Aménôthès Ier»; en foi de quoi on écrivit le troisième et
   dernier procès-verbal. La momie était enveloppée d'une forte toile jaunâtre et ne
   portait aucune inscription apparente» (*Guide du Visiteur*).

At present the whole surface of the body, excepting the head only, is covered with a
   black mass of bandage impregnated with resinous material. All the exposed areas of
   skin, including the face, are quite black; but M. Maspero informs me that when
   the head was first exposed in 1886 the skin was distinctly brown and not black.

The hands are folded in front of the chest. The upper arms are vertical and each forearm is flexed so that the hand is placed in front of the opposite shoulder. The left
   forearm is placed in front of the right.

The left side of the chest is stuffed with black masses of resin-impregnated linen, now
   of stony hardness. In the apex of the right side of the thorax there is a solid black

mass about the size of a closed fist. It is not linen, but some brittle jet-black material, with a shining surface when fractured. Below this and separated from it by a wide interval there is a large heart-shaped mass of stony consistency, which has a dull brown colour when scraped. It seems to be a viscus, perhaps the heart, but it is not possible to express any positive opinion without cutting it and submitting a piece of it to microscopical examination. It was the usual custom at all periods to leave the heart in the body. The fact that the object under consideration is in the right side of the thorax cannot be urged as a reason against its identification as the heart, because it usually happened that the embalmer, operating through the embalming wound in the left flank, pushed the heart over to the right side of the body, when he was excising the other viscera.

The common statement that the heart was placed in a Canopic Jar is due to a mistaken generalisation from isolated cases, in which the heart, or some fragment of it, was cut out accidentally by a careless embalmer. There can be no doubt that it was the usual procedure to leave the heart in the body attached by the great vessels.

Packed around this mass, which is probably the heart, there is a considerable quantity of resin-impregnated linen.

The abdominal cavity was partially filled with black masses of similarly treated cloth, but there is no trace of any viscus. Whether the kidney was left, as Diodorus, writing many centuries later, described, it is impossible to say.

Seti I was probably 1 m. 665 mill. in height when alive. That is the present height of his mummy together with a thin layer of wrappings on the feet, which are approximately of the same thickness as the skin on his heels was. The height of the symphysis pubis (with the same reservation) is o m. 897 mill. [probably a mistake? o m. 797 mill.]; pubes to chin, o m. 578 mill.; pubes to nose, o m. 644 mill.; breath of shoulders, o m. 400 mill.; breadth at iliac crests, o m. 295 mill.; intertrochanteric breadth (with wrappings); estimated length (axial) of tibia, o m. 375 mill.; distance from upper surface of tibia to middle of Poupart's ligament, o m. 461 mill.; estimated length of humerus, o m. 335 mill.; and estimated length of radius, o m. 264 mill. The toes are broken off, but the foot must have been about o m. 230 mill. in length : the maximum length of the hand is o m. 220 mill.

The length of the head (with a thin layer of bandages on the occiput) is o m. 196 mill.; breadth (without bandages), o m. 143; minimal frontal breadth, o m. 101 mill.; total facial height, o m. 128 mill.; upper facial height, o m. 080 mill.; length and breadth of nose, o m. 060 mill. and o m. 033 mill.; right orbit, o m. 050 mill. by o m. 030 mill.; left orbit, o m. 047 mill. by o m. 031 mill.; bizygomatic breadth, o m. 138 mill.; bigonial breadth, o m. 101 mill.; cranial circumference, o m. 550 mill.; auricular height, o m. 122 mill.; height, chin to vertex, o m. 208 mill.

The face is ovoid, but so nearly ellipsoid that when the lower half of the face was filled out by the jaw muscles in life it must have been ellipsoid.

The superciliary eminences are fairly prominent and the forehead sloping. The eyelids

are closed and, so far as one can tell, no packing material has been inserted be-
neathe them. No hair is visible, either on the scalp or face, excepting the eyebrows.
The big heavy jaw, with its wide and strong chin, as well as the more robust build
of the whole face, present a marked contrast to the features of the XVIIIth Dynasty
rulers, which were cast in a smaller and more refined mould than the big-featured
Pharaohs of the XIXth Dynasty. Not only in the features of jaw, face and forehead,
but also in his cranial form, Seti I differs from his predecessors of the XVIIIth
Dynasty; and the contrast is not merely an individual, but largely a racial one also.
Although the members of the royal family in the XVIIIth Dynasty present features
which it is difficult to reconcile with the Egyptian type, on the whole they conform
to that physical type; but in Seti I many more alien (Asiatic) traits in face and
cranium are manifested and there can be no doubt that he and his successors are
less characteristically Egyptian than his predecessors were.

M. Maspero realized these facts when he wrote the following sentences in his *Procès-
verbal de l'ouverture des Momies de Ramsès II et Ramsès III* (Bulletin de l'Institut
égyptien, 1886). «Séti Ier et Ramsès II sont d'un type assez différent. Ils se ratta-
chaient par les femmes à l'ancienne lignée; mais ce qu'ils avaient en eux de sang
royal ne leur avait donné aucun des traits qui distinguent les Thoutmos et les Amenhotpou» (p. 269).

I quote the following remarks from Professor Virchow's account (*op. cit. supra*) of this
mummy. «Sie ist die besterhaltene der ganzen Reihe und macht noch jetzt den
Eindruch eines kräftigen, vollendet schönen Mannes». «Der feingeschnittene und
fast europäisch aussehende Kopf ist gestrecht und ein wenig nach hinten zurück-
gebogen; die kahle und etwas niedige, sehr breit (106[mm]), voll gerundete, aber
etwas zurückgelegte Stirn ganz glatt, nur die Orbitalwülste leicht vortretend. Die
Augen geschlossen wie eines Schlafenden. Der Kopf lang und etwas flach gewölbt,
dolichochamaecephal (Längenbreitenindex 74.7, Ohrhöhenindex 58.2). Das
Gesicht hoch und oval, an der Grenze der Leptoprosopie (Index 89.9). Die Nase
fein, schmal, lang, aquilin, wie in den alten Abbildungen; nur an der Grenze des
knöchernen und knorpeligen Theils liegt ein, durch das Eintrocknen entstandener
Absatz; Index 54.3». «Der Unterkiefer hoch, das Kinn sehr breit, dreiecking,
etwas vortretend, in der Mitte des unteren Randes gebuchtet» (p. 773).

On p. 786 of the same work Professor Virchow sets forth a large series of measurements of this mummy, many of which reveal wide discrepancies, when compared
with the figures I have recorded above, as the results of measurements made by
Dr. Derry and myself.

61078. The mummy of Ramses II (pl. XLII, XLIII and XLIV).

«Le 1er juin 1886, sur l'ordre et en présence du Khédive (Tewfik), la momie de
Ramsès II fut ouverte solennellement» (*Les Momies royales*, p. 560 — see also
p. 765-767 and 773-775).

8.

Upon the coffin was inscribed the name of the Pharaoh in hieroglyphs, as well as reports written in hieratic analogous to those found on Seti I[er's] coffin informing us that in «l'an X du grand prêtre Pinotmou, on transporta Ramsès II dans le tombeau d'Aménôthès, en même temps que son père Séti Ier» (*Guide du Visiteur*).

«Le style du monument et certains détails d'orthographe nous reportaient à la XXe dynastie plutôt qu'à la XIXe. Pour savoir si la momie était bien celle de Ramsès II, comme le prétendent les inscriptions du couvercle, M. Maspero fit enlever une partie des bandages qui paraissaient être mal attachés, et il trouva, sur la poitrine du maillot original, une inscription à l'encre en hiératique, dont la teneur ne laisse subsister aucun doute; le grand prêtre Pinotmou Ier y déclare qu'il a fait réparer l'appareil funéraire de Ramsès II en l'an XVI» (*Guide du Visiteur*).

M. Maspero's account of the unwrapping of this mummy (*Bulletins de l'Institut égyptien*, 1886, p. 253-255) is as follows. «La présence de cette dernière inscription une fois constatée par S. A. le Khédive et par les hautes personnes réunies dans la salle, la première enveloppe fut enlevée, et l'on découvrit successivement une bande d'étoffe large d'environ o m. 20 cent., enroulée autour du corps, puis un second linceul cousu et maintenu d'espace par des bandes étroites, puis deux épaisseurs de bandelettes et une pièce de toile fine tendue de la tête aux pieds. Une image de la déesse Nouït, d'environ un mètre, y est dessinée en couleur rouge et noire, ainsi que le prescrivait le rituel; le profil de la déesse rappelle, à s'y méprendre, le profil pur et délicat de Séti Ier, tel que nous le font connaître les bas-reliefs de Thèbes et d'Abydos. Une bande nouvelle était placée sous cet amulette, puis une couche de pièces de toile, pliées en carré et maculées par la matière bitumineuse dont les embaumeurs s'étaient servis. Cette dernière enveloppe écartée, Ramsès II apparut. Il est grand, bien conformé, parfaitement symétrique [1]. La tête est allongée, petite par rapport au corps. Le sommet du crâne est entièrement dénudé. Les cheveux, rares sur les tempes, s'épaississent à la nuque et forment de véritables mèches lisses et droites, d'environ o m. o5 cent. de longueur : blancs au moment de la mort, ils ont été teints en jaune-clair par les parfums. Le front est bas, étroit, l'arcade sourcilière saillante, l'œil petit, le nez long, mince, busqué comme le nez des Bourbons, légèrement écrasé au bout par la pression du maillot, la tempe creuse, la pommette proéminente, l'oreille ronde, écartée de la tête, la mâchoire forte et puissante, le menton très long. La bouche, largement fendue, est bordée de lèvres épaisses et charnues; elle était remplie d'une pâte noirâtre, dont une partie, détachée au ciseau, a laissé entrevoir quelques dents très usées et très friables, mais blanches et bien entretenues. La moustache et la barbe peu fournies et rasées avec soin pendant la vie, avaient crû au cours de la dernière maladie ou après la mort; les poils, blancs comme ceux de la chevelure, mais rudes et hérissés, ont une longueur de 2 ou 3 millimètres. La peau est d'un jaune terreux, plaquée de noir. En résumé, le masque

---

[1] Même après le tassement des vertèbres et la rétraction produite par la momification, il mesure encore 1 m. 72 cent.

de la momie donne très suffisamment l'idée de ce qu'était le masque du roi vivant : une expression peu intelligente, peut-être légèrement bestiale, mais de la fierté, de l'obstination et un air de majesté souveraine qui perce encore sous l'appareil de l'embaumement. Le reste du corps n'est pas moins bien conservé que la tête, mais la réduction des chairs en a modifié plus profondément l'aspect extérieur. Le cou n'a plus que le diamètre de la colonne vertébrale. La poitrine est ample, les épaules sont hautes, les bras croisés sur la poitrine, les mains fines et rougies de henné, les ongles très beaux, taillés à la hauteur de la chair et soignés comme ceux d'une petite maîtresse : la plaie par laquelle les embaumeurs avaient ôté les viscères s'ouvre béante au flanc gauche. Les parties génitales ont été enlevées à l'aide d'un instrument tranchant, et probablement, selon un usage assez répandu, ensevelies à part dans le creux d'un Osiris en bois. Les cuisses et les jambes sont décharnées, les pieds longs, minces, un peu plats, frottés de henné comme les mains. Les os sont faibles et fragiles, les muscles sont atrophiés par dégénérescence sénile : on sait, en effet, que Ramsès II régna nombre d'années avec son père Séti Ier, soixante-sept ans seul, et dut mourir presque centenaire. »

It is open to question whether the discolouration of the finger and toe-nails may not be due to the staining by resinous embalming-materials and not to henna : and it is also not altogether certain that the genital organs were intentionally ablated. It is quite possible that they may have been broken off accidentally by the tomb-robbers who stripped the mummy in search of spoil (pl. XLII). It has already been pointed out that the pudenda were not removed in Ahmôsis I, Thoutmosis I, Thoutmosis IV, Amenothes II, and Yuaa, but that the state of affairs in Thoutmosis II, Thoutmosis III and the unknown man in Nibsoni's coffin was uncertain. In the case of Seti I the wrappings were not removed, so that no positive statement of the mode of treatment of the pudenda can be made. In Ramses IInd's successor Menephtah, the penis was left but the scrotum removed; and in all the later Pharaohs the genital organs were left intact.

It seems unlikely that in so important a matter as the treatment of the genital organs the embalmers should suddenly have broken away from the convention of their time in the case of Thoutmosis II and III, but not in their immediate predecessors and successors, and again in the succeding dynasty in the case of Ramses II. The absence of the genital organs in the latter Pharaoh seems to me to be due to accidental circumstances (see pl. XLII).

In support of this contention I would call attention, not only to the broken edges of the area from which the organs have been removed, but also to the fact that the wrappings (resin-impregnated bandages) cease abruptly at the edges of this patch (i. e. do not cover it) and have broken edges.

It is curious that in the cases of Seti I and Ramses II the embalmers should have departed from the usual practice (both in the late XVIIIth and the XIXth dynastic periods) of placing the right forearm in front of the left.

The measurement of Ramses IInd's height made by Dr. Derry and myself was 1 m. 733 mill.; but Professor Virchow says «die ganze Länge der sehr mageren Mumie maass

H^r Brugsch-Bey zu 1 m. 720 mill., also um 0 m. 155 mill. länger als die seines Vaters » (*op. cit.,* p. 774).

Height of upper margin of symphysis pubis..............	o m.	871 mill.
Height of chin above symphysis pubis.................	o	668
Height of suprasternal notch above pubis..............	o	525
Height of nasal spine above pubis	o	736
Breadth of shoulders................................	o	381
Interacromial breadth...............................	o	337,5
Estimated length, right humerus	o	332
Estimated length, left radius	o	247
Estimated length, left femur.........................	o	460
Estimated length, left tibia..........................	o	358
Distance from middle of Poupart's ligament to upper surface of tibia	o	468
Breadth at iliac crests..............................	o	312
Bitrochanteric breadth	o	310
Length of foot.....................................	o	234
Breadth of foot	o	074

The cranium is a long narrow ovoid, with a prominent occiput, and without any depression to interrupt the sweep of the curve from the parietal to the occipital region (pl. XLIV, fig. 1).

The maximum length of the cranium is o m. 195; breadth (including a thin layer of hair, — see pl. XLIV), o m. 136 mill.; minimal frontal breadth, o m. 091 mill.; auricular height, o m. 121 mill.; circumference (inclusive of a thin layer of hair), o m. 526 mill.; total facial height, o m. 136 mill.; upper facial height, o m. 080 mill.; nasal height, o m. 061 mill.; nasal breadth, o m. 029 mill.; bizygomatic breadth, o m. 132 mill.; bigonial breadth, o m. 097 mill.; right orbit, o m. 042 mill. × o m. 038 mill.; left orbit, o m. 042 mill. × o m. 036 mill.; right palpebral cleft, o m. 032 mill. long, eyelids 3 millimetres apart : left palpebral cleft, o m. 033 mill. long, eyelids, 7 millimetres apart; and interorbital breadth, o m. 021 mill.

The temples and the back of the head are covered with fine silky hair, about o m. 060 mill. long, which originally must have been quite white, but now is yellow. The upper part of the scalp was quite bald, although there are still scanty hairs on the frontal region. Amongst them are some « blackheads », due to the plugging of the orifices of sluggish sebaceous glands, such as one frequently sees in old men. The superficial temporal arteries are very prominent and tortuous and there can be no doubt that their walls are calcareous (pl. XLIII and XLIV). On the vertex (pl. XLIII, fig. 2), near the extremity of the greatly enlarged anterior branch of the right superficial temporal artery, there are curious markings upon the bald scalp. There is a well-marked white line, running in the mesial sagittal plane, and a fainter transverse mark, forming a pattern which in some lights looks like a cross. Between this and the prominent artery there is a crescentic mark. Whether these marks are painted on the scalp, or only scratched, and whether they are intentional or only accidental are questions which I am unable to answer.

Ramses II had a low sloping forehead (pl. XLIV) and moderately prominent superciliary eminences. The eyebrow (scanty grey hairs about 6 millimetres long) is preserved only on the right side. Traces of a layer of dark brown or black paint still persist on the superciliary ridges. The skin of the forehead is of a light yellow colour, thickly spotted with reddish brown patches. This mummy reveals a distinct advance in the technique of the embalmer's art — for the first time it became possible to preserve the skin without the dark brown or black discolouration that occurred invariably in earlier attempts at mummification. It is true that in some cases, Raï, Amenothes II, Thoutmosis IV, Iuîya and Thouîyou a only a moderately dark brown tint was given to the skin; but from the time of Ramses II onward a much more uniformly light colour was attainable.

The most outstanding feature of Ramses IInd's long narrow ovoid (or perhaps ellipsoid in life) face is the large, narrow, prominent nose. The mesial suture between the nasal bones is o m. o29 mill. long; and its lower (anterior) extremity is o m. o25 mill. in front of the inner margin of the orbit. The soft parts of the nose have been carefully moulded, each nostril having been stuffed with resin, which, in addition to being part of the antiseptic toilet of the face, helped to preserve the form of the nose.

In its present condition the upper lip is exceptionally long, the distance from the lateral nasal cartilage to the edge of the lip being o m. o28 mill. The lip is thickly studded with white hairs varying in length from 1 to 3 millimetres. There are also a few scattered hairs around the angles of the mouth and on the lower lip and chin; but the masseteric regions appear to be wholly devoid of hair. There is a thick patch of about thirty hairs on the edge of the jaw about 3 centimetres to the left of the middle line; and the whole submaxillary region is studded with sparsely scattered hairs.

The lips are slightly separated and the mouth appears as a transverse fusiform slit, o m. o85 mill. long (measured around the arc). The opening was filled with a dark brown resinous paste, some of which was removed in 1886, exposing parts of two teeth on the right side. Both of these teeth have been broken recently (? when the resin was being removed). There is a gap between the teeth, suggesting that the first bicuspid tooth had been lost. The teeth are clean and in an excellent state of preservation : they were only slightly worn. It is a curious problem to determine why this exceedingly old man should have healthy and only slightly worn teeth, whereas his younger predecessor Amenothes III was the victim of severe dental caries and alveolar abscesses and had much worn teeth. The difficulty of explaining Ramses' immunity from these dental troubles is increased by the fact that the vast majority (over 90 o/o) of the aristocracy of Memphis in the times of the Pyramid-builders suffered severely from tooth-affections.

The ears had been smeared with a thick layer of resinous paste. Both lobules (now broken) had been pierced. A bunch of long grey hairs projects from each meatus.

Although the skin of the face is shrunken and parchment-like its form is fairly well preserved : but in the case of the neck it clings around the vertebrae and larynx, forming an irregular column, only o m. 195 mill. in circumference, with little resemblance to the form it had in life, even in an extremely emaciated body. Many details of the transverse processes and spines of the vertebrae are reproduced in the form of the skin; and in front the thyroid cartilage and the hyoid bone are exceptionally prominent.

The great part of the body is still enclosed in a hard shield of linen impregnated with resinous material. A piece of this carapace with the skin and part of the sternum had been broken off the upper part of the thorax. On raising this I was very much surprised to find that, in spite of the great age to which Ramses had attained, the manubrium sterni was not ankylosed to the gladiolus, and the ossified 2nd costal cartilages still articulated by joints with the sternum.

The scale of an onion was found adhering to the resin in the neighbourhood of the left axilla. This is of some interest, for in the succeeding three dynasties onions were used freely in the process of embalming, whether as deodorants or antiseptics, or for some unknown symbolic reason must remain a matter of conjecture. But even in the present day the modern Egyptians, and especially the Copts, attribute many virtues to the onion.

The embalming-wound (pl. XLII) placed in front of the left flank, is a large elliptical gaping wound, o m. 165 mill. long and o m. 055 mill. broad. It begins above the middle of Poupart's ligament, o m. 033 mill. below the level of the anterior superior spine of the ilium, and passes vertically upward to a point at the anterior extremity of the 9th rib. Its mesial edge is o m. 063 mill. from the mesial plane. Its margins are thickly smeared with a paste of reddish resin.

The position of the embalming-wound in thus different from those distinctive of both the early (high) and late (low) XVIIIth Dynasty. The altered site is a development of the latter (or low) position; but in order to afford more room for the manipulations inside the body the low incision has been prolonged upward so as secondarily to occupy the high (early XVIIIth) position, but slightly further forward than was customary at the beginning of the XVIIIth Dynasty (compare Diagram 3, p. 34).

The skin of the hips and buttocks is thrown into a series of longitudinal folds.

The legs are still encrusted, in the greater part of their extent, with a resinous mass 6 millimetres thick. Where the limbs are exposed they seem to consist merely of a layer of skin closely clinging to the bones.

A thick resinous layer fills up the concavities of the arches of the feet. The toe-nails are long and incurved : the overgrown edge of the great-toe-nail is 4 millimetres long.

The right hand is completely flexed but the left hand only semi-flexed. A similar state of affairs is found in Menephtah's mummy, which however differs from Ramses' in having the right forearm in front of the left. They resemble one another however in that the right hand, instead of being in front of the left shoulder, as is customary, is placed near the middle of the left humerus.

The finger nails exhibit very distinct longitudinal ridging. In the case of some of the finger-nails the overgrown edges are more than 5 millimetres long. Length of hand, from wrist along middle finger, o m. 222 mill.

The skin of the face and neck was very much wrinkled, but most of the folds, especially the transverse wrinkles on the forehead, have been smoothed out by the embalmers.

The eyes have been smeared with resinous material, so that it is not possible to say with certainly whether or not any foreign material has been introduced underneath the eyelids.

In the general features of the form of cranium and face Ramses II conforms to the Egyptian type; but the sloping forehead, the prominent superciliary ridges, the narrow, high-bridged, outstanding nose, and especially the great jaw with its large and massive ascending ramus (pl. XLIV, fig. 1) are alien characters, to which I shall refer again when discussing the features of Ramses II[nd's] son and successor Menephtah.

Professor Virchow's measurements (*op. cit.*, p. 774 and 786) again present many discrepancies in comparison with mine. Perhaps the most surprising of his figures is the cranial length, which he makes 6 millimetres less than my estimation; but this makes the long-headed Ramses II (see pl. XLIV) appear the shortest-headed of the Pharaohs measured by Professor Virchow!

61079. The Mummy of Menephtah (pl. XLV, XLVI, XLVII, XLVIII and XLIX).

Acting on the instructions of M. Maspero, *Directeur général du Service des Antiquités*, I removed the wrappings from the mummy of Menephtah on July 8th, 1907, in the Cairo Museum (*Annales*, 1907).

The mummy of this Pharaoh was found in 1898 by M. Loret in the tomb of Amenothes II at Bibân el Molouk, Thebes, and was brought to the Museum in Cairo in 1900. In his *Guide du Visiteur au Musée du Caire*, M. Maspero makes the following remarks : «Momie du Pharaon Ménéphtah, fils et successeur de Ramsès II, trouvée dans le cercueil de Setnakhîtî. M. Loret crut y reconnaître la momie du Pharaon hérétique de la XVIIIe dynastie, Khouniatonou. M. Groff affirma le premier que c'était Ménéphtah, et la lecture du cartouche, tracé en écriture hiératique sur la poitrine de la momie, démontra la justesse de son opinion. Le fait était d'autant plus intéressant à constater que Ménéphtah serait, d'après une tradition d'époque alexandrine, le Pharaon de l'Exode, celui qui, dit-on, aurait péri dans la mer Rouge. »

Even without the evidence of the writing on the shroud many details of the process of mummification would have enabled us to put this mummy into the same group as those of Ramses II (unrolled by M. Maspero in 1886) and Siptah and Seti II (unrolled by me in 1905) : and the physical characters of the mummy itself are such as to suggest a near affinity to Ramses II and Seti I[st]. On these grounds there can be little doubt as to the correctness of the identification of this mummy as Menephtah.

The mummy was wrapped in a sheet of fine linen, which covered the front and sides of the body, but not the back. It passed over the head and extended behind the neck : at the other end it enclosed the feet and ended behind the ankles, its two lower corners being drawn forward and tied in front of the ankle joint. The name was

written in ink on this sheet in hieratic characters across the chest. It was very much
faded, and cannot be seen in plate XLV, fig. 1.

This outer sheet was fixed in position by three bandages — one around the neck, one
around the hips and the third around the knees. Each bandage passed around the
body three times and its end was passed under the rest of the bandage.

When the covering sheet was removed the mummy was found to have been very carelessly and hastily wrapped in a series of broad bandages, which only partially covered
the body. In many places masses of loose rags projected between the bandages and
parts of the skin of the right side of the face were exposed to view.

The first bandage ended on the knees and was found to invest the thighs three times
from its beginning at the hips. Then a second bandage of a similar character was
removed from the thighs.

Then a very loose bandage of fringed linen, arranged in a figure-of-8 pattern around
the neck and head, was removed. When two more short pieces of linen were removed
from the neck and face a loose mass of rags that partially covered the face and head
was freed and dropped off the head, leaving it completely bare.

Then a broad bandage was removed from the chest and two very loosely arranged
bandages of a dark, reddish-brown, fringed material were unwound from the neck
and thorax. Then I removed a series of four broad bandages, which formed a covering
for the body from the neck to the feet — the first one surrounding the shoulders,
chest (including the folded arms) and abdomen, the second enclosing the thighs,
the third the legs from knees to ankles, and the fourth the feet.

When these were removed a great mass of loose rags of fine linen — clearly part of
the original wrappings — was exposed and then removed. A loose reddish-brown
bandage was then removed from the arms, which were thus almost completely
exposed, folded ×-wise in front of the chest, the right forearm being in front of the
left. Another broad bandage was found wrapped around the abdomen and thighs :
when this was removed, another mass of loose rags that filled up the widely-gaping
abdominal wall was taken away. The whole body was thus exposed covered in parts
by a thin layer of very fine linen impregnated with a bright yellow resin-like material.
Dr Charles Todd kindly examined this material, which proved to be a balsam. When
dissolved in alcohol it has a pleasant odour like Friar's balsam. The arms, the chest
wall, parts of the leg and feet were enclosed in this balsam-impregnated carapace
of fine linen.

Not a fragment of writing, nor ornaments of any kind, were found on the mummy.

The body is that of an old man and is 1 m. 714 mill. in height. Menephtah was almost
completely bald, only a narrow fringe of white hair (now cut so close as to be seen
only with difficulty) remaining on the temples and occiput. A few short (about
2 mill.) black hairs were found on the upper lip and scattered, closely-clipped hairs
on the cheeks and chin.

The general aspect of the face recalls that of Ramses II, but the form of the cranium
and the measurements of the face much more nearly agree with those of his grandfather, Seti the Great.

The process of embalming has been eminently successful, the body being well preserved
without much distortion and without the dark discolouration seen in the mummies
of the XVIIIth Dynasty.

The soft parts of the nose have become somewhat flattened, thus spoiling the appearance
of the face. After the brain had been removed the embalmers packed the cranial
cavity with small pieces of fine linen and some balsam; the nostrils were then plugged
with a resinous paste, and the same material was spread over the mouth and ears.
A semilunar patch of black paint was then applied in the situation of the eyebrows.
Beyond this a thin layer of red paste had been applied to the face. In places this has
now peeled off leaving white patches. The ears were pierced in life, but the holes
are quite small.

The embalming wound is almost vertical and situated just in front of the anterior
superior iliac spine, which is opposite its midpoint. The wound was smeared with
resinous paste and a plate applied to its surface, but only a part of the impression
of the plate is now evident.

All the viscera were removed from the body-cavity, except (possibly) the heart. I was
able to recognise part of the heart pushed far up into the thorax, but still attached
to the aorta. Whether or not it was intended to leave the whole heart in the body,
as the practice was in the time of the XXIst Dynasty, I cannot say.

The aorta was in an extreme stage of calcareous degeneration, large bone-like patches
standing out prominently from the walls of the vessel. Mr. S. G. Shattock, the
Curator of the Pathological Section of the Royal College of Surgeons' Museum in
London, has made an exhaustive study of a piece of this artery and found it to be
affected by the ordinary senile form of calcareous degeneration.

The body had been packed with that white cheesy material, such as I found in many
mummies of the priests of Amen (of the XXIst Dynasty). My colleague, Professor
W. A. Schmidt, considered the material (in the case of the latter mummies) to
consist of the decomposition-products of a mixture of butter and soda.

A very curious feature of this mummy is the complete absence of the scrotum, although
the penis was left. Midway between the root of the penis and the anus (pl. XLV,
fig. 2) a transverse scar is visible. It represents the place from which the scrotal sac
was cut away, but as it is now thickly smeared with balsam it is not possible to say
whether it was removed during life or after death. It was certainly done before the
process of embalming was completed because the wound is coated with balsam. The
fact that there is a wound suggests that Menephtah was castrated either after death
or a within a short time of death.

The distal portion of the penis is broken off and is missing. This, however, was done
long after the body was mummified, no doubt by the tomb-robbers, who inflicted
such severe injuries on the mummy.

The hands were placed in the position of grasping sceptres, each 15 millimetres in
diameter, the thumbs being in the position represented in the bas-reliefs.

The skin of the body is thickly encrusted with salt, which my colleague, Mr W. M. Colles,
has examined and found to be sodium chloride.

The mummy has suffered considerably at the hands of plunderers.

The skin is shaved off the right zygomatic arch (Diagram 12, *a*) with a sharp instrument and scraped off a small spot on the forehead. The left side of the chin is cut through to the bone (pl. XLVIII and Diagram 12, *b*).

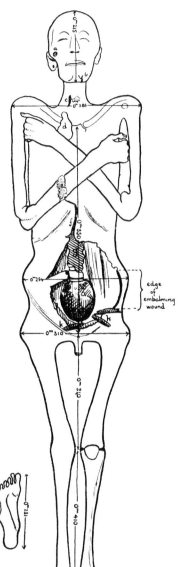

Diagram 12.

There is a deep gash on the right side of the larynx, breaking through the right ala of the completely-ossified thyroid «cartilage», and there are other smaller gashes in the larynx (pl. XLVIII and Diagram 12, *c*).

A deep axe-cut over the situation of the right sterno-clavicular joint (*d*) has broken through the chest wall, severing the inner ends of the clavicle, first rib (whose «cartilage» is ossified throughout) and part of the sternum. This separated part of the chest wall, was lying free in the body-cavity, but I have now replaced it (pl. XLVI and XLVIII).

The right arm was broken midway between the elbow and wrist (Diagram 12, *e*) and was held together only by the tendons and muscles (pl. XLVI).

Almost the whole of the anterior abdominal wall has been chopped away, a few ribbons of skin being practically all that is left of it. The axe-cuts passed right through the body to the spine, large pieces being chopped away from the lower two lumbar vertebræ (Diagram 12, *g*). The left iliac bone and the pubes are smashed by transverse axe-blows (*h* and *k*). Part of the phallus was also broken off. There were also numerous small gashes in the skin of various parts of the body and especially on the legs. The toes of the left foot were broken and two of them were missing.

On the right side of the back there is a large vertical oval opening in the body-wall o m. 93 cent. × o m. o53 mill. Its edges are eroded as though it had been eaten by mice, possibly attracted by the smell of the cheese-like material inside the body.

On the back of the head there is a hole (37 × 23 millimetres in size) in the right parietal bone. It has been deliberately made by means of blows from some sharp instrument. In the case of similar openings that I found in the mummies of Seti II, Ramses IV, Ramses VI (and possibly that of Ramses V also) I was inclined to look upon them as wounds accidentally made by plunderers, who, in their haste to remove the wrappings from the head and neck, chopped through the bandages and so damaged the cranium. I still think there is a good deal to be said in favour of this view; but the nature of the opening in Menephtah's skull seems to point to the possibility of it having been deliberately made — perhaps for some occult reason.

By scraping away a small piece of skin alongside this opening I was able to expose the upper three centimetres of this right lambdoid suture, which shows no sign of closing (pl. XLIX).

The patency of this suture is unusual in a man of the age that Menephtah is supposed to have reached. That he was a man of great age is shown by his baldness, the whiteness of the little hair left, the complete ossification of the thyroid cartilage and especially the ossification of the cartilage of the first rib (not its sheath only).

The calcareous patches in the aorta also point to the same conclusion.

Only one tooth is visible — the upper, right, median incisor, the others being hidden by the resinous paste filling the space between the lips.

Although the body is now reduced to little more than skin and bone, the redundancy of the skin of the abdomen, thighs and cheeks indicates that Menephtah was a somewhat corpulent old man.

Most of the foregoing account has been published in the *Annales du Service* (1907); but there are a number of features that call for further comment.

Seti I and Ramses II exhibit in their cranial and facial features many alien traits, curiously blended with Egyptian characters : but in Menephtah the foreign element in his composition is more obtrusively shown than it is in either his father or his grandfather. He has the prominent, high-bridged nose of his father, but a shorter and much broader cranium than either of his predecessors.

In norma verticalis his head is of a broad beloid form and is distinctly asymmetrical, the left side of the occiput being more prominent (Diagram 13).

The cranial length is only o m. 185 mill., a whole centimetre less than his father's; but the breadth is o m. 150. 14 millimetres greater than in the case of Ramses II and 7 millimetres greater than Seti I.

Diagram 13.

The mere comparisons of lengths and breadths of the cranium might lead one to imagine that the feeble successors of Menephtah, Siphtah and Seti II, retained something suggestive of Menephtah's cranium, for the measurements are respectively o m. 189 mill. × o m. 147 mill. and o m. 187 mill. × o m. 141 mill.; but the breadths of the forehead and face at once reveal the differences. Menephtah resembles his grandfather Seti I in having a wide face and forehead; minimal frontal diameter, o m. 101 mill. (Seti I, o m. 101 mill.; Ramses II, o m. 091 mill.; Siphtah, o m. 091 mill.; and Seti II, o m. 097 mill.); bizygomatic diameter, o m. 141 mill. (Seti I, o m. 138 mill.; Ramses II, o m. 132 mill.; Siphtah, o m. 129 mill.; Seti II, o m. 129 mill.). Total facial height o m. 129 mill. (Seti I, o m. 128 mill.; Ramses II, o m. 136 mill.; Siphtah o m. 127 mill.; Seti II, o m. 130 mill.). Estimated upper facial height, o m. 077 mill. (Seti I, o m. 080 mill.; Ramses II, o m. 080 mill.; Siphtah, o m. 078 mill.; Seti II, o m. 065 mill.). Bigonial breadth, o m. o99 mill. (Seti I, o m. 101 mill.; Ramses II, o m. o97 mill.; Siphtah, o m. 100 mill.; Seti II, o m. 102 mill.). Circumference, o m. 53o mill. Nasal height and breadth, o m. o6o mill. × o m. o32 mill. (Seti I, o m. o6o mill. × o m. o33 mill.; Ramses II, o m. o61 mill. × o m. o29 mill.; Siphtah, o m. o6o mill. × o m. o3o mill.; and Seti II, o m. o59 mill. × o m. o26 mill.). Right orbit, o m. o47 mill. × o m. o38 mill. : left orbit, o m. o46 mill. × o m. o37 mill.

In height Menephtah is intermediate between his father and grandfather, 1 m. 714 mill. (Seti I, 1 m. 665 mill.; Ramses II, 1 m. 733 mill.; Siphtah, 1 m. 638 mill.; and Seti II, 1 m. 64o mill.).

61080. The Mummy of Siphtah (pl. LX, LXI, LXII and LXIII).

This is one of the mummies found by M. Loret in the tomb of Amenothes II in 1898. I began the process of unwrapping it in the Cairo Museum on August 29th, 1905.

After photographs had been made of the coffin (pl. LX, fig. 1), the enshrouded mummy (pl. LX, fig. 2), and the writing on the shroud (pl. LXI, fig. 1), the unrolling of the bandages was commenced. Three days were devoted to this process.

1. The whole body was wrapped in a large sheet of cloth, which covered the head and feet and the front and sides of the body, overlapping behind. It was kept in position by three circular bandages, one passing around the neck, a second around the thighs and the third around the ankles. Midway between the latter two bandages there was a hieratic inscription in ink on the front of the large shroud. Much of the ink had scaled off so that the writing has became very indistinct.

The large investing sheet is a long narrow bandage of very fine linen, about two and a half times as long and broad respectively as the mummy itself. It is folded on itself from end to end so that the two ends, which are both tasselled, come together behind the ankles. This doubled sheet was wrapped around the body in the way already mentioned.

2. The circular neck-bandage passed obliquely around the head and covered the face and then encircled the neck twice, its end being tucked under the penultimate turn.

3. The circular thigh-bandage invested the legs three times passing from right to left in front. Its end was tucked under the rest of the bandage.

4. The ankle-bandage is like that just described but passed around the legs five times.

5. After removing these wrappings the body was found to be invested by a large series of very irregularly-disposed bandages (pl. LXI, fig. 2).

The forearms occupy a peculiar position, which was evident even before the outer shroud was removed. Both upper arms are placed vertically at the sides of the body : the forearms are disposed transversely in front of the thorax and epigastrium, the right being higher up than the left : both hands are clenched.

The loose ends of two bandages were placed just above the right hand. One of these (5) passed across the chest to the left shoulder; once around the neck; once around the head across the face; across the chest toward the right; then around the back; then up in front of the left side of the chest and around the neck to end in front of the right side of the chest. The other (6) passed twice around the chest and then behind the neck to the left shoulder, thence vertically down the left arm, around the elbow obliquely across to the front of the pubes and right thigh, where it ended without being fixed in position in any way. Where this bandage (6) ended another (7) began; it passed around the hips (from right to left in front) and then across the left hand; thence obliquely to the left shoulder, across the back to the right shoulder and obliquely across the front of the chest to a point underneath the left elbow : thence it passed around the hips where it ended by being intertwined with the end of the next bandage (8). This passed obliquely across the chest above the right hand, then transversely behind the chest and across the right elbow to the left hip, then behind the hips and in front of the left hand and around the right forearm to end on the left hand.

A bandage (9) began on the chest and passed to the right twice (alternately) around the neck and chest before it ended on the right shoulder. The next bandage (10) began in front on the chest and passed (toward the right in front) twice around the shoulders. The next (11) passed in the same direction transversely around the chest to the right hand and then circularly around the chest. Its two ends were knotted under the left hand. N° 12 started at the right hand (on the left elbow) and passed spirally around the arms and thighs as far as the knee, where it ended on the right side of the leg. Where it ended the next bandage (13) began and passed spirally down the leg and described a figure of 8 around the ankles and feet. These two bandages passed from right to left in front. Where the last bandage ended another (14) began and after forming a figure of 8 around the ankles and feet, it wound spirally up the leg as far as the knee, where another bandage (15) began and wound around the knees (from left to right in front) and then spirally around the left leg only. When his wrapping was removed the left foot, distorted in the manner know as talipes equino-varus, was exposed in its original wrappings. Another bandage (16) began between the forearms and, passing from right to left in front, wound around the body as far as the knees.

The right forearm had been broken, presumably by plunderers, long after mummification, and when the priests rewrapped the body, the forearm was fixed with splints. A ragged piece of linen (17) was wrapped around these splints (diagram 14 and pl. LXII).

All of the bandages enumerated above were put on the mummy by the priests of a later dynasty, after the mummy had been plundered. When these eighteen strips of linen had been removed the mummy itself was exposed partly wrapped in the torn fragments of its original bandages.

Each foot was partially wrapped in a large quantity of soft muslin of exceedingly fine texture, and the surface of this covering was smeared with a thick layer of resinous paste.

A considerable quantity of similar bandage was wound around the left thigh and connected by numerous 8-shaped loops across the perineum to the right leg. After removing this the selvedged end of a sheet of linen (0 m. 31 cent. wide) was found

wrapped around the left thigh and the left side of the body, its ragged torn end
being alongside the shoulders. It was inscribed with a series of lines of red paint.
After removing a small spiral bandage from the left thigh a similar bandage was
found : it was inscribed with hieroglyphic signs in black and lines in red (pl. LXIII,
fig. 1). It was arranged like the other painted sheet just mentioned. Similar bandages
and painted sheets of linen were found on the right thigh and side of the body.

Each arm was wrapped in a large mass of bandages of exquisitely fine linen smeared
on its surface with a layer of resinous paste.

Lying on the front of the chest there was a mass of torn bandages with strips passing
over the shoulders. The whole mass was thickly plastered with resinous paste, in
which the impression of part of the usual pectoral ornament could be plainly seen.
In front of the right elbow there was a cake of resin (adherent to the bandages)
in which there was a vertical groove o m. o15 mill. in diameter lined with gold
foil (Diagram 14). It was evidently the
impression of a gilded staff originally placed in the left hand of the mummy.

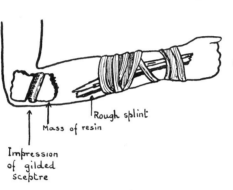

Rough splint

Mass of resin

Impression
of gilded
sceptre

Diagram 14.

The plunderers broke off the right hand at
the wrist-joint. When the mummy was being
rewrapped one third of a piece of a ragged
bandage. o m. 99 cent. by o m. 22 cent.,
was wrapped around the separated hand
leaving the other two-thirds free : this was
split into two bands, one of which was
wound around the forearm and a ventral

splint — a rough piece of wood o m. 15 cent. long — and the other encircled
the forearm and the dorsal splint — a rough piece of coffin o m. 25 cent. long. In
this way the hand was fixed to the forearm; and to render it more secure another
bandage was wound around both splints and the hand and forearm. Two strips of
bandage, each o m. 132 mill. long — one of them 1.5 cm. and the other 3.3 cm.
wide with a fringe of strings 8.5 cm. long on each — were intertwined to form
one cord, which was wound spirally round the two splints, beginning at the hand.
At the other end of the splints the two strips were separated and after being passed
in opposite directions around the forearm, were tied together.

The mummy is that of a young man 1 m. 638 mill. in height, with a thick crop of
short, reddish brown, curly hair. When the ringlets are unrolled the hair is o m.
o36 mill. long.

The cheeks were very carefully packed with long, narrow strips of very fine muslin.
The face was entirely hidden by a thick mass of resin firmly .adherent to the skin
and to the cloth covering it. Some of this I removed to expose the features of
the face.

The right cheek and the front teeth had been badly broken by a blow long after the
embalming process; and at the same time the lips and the whole right side of the
cheek down to the chin had been broken away. This was done before the mummy

was rewrapped, because the missing parts were not in the bandages. The ears were broken off.

The plunderers, who had done this damage to the face, also broke off the right arm at the shoulder and the right hand from the forearm.

In hacking through the bandages on the legs they had also shaved the skin off two spots on the outer side of the left knee.

They had also broken through the body wall, making an irregular hole o m. 15 cent. long above the umbilicus.

The abdomen was packed with lichen, and the embalming-incision was made along-side Poupart's ligament and was sewn up with narrow strips of linen.

Siphtah was 1 m. 638 mill. in height.

His cranium is of the form that Sergi calls «pentagonoid» (diagram 15) : it is o m. 189 mill. long and o m. 147 mill. broad : minimal frontal diameter, o m. 094 mill. : circumference, o m. 530 mill. : bizygomatic breadth, o m. 129 mill. : bigonial breadth, o m. 100 mill.; total facial height, o m. 127 mill.; upper facial height, o m. 078 mill.

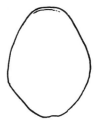

Diagram 15.

The nose is o m. 060 mill. in height and o m. 030 mill. broad. It has a moderately high bridge : the cartilaginous part has been flattened and distorted by the bandages, but there can be no doubt that it was small, narrow, aquiline and graceful in form. Across the forehead extends a broad (vertical measurement 16 millimetres), crescentic band of black paint, the lateral extremities of which are situated just above the external canthi. In the mummy of Siphtah several innovations in the technique of embalming make their appearance. The cheeks are filled out with linen packing and the body cavity is stuffed with dried lichen.

The embalming wound was sewn up. Although this method of dealing with it is not new, since I have seen it in the XVIIIth Dynasty mummy of Thuaa, it now became the custom and apparently remained so until the death of Ramses IV.

61081. The Mummy of Seti II (pl. LXIV, LXV and LXVI).

This mummy is one of those found in 1898 by M. Loret in the tomb of Amenothes II in the Bibân el Molouk. I began unrolling the bandages of this mummy in the Cairo Museum on September 3rd, 1905, and devoted several days to the process. At various times I was assisted by Mr. J. E. Quibell, Mr. Percy E. Newberry and Professor A. R. Ferguson; and M. Emil Brugsch pacha was present throughout the work of unwrapping.

Seti II was a young or middle-aged man, 1 m. 640 mill. in height. Both Siphtah and Seti II were thus decidedly smaller in stature than the three, great, old men who preceeded them in the XIXth Dynasty. Neither of them exhibits any trace of that decision and strength, which are so strongly imprinted on the faces of Seti I[st], Ramses II and Menephtah.

The body had been most carefully and successfully mummified, and wrapped in exceptionally fine, gauzy muslin of very soft texture. Successive layers of bandage were smeared with resinous paste, and in some places quite a thick layer of this material was found; it exhibited on its surface the imprints of the skin patterns of the fingers of the man who had moulded it into shape. Embedded in this resin I found around each leg a piece of string (on which a series of blue-glaze «eyes», of the usual pattern, were threaded) wound spirally around the leg from ankle to knee. At each end of the string there was a blue-glaze scarab. In front of the right knee, lying in the groove between the patella and tibia, there were three small sphinxes threaded on strings (Diagrams 17 and 18).

The mummy had suffered considerably at the hands of its plunderers. The head was broken off from the body, carrying with it the axis and atlas : the neck was broken at the cervico-thoracic junction.

Both arms were separated from the body and both forearms from the upper arms. The right forearm and hand were missing, and also the index, ring and little fingers (in part) of the left hand. The arms had originally been placed in the folded position over the chest and the left hand (and possibly the right also, if we can judge from the analogy of other royal mummies) was in the position of grasping a sceptre.

A large part of the anterior wall of the body was broken away; and that this was done before the rewrapping is clearly shown by the fact that part of the wall of the chest was found among the superficial bandages, as though it had been forgotten and had been put in just before the wrapping-process was completed.

The plunderers, when cutting through the original wrappings with some sharp instrument (? knife or perhaps axe), had gashed the skin in various parts of the body. The embalming wound resembles that of Siphtah in position and the manner in which it was treated.

The body had been packed with pieces of linen soaked in a solution of resin, which set into a stone-like mass filling the whole cavity.

The features were well-preserved and were not distorted, but the face is thickly encrusted with resinous paste. The scalp was not treated in this manner, so that it is possible to see that it was studded with short, closely-clipped, dark brown hair.

On the vertex of the skull, to the left of the sagittal suture, there is an irregular hole (0 m. 050 mill. × 0 m. 015 mill.) in the left parietal bone. The skin at its edge is cut into ribbons showing that the damage was done by numerous blows with some sharp instrument. It was certainly done *after* mummification.

Both ears were pierced.

Amongst the wrappings there was an unusually large quantity of the materials originally used for this purpose when the body was embalmed. There were fragments of several garments and two perfectly intact shirts of very fine muslin. Each of these shirts was made from a strip of fine linen 1 m. 25 cent. wide and 2 m. 54 cent. long, folded lengthways on itself, and its edges sewn together except in the upper 0 m. 31 cent. of its extent. This was left unstitched and was hemmed to form an arm-hole on each side. On the front of the square shirt thus made a circular neck-hole was cut near the upper edge and hemmed around. Its circumference is 0 m. 40 cent. In the middle line in front a slit o m. 090 mill. long was cut from this neck-hole vertically downward and hemmed like the rest.

In the lower (right-hand in one, left hand in the other) corner of the front of the shirt there was embroidered in red and blue thread a vertical cartouche and name, which Brugsch Pasha tells me is that of Menephtah. Alongside this (nearer the edge) in one of the shirts is a long vertically-placed hieratic inscription in ink : and on the left corner, another, shorter, badly-corroded inscription (Diagram 16).

[I regret that it is not possible to give a fuller description of these shirts and of the writing upon them. At the time when I unwrapped this mummy the shirts were handed over to the Conservator of the Museum, but when I came to write this Catalogue they were not to be found in the Museum].

The mummy was wrapped in a large shroud investing the whole body (pl. LXIV, fig. 1). Its tasselled ends were found behind the feet tied in a knot. It was composed of fine linen (warp 13, woof 23 to the centimetre) with both margins selvedged and one end string-fringed. It measured 3 m. 14 cent. × 0 m. 85 cent. It was very much torn and had been repaired in many places.

There was a faint traces of the name written (in ink) in hieratic on the front of this sheet of linen.

This sheet was held in position by four strips of linen wrapped in a circular manner around the mummy — neck, hips, thighs and ankles respectively — and knotted behind.

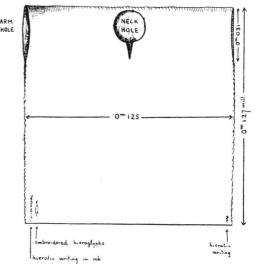

Diagram 16.

When these five pieces of linen — the shroud and the four circular bandages — were removed, I found a loose piece of very fine, gauzy muslin (6) placed in front of the body. Then beginning to unroll the bandages I found the end of the first (7) in front of the right elbow and it was unwound from the body, around which it passed in a circular manner twice.

Bandage number 8 had been applied as a spiral beginning at the hips and ending on the ankles. It consisted of a piece of loose-textured linen 3 m. 75 cent. × 0 m. 33 cent., with string-fringe at both ends. It had 8 threads to the centimetre warp and 16 woof. Then we found a pad (9) on the right hip, consisting of three ragged pieces of very fine linen (warp 23 woof 51), one of them smeared with resin-paste. Undoubtedly all three were parts of the original wrappings of Seti II.

Bandage number 10 was a sheet 3 m. 45 cent. × 0 m. 17 cent., with one end and one edge selvedged and the other end converted into string tassels 0 m. 015 mill. long, each string consisting of two strings intertwined and knotted at the end — texture of linen, 14 warp and 20 woof to the centimetre. This bandage was applied as a figure of 8 around the feet and ankles and then spirally around the legs up to the knees.

Bandage 11, a long ragged strip 3 m. 45 cent. × 0 m. 16 cent. selvedged on one side — texture like n° 10 — was put on spirally around the legs from the knees to the ankles.

Bandage 12, a piece of the same sheet as n°s 10 and 11, 0 m. 017 mill. wide, was put on spirally around the legs from the knees to the hips.

N° 13 is a pad placed in front of the thighs.

N° 14 consisted of two pieces of bandage, one (a) 3 m. 60 cent. × 0 m. 19 cent. and texture 10 × 20 and the other (b) 2 m. 05 cent. × 0 m. 19 cent. and texture 15 × 24. One end of a had been torn and darned with a rope-like seam.

It was applied in a spiral course completely covering the legs from the ankles to the thighs and then down again as far as the knees.

N° 15 is a sheet 3 m. 60 cent. × 0 m. 19 cent. with one end selvedged — texture : warp 13, woof 18 to the centimetre. It was applied circularly around the abdomen and thorax.

Underneath this bandage a large piece of the wall of the chest was found lying loose on the surface of the deeper bandages.

N° 16 consists of a pad of linen placed on the right side of the abdomen. It includes five pieces of material : (a) a sheet of very fine, gauzy muslin 1 m. 73 cent. × 0 m. 20 cent. — one end tasselled. At the attachment of the strings of the tassel there are six transverse string-like bands in the cloth, of which the middle two are green (probably blue originally). The threads are too fine and irregular to count. Three of the rest are scraps of similar, though not identical, material; and the fifth (e) is a closely-woven sheet 1 m. 47 cent. × 0 m. 22 cent. of the texture, warp 20 woof 37 to the centimetre.

N° 17 is a very ragged bandage 3 m. 50 cent. × 0 m. 21 cent. on end and edge selvedged and the other end string-fringed like n° 16 — texture 20 × 21.

It was applied to the right side of the head, then in a series of spirals around the neck and thorax.

N° 18 is a mass of rags placed in front of the neck, held in position by n° 17.

N° 19 is a very ragged bandage (3 m. 76 cent. × 0 m. 16 cent.) of close textured cloth (warp 11 woof 23), both ends converted into string-fringe. It was put on in a circular manner around the hips, abdomen and thorax.

N° 20 is a bandage (3 m. 56 cent. × 0 m. 27 cent.) of fine, regular thread (13 × 24), with one end selvedged. It was applied in a circular manner once around the abdomen, then obliquely from the left elbow to the right shoulder in front, then behind the back to the left shoulder and obliquely across the body to the right hip.

N° 21 is a bandage (3 m. 11 cent. × 0 m. 15 cent.) composed of material like n° 20, but with strings-tassels like n° 16. It was applied in a circular manner around the chest and shoulders.

N° 22 is a large mass of loose rags placed in front of the chest, parts of shirts of very fine linen.

N° 23 is a bandage (3 m. 48 cent. × 0 m. 19 cent.) of very regular even texture (warp 16 woof 25), with torn ends and sides. It was applied circularly around shoulders, neck, head, neck and thus back to the shoulders.

The left forearm was then exposed lying separate on the left side of the abdomen, the hand being downwards towards the pubes and the upper ends of the radius and ulna over the lower left ribs. The right forearm is missing. The left upper arm could not be found at this stage, but it came to light later on, lying between the thighs.

N° 24. Two pieces of coarse cloth (warp 12 woof 17), each of them 0 m. 53 cent. × 0 m. 60 cent. sewn together along the two shorter borders to form an open tube. It was placed around the head and neck.

N° 25 is a fine bandage (3 m. 50 cent. × 0 m. 18 cent.) with one end fringed, the other selvedged — texture 15 × 24. Beginning on the top of the head it was applied in the following manner : — it was brought down through the right armpit across the back into the left armpit, thence across the top of the head in a transverse direction, being split to enable it to hold more firmly on the arched vertex of the skull : then it passed through the right armpit (forwards) across the front of the chest to the left armpit, thence vertically upward behind and then above the head (where it is again split) and finally downward into the right armpit.

The object of this bandage is probably twofold : — to fix the head more firmly on the body; and to bridge over the gap between the head and the body and facilitate the attainment of the customary form of the wrapped mummy.

N° 26 is a small sheet of fine linen (0 m. 75 cent. × 0 m. 62 cent.) placed in front of the thighs — texture, 22 × 31.

When these twenty six bandages were removed a large mass of pieces of exquisitely fine muslin (many pieces with elaborately fringed and coloured — red and blue — borders) and clothes was exposed loosely thrown around the body in the most irregular and disordered manner (pl. LXIV, fig. 2). In addition to the two shirts, to which I have already referred earlier in this account, there was found in contact with the body a large loose mass which consisted of the original wrappings of the thorax and abdomen of the mummy. It consisted of a large sheet of very fine, soft muslin composed of particularly delicate threads, of which there were 46 to the centimetre in the warp and 24 in the woof. It was folded on itself longitudinally and also transversely. As the lower part of the sheet is destroyed its length cannot be estimated. It is 0 m. 95 cent. wide and 0 m. 35 cent. of this breadth is folded over. Outside this fine muslin there was a sheet of coarser, very close-textured linen (warp 18 woof 30); and on the surface of this there was a layer of resin-paste 0 m. 001 mill. thick. On the surface of this there was originally a large series of bandages of soft muslin, 0 m. 042 mill. wide, but so puckered and folded (longitudinally) as to be only 0 m. 05 cent. wide, when not flattened out. Each leg had been wrapped in large quantities of very fine muslin bandages. When the leg was completely covered, a layer of resinous paste 0 m. 002 mill. thick was spread over the whole surface : another series of bandages was then applied and another layer of paste and so on until eight layers of alternate muslin and resinous paste (four of each) were put on. The arms were treated in a similar manner and every finger and toe was wrapped separately.

The plunderers made large gashes through this eight-fold carapace on both sides of the right knee, in front of the right tibia near the ankle, on the outer side of the left ankle and in both thighs. By means of these openings they obtained a number of small charms, but at the same time they left some of these objects, which I found firmly embedded in the re-sinous capsule which enclosed the two legs.

These consist of portions of long strings of blue-glaze eye-amulets and beads on both legs and three small human-headed sphinxes from the front of the right knee. These objects were firmly embedded in the resinous paste and it was im-possible to expose them in such a manner as to photograph them *in situ*. In lieu of this I have carefully determined the position of each ob-ject in turn and constructed the two accompanying plans, drawn to sca-le. In diagram 17 the outlines of the right knee-cap (patella) and the upper ends of the tibia and fibula are indicated, as seen from the front. Each of the three sphinxes (A, B and C) was mounted on its own string and the ends of the strings were knotted behind the

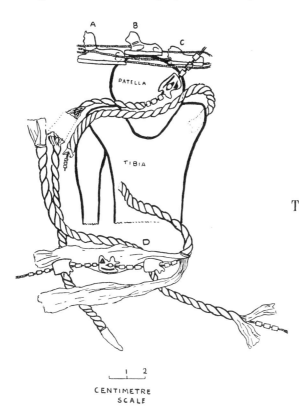

Diagram 17. A diagram, accurately drawn to scale, to illus-trate the arrangement of the objects found around the right knee and leg. The outlines of part of the skeleton are seen.

Above the knee-cap (patella) are seen three sphinxes (A, B and C) each threaded on its own string. Lower down are seen two ropes, the upper are joined to a string bearing six blue-glaze «eyes».

The group of ropes and the string of beads at D are on the back of the leg and are seen from in front. The bones are not represented there, so as to show these ropes. The «face» of one of the three «eyes» was applied to the skin : the plain surface of the other two is seen.

knee. One of them (C) is made of frit with a bright green glaze and the other two are made of Amazonite. This determination of materials is M. Maspero's.

On each leg there were portions of a long rope, formed by intertwining two strips (each o m. o3 cent. wide) of longitudinally rolled bandage — each roll being 2.5 mill. in diameter and the rope o m. oo5 mill. Although only a few torn fragments have been left by the plunderers, yet their united length on the right leg is o m. 62 cent. and even more on the left. So that originally there must have been quite a long rope wound around the leg between the ankle and the knee.

At one end the rope is finished off in a conical form (Diagrams 17 and 18), the extremity of one of the bandages being wrapped around it and tied in position. From the other end a string (on which beads and « sacred eyes » are threaded) emerges from the rope. One of the two bandages from which the rope is formed is wrapped around the string for a distance of more than three centimetres. The objects threaded on the string are not arranged in the same manner on the two sides. On the right leg the series begins with three cylindrical, blue-glaze beads (each 3 millimetres long), then a blue-glaze « eye », then three beads and so on to the end. On the left leg the series commences with three smaller beads, then a small blue-glaze scarab (Diagram 18, S),

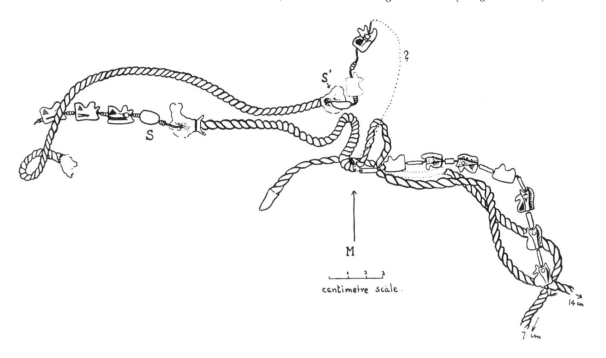

Diagram 18. The ropes removed from the left leg spread out it one plane. M represents the mesial line in front of the leg. S is a scarab (plain face) with the beetle-surface toward the skin. S' is another scarab turned sideways. 21 centimetres (7 + 14) of the rope were left out of the drawing at the lower right hand corner for want of room.

then three small beads, then an « eye » and the series of alternate groups of three small beads and « eyes » until the other end is reached. There (Diagram 18, S') we find another scarab, but no small beads beyond it. Either in the middle of this string or perhaps on a second string we find long, cylindrical, blue-glaze beads instead of the three small beads (diagram 18).

The features of the face have been well preserved without much distortion; but the face (pl. LXVI) is thickly encrusted with resinous material as far up as a line crossing the frontal eminences and running obliquely downward on each side to the upper margin of the external ear. Unlike the case of Siphtah's mummy where the features were completely hidden and disguised by the paste covering it, the contour of Seti II[nd's] face is quite evident, and its life-like appearance is enhanced by the fact that the resin has cracked along the lines of the palpebral clefts.

There is little resemblance to the other XIXth Dynasty Pharaohs in Seti II[nd's] features, but they recall in a striking manner those of the XVIIIth Dynasty. The small, narrow, high-bridged aquiline nose is not unlike that of Amenothes II and Thoutmosis IV. The marked projection of the upper teeth and the hanging lower jaw are other points of resemblance to the royal family of the preceding dynasty, and of contrast to the orthognathous heavy-jawed XIXth Dynasty rulers.

In the intervals where the resin has peeled off the lips, chin and cheeks no trace of hair is visible except on the right edge of the mandible, where I was able to detect (with the aid of a lens) eight hairs a little more than one millimetre long.

The scalp is studded with closely-clipped (less than 3 millimetres long), dark brown, straight hair.

Although the skin of the cheeks, so far as it is visible, is quite smooth and unwrinkled, there are several folds of skin below each ear parallel to the posterior margin of the mandible.

The cranium is a small pentagonoid (Diagram 1 9) o m. 1 8 7 mill. long and o m. 1 4 1 mill.

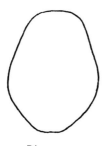

Diagram 19.

broad : the minimal frontal breadth is o m. o 9 7 mill.; and the circumference, o m. 5 2 o mill.

There is marked flattening of the left side of the chest.

The ensiform cartilage is ossified and completely ankylosed to the mesosternum. This suggests that Seti II must have been a middle-aged man.

The embalming incision (now in great part destroyed, as the result of the destructive work of the tomb-robbers) was situated alongside the outer half of the left Poupart's ligament and on the inner side of the iliac crest. It had been sewn up with a narrow strip of bandage as in the case of Siphtah's mummy.

The whole scrotum and the greater part of the penis have been broken off and lost. This was not done by the embalmers, but is one of the many injuries inflicted upon this body by the tomb-robbers. The penis was hanging vertically and was bandaged. The left side of the pubes and the skin covering it were knocked off and lost. The anus is plastered over with resinous material.

The undue prominence of the head of the astragalus and the antero-lateral edges of the calcaneum seems to indicate that the feet were forcibly bent straight after the tissues had become softened. This must not be confused with the condition of talipes equino-varus seen in Siphtah, nor does it justify the statements of certain writers that the embalmers deliberately and of set purpose dislocated the feet of mummies, «to prevent them from walking». There is no dislocation, in the proper sense of the term; and what displacement there is has obviously been produced simply by forcing the feet into the conventional mummy-position.

That this explanation is the true one is shown by the fact that there is an analogous displacement of the carpus. The hand and wrist are twisted much further forward (in relation to the carpal extremity of the radius) than is possible naturally in the living body.

The right forearm and hand are missing. When I restored the fragments of the left arm to the positions they had occupied when the body was mummified, the hand came to lie in front of the right shoulder. It was bent back 45° from the line of the forearm. The thumb was placed in close approximation to the index and fully extended : but the four fingers were flexed at the metacarpo-phalangeal and proximal interphalangeal joints and extended at the distal interphalangeal joints.

The following measurements will enable the reader to reconstruct from plate XLV the exact proportions of the body and compare them with the various canons :

	Metre	mill.
Height..	1	640
Height of suprasternal notch...........................	1	304
Height of upper margin of the symphysis pubis...........	0	850
Height of nasal spine above the symphysis pubis...........	0	680
Left tibia (with internal malleolus).....................	0	370
Left tibia — estimated length (without malleolus)	0	355
Height of upper border of the right great trochanter above the external condyle of the femur.......................	0	427
Bitrochanteric breadth................................	0	273
Bi-iliac breadth....'..................................	0	256
Distance between anterior iliac spines...................	0	198
Maximum breadth of chest.............................	0	245
Biacromial breadth...................................	0	325
Height, chin to vertex................................	0	192
Height, chin to glabella...............................	0	130
Height, upper lip to glabella...........................	0	087
Height, nasal spine to glabella.........................	0	065

61082. Mummy of an unknown woman «D» found in the coffin-lid of Setnakhiti (pl. LXVII and XLVIII).

This is one of the mummies found by M. Loret in the tomb of Amenothes II in 1898. It was lying in a broken coffin-lid bearing the name Setnakhiti and was supposed to be the mummy of that king, until the year 1905, when I removed the wrappings (July 5th) and found it to be the body of a woman.

In the process of unwrapping the mummy I was assisted by M. Daressy and Mr. Howard Carter.

The condition in which the mummy was found is shown in plate LXVII, fig. 1.

The roughly applied bandages had been disturbed (by ancient tomb-robbers) in the front of the body and on the head; and through the wrappings a bunch of curls projected from the left side of the head (compare figs. 1 and 2, pl. LXVII).

The bandages had been applied so carelessly that there is no need for a detailed account of their arrangement.

A large quantity of bandage (0 m. 180 mill. wide) was unrolled from the legs and body. The inner sides of the thighs were padded with large quantities of coarse cloth of different textures. Underneath these there were spirally-wound bandages on each leg, starting at the thigh on the left leg, and the ankle on the right. Under these a shirt had been placed in front each leg; and underneath there was a second shirt, one of the ends of which was on the side of the thigh : it was brought round the foot and up on the other side of the leg.

On the sole of each foot there was a large mass, wrapped in coarse cloth, and fixed in position by bandages of the leg which passed around it. The parcel on the right foot contained a mass of epidermis mixed with large quantities of natron : that on the left portions of viscera with similar preservative material. The epidermis had been removed from the soles of the feet for the most part and the small remaining fragment had a clean-cut edge.

After removing a series of bandages from the head, some of which had been wound in a circular manner and others forming a figure-of-8 around the head and neck, the hair was found to be enclosed in cloths tied like those of modern Egyptian girls. A piece of linen about the size of an ordinary handkerchief was placed upon the head and its lateral corners brought round to the forehead and tied in a knot.

Neither the fingers nor the toes were wrapped separately.

The body is 1 m. 589 mill. high. The head is o m. 190 mill. long and o m. 148 mill. broad — exceptionally large figures for a woman — and its shape was beloid. The arms were placed vertically at the sides, the hands being upon the lateral surfaces of the thighs.

The mummy had escaped all damage at the hands of tomb-robbers, excepting that a large rounded hole had been made through the brittle anterior abdominal wall in the epigastrium (pl. LXVII, fig. 2).

The second and third toes of the left foot were bent sharply upward; but this had been done when the body was still plastic.

The right foot is o m. 211 mill. long and o m. 058 mill. broad.

The oblique length of each femur is estimated at about o m. 436 mill.; the axial length of the tibia at o m. 336 mill.; the oblique length of the humerus at o m. 295 mill.; and the axial length of the radius, o m. 230 mill.

The left hand is o m. 170 mill. long. The breadth across the iliac crests is o m. 245 mill.

The body is that of an extremely emaciated woman with apparently complete atrophy (? senile) of the breasts. Her hair is well preserved and has been made into a series of sharply-rolled curls, of the variety distinguished by modern ladies by the name «Empire» (pl. LXVII). She had a prominent, narrow, high-bridged, «Ramesside» nose; but the pressure of the bandages has distorted the cartilaginous part and marred its beauty. She had a straight line of brow, and a long hanging jaw. The packing of the mouth has given the lips a pouting expression and further disturbed the natural profile of the face.

There is a large widely-gaping elliptical embalming-wound (pl. LXVII, fig. 2) placed obliquely, with its long axis parallel to Poupart's ligament. It extends as far as the symphysis pubis below (internally) and beyond the anterior superior spine of the ilium above (externally). A large pad of linen had been pushed against the perineal region — not the perineum proper, so much as the neighbourhood of the obturator foramina — producing large depressions (pl. LXVII, fig. 2) at the inner side of each femoral neck.

There was no sign of any writing or any inscription that might indicate the identity of this woman.

The complete absence of any attempt at packing the limbs or trunk, as well as the situation of the embalming wound, demonstrate that the body was mummified before the beginning of the XXIst Dynasty.

The texture of the tissues, the light colour of the skin, and the absence of any of the discoloration that was the rule up till the time of Seti I, and other details of the embalmer's technique, indicate that this body was not mummified before the latter part of the XIXth Dynasty.

The position of the arms gives us no information, for I have already called attention to the fact (see the accounts of the mummies of the women in Amenothes II$^{nd's}$ tomb and that of Thuaa) that the conventions adopted in the case of men did not apply to women. At all periods the mummies of women had their hands alongside the thighs, although there were occasional exceptions to this rule (as for example the elder woman in Amenothes II$^{nd's}$ tomb).

The nature and situation of the embalming-wound varies a good deal from reign to reign. In this mummy it is placed alongside Poupart's ligament, as was customary in the latter part of the XVIIIth Dynasty. But the state of preservation of the mummy puts this period out of the question. In the early part of the XIXth Dynasty it was the rule to extend the embalming wound upwards into the iliac region; but at the close of that Dynasty (in the mummies of Siphtah and Seti II) the embalmers returned to the late XVIIIth Dynasty convention, as in this mummy; and in the XXth Dynasty (Ramses IV and V) the early XIXth Dynasty (Ramses II and Menephtah) site once more becomes the fashionable one. In the XXIst and XXIInd Dynasty the early XVIIIth Dynasty site (high or suprailiac incision) comes into vogue.

Thus on the evidence of the site of the embalming incision one might be inclined to put this mummy into the same group as Siphtah's and Seti II$^{nd's}$. But in the case of both of these mummies, as well as in that of Ramses IV (it is not known how the wound was treated in Ramses III) the incision was stitched up, whereas it is gaping in this woman's mummy. However two mummies of the same date (for instance, Iouïya's and Thouïyou's) may be treated in different ways.

Then again there is the nature of stuffing-material in the body cavity — the use of strips of linen. Seti II had hard resin-impregnated linen, like the XVIIIth Dynasty mummies, whereas Siphtah and Ramses IV had dried lichen. From this it seems that the end of the XIXth and the commencement of the XXth Dynasties represent a transition period when experiments were being made in new forms of packing-material. In the mummy under consideration ordinary linen bandages, not treated with resin, were employed. The fact that no attempt was made to make artificial eyes favours the view that the mummy was earlier than Ramses IV, although this kind of evidence is not altogether conclusive, as the mummy of Ramses V shows.

On the other hand the practice of stuffing the cheeks (pl. LXVIII) does not begin until the time of Siphtah, so far as I am aware.

The evidence is quite conclusive that this mummy belongs to the XIXth-XXth epoch and there is a good deal to suggest that it was either very late XIXth or very early XXth.

The fact that it was associated with a group of mummies of kings suggests that this lady was also a member of the royal family.

It is a very suggestive fact — though it may be a mere coincidence — that the only woman's tomb of the XIXth-XXth date that is known in the Bibân el Molouk was made for Tauosrît, the consort in succession Siphtah and of Seti II, to whose times the technique of the mummification has led us to assign this body.

61083. The Mummy of Ramses III (pl. L, LI and LII).

The account of the unwrapping of this mummy, which took place on June 1st, 1886, in the presence of His Highness the Khedive Tewfik, is given in *Les Momies royales*, p. 563-566 (see also p. 767), and also in the *Procès-verbal de l'ouverture des Momies de Ramsès II et Ramsès III* (Bulletin de l'Institut égyptien, 1886), from which the following account is taken, and reproduced in M. Maspero's words.

«Vers dix heures moins dix minutes, la momie n° 5229 fut retirée à son tour de la cage en verre. Elle avait été trouvée dans le grand sarcophage n° 5247, ainsi qu'une autre momie sale et déguenillée. Comme le sarcophage porte le nom de Nofritari, femme du roi Ahmos Ier de la XVIIIme dynastie, on en avait conclu que la momie n° 5229 était celle de cette reine. L'autre momie aurait appartenu à une princesse encore inconnue, et aurait été placée à côté de Nofritari par les prêtres chargés de cacher les cercueils royaux dans le trou de Dêir-el-Baharî. Reléguée aux magasins du Musée, elle acheva de s'y corrompre et répandit bientôt une telle odeur qu'il devint nécessaire de s'en débarrasser. On l'ouvrit donc et on reconnut qu'elle était emmaillotée avec soin, mais le cadavre fut à peine exposé à l'air qu'il tomba littéralement en putréfaction et il se mit à en suinter un pus noirâtre d'une puanteur insupportable. On constata que c'était une femme d'âge mûr et de taille moyenne, appartenant à la race blanche. Les bandelettes n'avaient aucune trace d'écriture, mais un lambeau d'étoffe, découvert dans le sarcophage n° 5247, avait une scène d'adoration du roi Ramsès III, à deux formes d'Amon. Une courte légende, mi-partie en hiéroglyphes cursifs, mi-partie en hiératique, nous apprit que le linge ainsi décoré était un don du chef blanchisseur de la maison royale, et on pensa que la momie anonyme était d'une des nombreuses sœurs, femme ou filles de Ramsès III.

La momie n° 5229 était enveloppée proprement d'une toile de couleur orange, fixée par des bandelettes de toile ordinaire. Elle ne portait aucune inscription apparente; on voyait seulement autour de la tête un bandeau couvert de figures mystiques. M. Maspero rappela à S. A. le Khédive que Nofritari est représentée peinte en noir dans certains tableaux, mais que d'autres monuments lui attribuent le teint jaune et les cheveux lisses des femmes égyptiennes. De là des discussions interminables entre les égyptologues, les uns prétendant que la reine était une négresse, les autres affirmant que la couleur noire de son visage et de son corps était une simple fiction des prêtres : son culte, très répandu à Thèbes, en faisait une forme d'Hathor, la déesse noire, la déesse de la mort et des ténèbres. L'ouverture de la momie n° 5229 allait probablement résoudre à tout jamais ce problème d'histoire. La toile d'orange détachée, on aperçut, sur le linceul en toile blanche qui venait immédiatement au-dessous, une inscription en quatre lignes : « L'an XIII et le second mois de Shemou, le 28, ce jour-là, le premier prophète d'Amon, roi des dieux, Pinotmou, fils du premier prophète d'Amon Piônkh, le scribe du temple Zosersoukhonsou, et le scribe de la nécropole Boutehamon, allèrent restaurer le défunt roi Ousirmarì-Miamoun et l'établir pour l'éternité. » Ce qu'on avait pris jusqu'alors pour Nofritari était donc le cadavre de Ramsès III, et la momie anonyme était sans doute Nofritari. Ce point constaté, Ramsès III fut dressé sur ses pieds et photographié dans son costume de bandelettes. Si courte que fût la pose, elle parut longue encore au gré des spec-tateurs. La péripétie qui substituait un des grands conquérants de l'Égypte à la reine la plus vénérée de la XVIIIme dynastie les avait surpris et excités au plus haut degré : le dépouillement recommença au milieu de l'impatience générale. Tous avaient quitté leur place et se pressaient pêle-mêle autour des opérateurs. Trois épaisseurs de bandelettes disparurent rapidement, puis on fut arrêté par un maillot de canevas cousu et enduit de poix, puis, cette gaine fendue à coups de ciseau, de nouvelles couches de linge se firent jour à travers l'ouverture; la momie semblait fondre et se dérober sous nos doigts. Quelques-unes des toiles portaient des tableaux et des légendes à l'encre noire : le dieu Ammon est assis sur son trône, et, au-dessus, une ligne d'hiéroglyphes nous apprend que cette bandelette a été fabriquée et offerte par un dévot du temps ou par une princesse de sang royal, « par la dame chanteuse d'Amon-Râ, roi des dieux, Faïtâatnimout, fille du premier prophète d'Amon, Piônkh, pour que le dieu Amon lui accordât vie, santé et force ». Deux pectoraux se dissimulaient sous les plis de l'étoffe : le premier, en bois doré, n'avait que la représentation ordinaire d'Isis et Nephthys adorant le Soleil; mais l'autre, en or pur, était Ramsès III. Une dernière gaine de canevas poissé, un dernier linceul de toile rouge, un désappointement vivement ressenti par l'assistance : la face était noyée dans une masse compacte de goudron qui empêchait de distinguer les traits. A onze heures vingt minutes, S. A. le Khédive quitta la salle.

Les opérations furent reprises dans l'après-midi du même jour et dans la matinée du 3 juin. Un nouvel examen des bandelettes a permis de reconnaître des inscriptions sur deux d'entre elles; la première est de l'an IX, la seconde de l'an X du grand prêtre d'Amon, Pitotmou Ier. Le groudron, attaqué prudemment au ciseau par M. Alexandre Barsanti, sculpteur adjoint au Musée, se détacha peu à peu. Les traits sont moins conservés que ceux de Ramsès II; on peut cependant recomposer jusqu'à un certain point le portrait du conquérant. La tête et la face sont rasées de près et ne montrent aucune trace de cheveux ou de barbe. Le front, sans être ni très large, ni très haut, est mieux proportionné que celui de Ramsès II; l'arcade sourci-lière est moins forte, les pommettes sont moins saillantes, le nez moins arqué, le menton et la mâchoire moins lourds. Les yeux étaient peut-être plus grands, mais on ne peut rien affirmer à cet égard : les paupières avaient été arrachées, la cavité avait été vidée, puis remplie de chiffons. L'oreille est moins écartée du crâne que celle de Ramsès II; elle est percée pour recevoir des pendants. La bouche est démesurément grande, les lèvres minces laissent apercevoir des dents blanches et bien rangées; la première molaire de droite semble s'être brisée à moitié ou s'être usée plus vite que les autres. Le corps, vigoureux et bien musclé, est celui d'un homme de soixante-cinq ans. La peau ridée forme derrière la nuque, sous le menton, aux hanches, aux articulations, des plis énormes imbriqués l'un sur l'autre; le roi était obèse au moment de la mort. Bref, Ramsès III est comme une imitation réduite et floue de Ramsès II; la physionomie est plus fine et, somme toute, plus intelligente, mais la taille est moins haute, les épaules sont moins larges, la vigueur était moindre. Ce qu'il était lui-même à la personne, son règne l'est au règne de Ramsès II : des guerres, non plus à distance, en Syrie ou en Éthiopie, mais aux bouches du Nil et sur les frontières de l'Égypte, des constructions, mais le mauvais style et d'exécution hâtive, une piété aussi fastueuse, mais avec des ressources moindres, une vanité aussi effrénée, et un désir tel de copier en tout son illustre prédécesseur qu'il donna à ses fils les noms des fils de Ramsès II et presque dans le même ordre.

Les deux momies, replacées dans leurs cages après une légère préparation, seront désormais exposées à visage découvert comme celle du prêtre Nibsoni. »

Professor Virchow makes the following statements, among others, in reference to this mummy. «Wie es scheint, stand dieser Pharao in einem Verwandtschafts-Verhältniss zu Nachkommen von Ramses II. In der That erinnert seine Mumie in ihrer ganz modernen Gesammterscheinung an der von Seti I. Der noch erhaltene innere Mumiendeckel is ähnlich, nur zeigt er eine am Rücken eingebogene Nase. Die äussere Hülse gehörte ursprünglich Nefert-ari an. Der Kopf ist von kräftigem Aussehen, die Stirn gross und hoch, mit schwachen Wülsten besetzt. Der Scheirtel hoch. Auch dieser Kopf ist dolicocephal (Index 73-9) und wahrscheinlich orthocephal (Ohrhöhenindex 63-5). Das Gesicht ist stark entstellt dadurch, dass man, wahrscheinlich bei der Einbalsamirung, die Mundwinkel durch lange, schräg nach unten gerichtete Schnitte verlängert hat. Der Gesichtsindex (89-6) erreicht fast die Leptoprosopie, dagegen hat die grosse und gekrümmte Nase einen verhältnissmassig hohen Index (58-9), abhängig von der grösseren Breite der Nasenflügel. Die oberlippe ist viel kürzer als die der früheren Könige. Die Kiefer orthognath. Das Kinn hoch angesetzt und etwas eckig. Körperlänge 1 m. 683 mill. » (*Die Mumien der Könige im Museum von Bulaq*, op. cit. supra, p. 776).

Virchow (p. 786) gives the following measurements : cranial length, 0 m. 192 mill.; cranial breadth, 0 m. 142 mill; auricular height, 0 m. 122 mill.; circumference, 547; minimal frontal breadth; total facial height, 0 m. 121 mill.; upper facial height (measured to lip), 0 m. 073 mill.; bizygomatic breadth; bigonial breadth, 0 m. 102 mill.; nasal height and breadth, 0 m. 056 mill. and 0 m. 033 mill.

As the resin-impregnated linen carapace investing this mummy is quite complete, excepting the head-portion, which was removed in 1886 (see M. Maspero's account quoted above) it was deemed undesirable to interfere with it. Hence we have no direct information concerning the treatment of the body of Ramses III; but the details of the embalmer's technique were so similar in the late XIXth (as revealed in the mummies of Siptah and Seti II) and the XXth (as seen in Ramses IV and his successors) that it is unlikely this mummy would have thrown any new light upon the methods of mummification. It would have been of same interest to learn whether any protecting plate was placed over the embalming wound; and if so whether it was of the oblong form (with the eye-design stamped upon it) as in the XXIst Dynasty or the plain leaf-life form used in the XVIIIth Dynasty.

Such a point as this would easily be determined by the use of the X-rays without damaging the mummy or its wrappings; and at the same time the question of the presence or absence of amulets analogous to those found on Seti II could be settled.

There are several features of this mummy that may be regarded as innovations.

The hands are not flexed as in mummies of the late XVIIIth, and XIXth Dynasties; but are fully extended with the palms resting upon the shoulders. As this full extension of both hands, in association with flexed elbows, occurs also in Ramses IV and Ramses V (and in all probability in the case of Ramses VI also, *vide infra*), but in no other mummies, it can be regarded as a distinctive feature of the XXth Dynasty mummification.

Artificial eyes are found in this mummy (pl. LI), and although it became the custom from this time onward to improve the appearance of the mummy's face by inserting linen, stone or some other material to fill out the eyelids and represent the eyes, the mummy of Ramses III is, I believe, the earliest in which such a device has been found.

In appearance Ramses III presents a considerable likeness to the three earlier kings of the XIXth Dynasty described in this Catalogue.

61084. The Mummy of Ramses IV (pl. LIII, LIV and LVII).

This is one of the mummies found by M. Loret in 1898 in the tomb of Amenothes II. The wrappings were removed by me in the Cairo Museum on June 24th, 1905.

The ancient grave-plunderers stripped this mummy of all its wrappings; and when it was reclothed in the succeeding dynasty all that was done was simply to throw around the body a mass of rags with a few simple bandages to hold them in position, and then place a shroud around it.

The name of Ramses IV was written in ink upon this shroud, as well as upon the lid of the wooden coffin in which it was found.

Ramses IV was a man 1 m. 604 mill. in height. He was almost quite bald, only a very narrow fringe of hair (cut quite close to the scalp) remaining on the temples and occiput. The complete closure of the lambdoid and posterior part of the sagittal sutures (the only regions available for examination) suggests an age of at least fifty years and probably more.

The body is in a good state of preservation, but the bandages are adherent to the skin in most places. The skin is darkened so as to be almost black in most regions of the body; but the face and scalp are quite a light brown colour.

The face was clean shaven and it requires a lens to detect the presence of the closely cut hair on the lips and chin.

A crescentic band of black paint (8 millimetres in vertical extent at its widest part) extends across the whole supraorbital area.

A great part of the skin of the forehead has been eaten by beetles or some other insects.

In front of each collapsed eye a small onion had been pushed under the eyelids to simulate the real eyes. The effect was more successful than one might imagine possible. The light brown colour of the dried onion distending the eyelids harmonises with the colour of the skin and lends quite a natural appearance to the whole face.

In placing the mummy in the vertical position for the purpose of photographing it (pl. LIII and LIV), the onions have fallen on to the lower eyelids.

In the account of Ramses III I referred to the use of artificial eyes as being an innovation in the XXth Dynasty, which became a regular custom afterwards.

Through the nostrils the brain was removed and the cranial cavity packed with a reddish resin in a state of powder. The nose was then packed with a resinous paste (which is now set into a mass of stony hardness), and the surface of this paste in each nostril was covered with the scale of an onion.

The pressure of the embalmer's bandages has flattened the cartilaginous part of the nose (pl. LIV); but there is no doubt that Ramses IV had the prominent aquiline nose suggestive of his forerunners of the XIXth Dynasty, associated however with a prominence of the upper teeth such as distinguished the royal family in the XVIIIth Dynasty and Seti II in the XIXth.

The mouth is filled with a black resinous paste, which is also spread over the lips in a band about 13 millimetres broad. Part of this mass was loose in the space between the lips and I removed it so as to expose seven of the upper teeth. They were regular and healthy, but well worn.

Ramses IV has a moderately long oval face.

The ears are small and shrunken. There is no definite evidence to prove that they were pierced, although analogy with other mummies suggests the probability that the lobules might have been perforated. The lobule of the right ear is represented by two small nodules. It is quite possible that they represent the remains of a greatly stretched ring of lobule, which has been torn right through.

In the left parietal bone, just in front of the lambdoid suture, there is a large irregularly triangular hole in the cranial vault : its edges measure 5, 4.9 and 4.8 centimetres respectively (pl. LVII, the figure on the right side). It is clear that it was done after the process of mummification. At one time I was inclined to regard this injury as the result of the attempts of plunderers to hastily remove the wrappings from the head by hacking through them with an axe and then hastily ripping them open; but the remarkable regularity with which such as injury occurs in the cases of Menephtah, Seti II, Ramses IV, Ramses V, Ramses VI and others raises some doubt as to the theory of accident. Moreover in the case of the mummy of Menephtah, which I have recently unwrapped, the hole is small and appears to have been deliberately made. What the explanation of this can be must be reserved for future discussion. M. Maspero puts forward the hypothesis that it was done for superstitious reasons, « to let out the evil spirits ».

Against the view of this injury being accidental is the fact that these mummies belong to one group chronologically, which may suggest that it was a practice to make such on opening in the late XIXth and XXth Dynasties. But the prince in Amenothes II^{nd's} tomb, whose body was certainly embalmed in the XVIIIth Dynasty, also has his cranium broken in. This suggests another possible explanation. The fact that the group of mummies in which this injury occurs were associated together in the tomb of Amenothes II, while the other royal mummies hidden elsewhere at Deïr el Bahari are exempt from it, may mean that these mummies were plundered by a band of robbers who made a practice of chopping the bandages of the head for the purpose of rapid stripping of the mummy.

There can be no doubt that in most cases (probably all excepting Ramses V only) the damage to the scalp and cranium was done long after the process of embalming was completed; and in view of this fact I am inclined to look upon these cranial injuries as having been accidentally inflicted by robbers. The cranium is o m. 194 mill. long; o m. 142 mill. broad : minimal frontal breadth, o m. 101 mill.; and circumference, o m. 545 mill.

The arms are flexed at the elbows and the hands are fully extended in the manner characteristic of the XXth Dynasty (pl. LIII). The right hand, however, is lower than is usual in the XXth Dynasty : instead of being in front of the shoulder, it is placed opposite the middle of the humerus. The left forearm is placed in the more usual position.

Four holes in the front of the neck (pl. LIII) are the work of some insect.

The embalming-wound (which is now torn open and its anterior lip broken) extends parallel to the left Poupart's ligament from the anterior superior spine of the ilium to the spine of the pubes. It was stitched up with a string consisting of a twisted piece of fine linen bandage.

The abdomen is packed with short stalks of dried lichen, probably *Parmelia furfuracea* Ab. Precisely similar material was found in the mummy of Siphtah.

The penis and scrotum, hanging vertically, were each bandaged separately (pl. LIII). The penis is o m. 091 mill. long, and the scrotum o m. 076 mill. long and o m. 030 mill. broad. An elliptical piece of skin, 18 × 7 millimetres, was cut off the right side of the penis at the junction of the glans with the body of the organ : this was done probably just after death and before the process of embalming, but it may possibly be an ulcer with clean-cut edges.

The problem of deciding whether Ramses IV and V were circumcised was not easy of solution, although the condition of other mummies makes it probable a priori that they were. However, I shaved off thin slices of the retroglandular skin and examined them with the help of a lens : this served to remove all doubt in my mind that circumcision had actually been performed.

A plug of resinous paste was placed in the anus.

Among the damage inflicted upon this mummy by the tomb-robbers, the right foot was broken off and the finger nails were displaced and lost.

61085. The mummy of Ramses V (pl. LV, LVI and LVII).

This is another of the mummies found by M. Loret in 1898 in the tomb of Amenothes II.

I removed the wrappings from it on June 25th, 1905, in the Cairo Museum.

After the outer shroud was removed the upper part of the body was found to be enveloped merely in a mass of torn bandages loosely thrown around it without any attempt at bandaging. Some of the linen was burnt by some corrosive agent. A series of simple bandages were then removed from the lower part of the chest, abdomen and legs, and then a bandage which described a figure of 8 around the feet and ankles before winding around the legs.

Then a sheet of linen, which extended from the neck to the knees, was removed, and after taking away a large mass of loose rags the body was found to be completely divested of all its coverings.

The embalming wound was a large (o m. 169 mill.) elliptical, widely gaping opening in the front of left side of the abdomen close to the ilium (pl. LV).

This is a sudden reversion from the late XVIIIth site for the embalming incision, seen in the mummy of Ramses IV, to the early XIXth site (see Ramses II, for example).

The abdomen contained sawdust with some unrecognisable viscera lying loose (without wrappings) in it. This fact is of interest, when it is recalled that during the time of the succeeding, or perhaps even in the latter part of the XXth dynasty, it became the custom to replace the viscera in the body-cavity, usually in a sawdust packing.

In contact with the skin over the anterior part of the second left intercostal space a lock of hair was found lying free. It was closely rolled in a narrow spiral (tubular) form o m. 060 mill. long and o m. 005 mill. in diameter.

The face was painted an earthy red colour, like that of the mummies of many priests of the XXIst Dynasty.

The cranial cavity was packed with 9 metres of soft linen o m. 031 mill. wide. This material was introduced into the cranial cavity (through a perforation in the ethmoid bone) by way of the right nostril. In the process the nose was not distorted in any way.

Both nostrils were plugged with discs of wax.

Linen was packed under the eyelids to form artificial eyes.

The lobules of the ears were perforated; and the holes were enlarged, so that the lobular tissue of each ear had become reduced to a more string surrounding a quadrilateral perforation.

The upper lip, the front of the chin and the submaxillary triangle are studded with

straight, dark brown, and some lighter-coloured hair, varying from 3 to 4 millimetres in length. The scalp is thickly covered with hair of similar length.

The lips are placed in exact apposition and the oral cleft filled with wax.

Ramses V was a much younger man than his predecessor. The mummy is 1 m.
726 mill. in height and is in an excellent state of preservation.

On the surface of the pudenda, lower part of the abdominal wall and the face
(pl. LVI) there is a very well-marked papular eruption, the distribution of which
my colleague, Professor A. R. Ferguson, states to be highly suggestive of small-pox.

The plunderers have done comparatively little damage to this mummy beyond completely stripping it of its original wrappings. The tips of the fingers of the left
hand were sliced off by a sharp instrument, as well as the skin from the knuckles
and the left zygomatic arch,

In the left parietal bone, just behind the coronal suture and close to the middle line,
there is an obliquely-placed irregularly-elliptical hole in the cranium (pl. LVII,
the figure on the left) o m. 034 mill. × o m. 019 mill. Behind it the scalp is
raised from the bone for a distance of about o m. 02 cent. and rolled back in a
manner which was possible only when the scalp was plastic i. e. either before or
just after death. In this respect it forms a marked contrast to the condition found
in the other mummies with perforated crania — Menephtah, Seti II, Ramses IV
and Ramses VI : in them the injury was inflicted when the scalp was dry and
paper-like i. e. after mummification. Moreover on the skull of Ramses V there is a
wide area of discolouration and a patch of black material around the hole. Although
the whole appearance of this discoloured area is suggestive of ante-mortem blood-
staining it is impossible to determine whether the black material is really blood,
because neither the chemical nor biological tests for blood can afford positive
evidence in the case of material that is more than a century, or at most two
centuries, old.

Unlike the state of affairs found in Ramses IVth mummy, the pudenda were not
wrapped separately in this mummy. The penis was dragged laterally into contact
with the right thigh (pl. LV). It is o m. 114 mill. in length. The scrotum is large
and baggy, o m. 014 mill. long and o m. 087 mill. wide, and has been pushed
back and pressed against the perineum, the whole of which (including the anus)
is covered by it. The great size of the scrotum suggests that Ramses V suffered from
inguinal hernia, or possibly hydrocele.

Immediately below Poupart's ligament in the right groin there is a large irregularly
triangular deep ulcer with thickened edges. It measures o m. 022 mill. by o m.
018 mill. It is smeared with a black resinous paste, which prevents a minute examination of the characters of the ulcer : but its situation and characters suggest
that it may represent an open bubo.

Certain injuries of the body suggest that the tomb-robbers used sharp-bladed instru-
ments to chop off the wrappings. The fingers of the left hand (pl. LV and LVI)
were sliced by a sharp blade. The skin covering the metacarpo-phalangeal joint of
the index finger was cut off by one stroke; a second raised the skin from the

proximal interphalangeal joints of the index and middle fingers; and a third cut
sliced off the tips of the index, middle and ring fingers.

Another cut removed the skin from the left zygomatic arch.

The arms are placed in the position characteristic of the XXth Dynasty (pl. LV).

Ramses V had a sloping forehead, a fairly prominent nose, and a big, heavy, square
jaw — features recalling those of the early XIXth Dynasty Pharaohs.

61086. The Mummy of Ramses VI (pl. LVIII and LIX).

This mummy was found by M. Loret in 1898 in the tomb of Amenothes II. I removed
the wrappings from it on July 8th, 1905, in the Cairo Museum.

Much as the royal mummies have suffered at the hands of ancient tomb-robbers, none
of them, not even that of Amenothes III, was so severely maltreated as that of
Ramses VI. The head and trunk were literally hacked to pieces and when the
mummy came to be rewrapped it was necessary to obtain a board — a rough piece
of coffin — on which to tie the fragments of the body and give them some semblance
of the form of a mummy (pl. LVIII).

The shroud of fine linen, which had enveloped the whole body, was already pulled
aside from the upper part of the mummy, where the underlying wrappings were
in a state of great disorder (fig. 1).

Amongst the mass of rags the broken pieces of the head and a woman's right hand
came to light. In removing the loose bundle of torn pieces of linen that were thrown
around the chest, I found a distorted and mutilated right hand and forearm of a
man, but they did not belong to this mummy. In the place where the neck of the
mummy should have been I found the separate left hip bone (os innominatum) and
the rest of the pelvis. The right elbow and the lower half of the humerus were
found lying on the right thigh and the head of the left femur was alongside the
upper end of this fragment in front of the abdomen.

When the bandages investing the right thigh were removed the right forearm (hacked
off at the elbow and wrist with axe-cuts) was found — still wrapped in its original
bandages. Although an attempt had thus been made to put the arm into the
position in which it was customary to place it at the time the rewrapping was done
(i. e. vertically at the sides — the XXIst Dynasty custom), it is interesting to note
that the folds of skin around the elbow make it clear that the arms were originally
folded over the chest, as the practice was in the XXth Dynasty.

The left upper arm was torn off at the shoulder and put in its proper place. The rest
of the arm had been chopped off at the elbow.

On removing the first bandage, which passed spirally around the lower parts of the
legs a broken piece of rib was found lying in front of the ankles.

This bandage was a tattered strip of fine linen 3 m. 005 mill. × 0 m. 19 cent. A
second similar bandage passed spirally around the legs upward beyond the knees
and a third continued the process upward to the hips.

A mass of loose rags was then removed from the front of the knees. Then was exposed

a longitudinal sheet of very coarse matting tied in front of the legs by irregular
scraps of fine linen in the form of circular ligatures. When this was removed I
found a series of short bandages of varied materials and sizes — but all of them
old tattered scraps — wound spirally around the legs. Then a mass of loose rags
were found packed around the left hand and forearm. There was then exposed a
complicated bandage intended to fix the head and the other loose fragments to the
legs — the only solid part of the body. [At this state the photograph shown in plate
LVIII, fig. 2, was taken]. A yellowish shawl was slung round the thighs fixing the
left forearm; it was looped in front and then passed obliquely downward, then
under the feet and up as far as the right knee, where it was tied to a reddish brown
scarf, which passed right up around the fragments of the head, down the left side
of the body and under the feet, reaching almost as far as the above-mentioned knot.

When this was removed three bandages were found fixing the legs to the board on
which the mummy was placed : a figure-of-8 around the ankles and feet, a
circular bandage below the knees and another around the thighs.

Then a peculiar sheet of linen (Diagram 20) — apparently the remains of a dress,
with two armholes (CC) — was wrapped around the mummy. The ends of the sheet
(for one third of the distance at each end) were torn into four strips of equal breadth :
at the head-end the outer pair of tails were torn off and the remaining two (AA)
were tied around the head. The tails at the other end
(BBBB) were wrapped in figures-of-8 around the legs.

Under these two bandages were found — one passing in a circular manner around the hips and the other around the ankles.

After removing a few loose rags the remains of the body were
exposed.

The separated anterior abdominal wall was turned inside out.

The neck was severed from the body at the sixth cervical vertebra. The lower jaw and the skin covering it were detached
from the head. The whole facial skeleton was broken off and
lost, only the skin of the face remaining. There is a large
gash caused by two axe-cuts just above the left ear and tem-
poro-maxillary joint, and a second vertical cleft through the
right side of the whole face and forehead in the mid-orbital
line. There are two knife-cuts below the left eye. A vertical
crack extends from the gash above the left ear to a large hole
o m. 144 mill. × o m. o9 cent. in the vertex of the skull.
The left hip-bone was broken. All the ribs were broken in
the mid-axillary line and the front of the chest-wall lost.

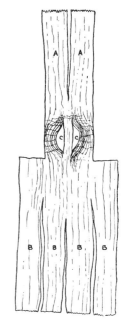

Diagram 20.

The right scapula and the upper part of the humerus were smashed off (not cut) in
their bandages. The elbow was hacked through with an axe, leaving the head of
the radius and part of the olecranon attached to the humerus. The wrist was
chopped through with an axe in an oblique direction. The right hand is missing;
but the right hands of two other mummies were found amongst the wrappings.

The left scapula and outer half of the clavicle are still attached to the body. The humerus was torn off at the shoulder joint and the middle of the shaft of the humerus (still in its wrappings) was broken across. The elbow was hacked through with an axe leaving the upper ends of the radius and ulna attached to the humerus. The left hand, fingers and the wrist exhibit numerous axe-cuts.

The cranial cavity had been packed with pieces of linen and resinous paste. The membranes of the brain were preserved. The nasal fossæ were packed with linen as far back as the pharynx.

Ramses VI was 1 m. 714 mill. in height and apparently middle-aged — probably older than Ramses V, but younger than Ramses IV.

His body was embalmed in the same manner as those of his two predecessors.

I have fitted together the pieces into which the tomb-robbers chopped his head (pl. LIX).

The cranium is beloid; length, o m. 182 mill., and breadth, o m. 148 mill. : circumference, o m. 545 mill.

No hair (excepting the eyelashes) are visible upon the face to the naked eye : but with a lens closely shaven hair of the beard and moustache can be detected.

The part of the scalp of the forehead that is visible is bald : but on the scalp elsewhere short hairs (about 1 millimetre long) are present.

The face, including the eyes and forehead, was thickly plastered with resinous paste. The ears were pierced.

The teeth are only slightly worn.

61087. The Mummy of Queen Notmît (pl. LXIX, LXX and LXXI).

This mummy was partially unwrapped by M. Maspero (*Les Momies royales*, pp. 569, 570 and 677) on June 1ˢᵗ, 1886, and on September 13ᵗʰ, 1906, I removed some more bandages, so as to expose the head and certain other parts of the mummy, concerning the treatment of which information was needed.

In *Les Momies royales* (p. 677) M. Maspero states that Notmît was the consort of Hrihorou. «Hrihorou was married to Notmît. To the probabilities that I have indicated above, M. Wiedemann has supplied the conclusive proof of this statement». But in his *Guide du Visiteur* (1905 Edⁿ, p. 336) M. Maspero refers to «la reine Notmit, mère du prêtre-roi Hrihorou».

In the account given in the *Guide* it is stated that «la momie avait été fouillée par les Arabes et le papyrus enlevé. Une partie du papyrus est déposée au Louvre, l'autre au British Museum».

The mummy of Notmit, being the earliest representative of the XXIˢᵗ Dynasty, which was a period when the whole technique of the embalmer's art underwent the most curious and profound modifications, is of peculiar interest in the study of the evolution of the new practices (see my memoir entitled *A Contribution to the Study of Mummification*, Mémoires de l'Institut égyptien, 1905).

It was during the reign of Hrihorou that great activity was displayed in restoring the plundered tombs of the rulers of the three preceeding dynasties, whose mummies have been under consideration in the foregoing part of this Catalogue.

Whether or not it was the contemplation of the shrunken and distorted forms of many of these mummies that impressed on the embalmers of Hrihorou's time the imperfections of their art it is, of course, impossible to decide. But we do know that immediately after the striking object-lesson afforded by the handling of these mummies of the XVIIIth, XIXth and XXth Dynasties (see in this connection pl. LIII, LV and LXVII, as examples of what the restorers of the XXIst Dynasty saw), the embalmers of the XXIst Dynasty set to work to devise some means of restoring to the embalmed body the fulness of limb and features that it had possessed during life but had lost during the process of mummification.

There were two possible ways of restoring the shape of the mummy (1) by applying materials to its surface or (2) by packing them underneath the skin. In other words the embalmer had the option of building up the shape of the wrapped mummy or of the body itself. The former method had been tried in the time of the Ancient Empire (the mummy supposed to be Ranofir, found by Professor Flinders Petrie at Medûm in 1892) and long afterwards had some vogue in Græco-Roman times. The second method had been tried in the case of the mummy of Amenothes III, but was abandoned immediately afterwards, until the embalmers of the XXIst Dynasty once more revived it.

It is of peculiar interest to note that in the case of Notmit's mummy only the former method (padding applied to the surface) was employed; but in the case of her successors of the XXIst and XXIInd Dynasties the process of packing the body itself was used, without any external padding.

There are certain indications that suggest a possible reason for the adoption of the much more difficult operation of stuffing the body in preference to the simpler procedure of padding. For many details of the technique of embalming that make their appearance for the first time in these XXIst Dynasty mummies go to prove that the idea of the embalmers was to make the body not only as life-like, but also as complete, as possible, so that it might represent the deceased, and take the place of both his actual remains and the funerary statue, which was placed in in his tomb in earlier times.

The body was painted with red or yellow ochre and gum just as the statues used to be treated : artificial eyes were inserted; the cheeks and neck were filled out with stuffing; the forms of the trunk and limbs were restored; and the viscera, which it had been customary to set apart in the four Canopic Jars, were now restored to the body so as to make it whole and complete.

That this idea of making the body itself complete determined the choice between «external» and «internal» padding in favour of the latter is suggested by the fact that the practice of replacing the viscera and inserting artificial eyes was already coming into vogue in the XXth Dynasty (vide supra : the mummies of Ramses IV and Ramses V), before any attempt was made to remedy the defects of its external form.

There was evidently already in the XXth Dynasty a feeling in favour of restoring to the body the viscera which had been removed for the purpose of mummification and so of making the body complete in itself; and when the pious labours of Hrihoru impressed upon the embalmers of the XXIst Dynasty the need for restoration of the *form* of the body also, they hesitated at first in their choice between the simple proceeding of external padding and the highly difficult operation of internal packing; but were eventually brought to adopt the latter by reason of their newly-acquired desire to make the body complete. They attempted to make the mummy not only structurally complete, but also to restore the form of the body itself.

In Notmit's mummy we have exemplified the transition-period, when the embalmers were trying to restore the form of the wrapped mummy.

There is no trace of any packing *within* the limbs or neck. The practice of stuffing the mouth, initiated apparently in the case of Siphtah and continued through the XXth Dynasty, was still in vogue. The back is not stuffed; but masses of sawdust wrapped in linen were placed upon each buttock; and a very large quantity of sawdust was packed around other parts of the body, and especially the legs and abdomen, and retained in position by means of bandages impregnated with resinous material so as to form a complete carapace, analogous to that seen in the mummy of Ramses III (pl. L).

No definite plate was placed over the embalming-wound; but an amorphous lump of wax, about the size of a hen's egg, was plugged into the wound.

Upon the head there is an artificial wig, consisting of an elaborate arrangement of long plaits, tied (as in the case of Hent-em-pet's wig, p. 21) to strings forming three sides of a square (pl. LXX). The wig consists of brown hair, but (pl. LXXI) I have drawn some of its strands aside to show some of Notmit's own scanty grey locks.

Instead of the paint which it was customary to apply to the eyebrow region, in Notmit's mummy a pencil of hair was applied longitudinally to the skin of each eyebrow-region and stuck there (pl. LXX).

The eyes, mouth, nostrils and ears were protected by wax plates, which I removed in order to display the features. Artificial eyes, made of white and black stone, were inserted under the eyelids. This is the earliest instance of the use of stone eyes or of the attempt to represent the pupil in an artificial eye in a mummy, although in statues such objects had been in use for more than fifteen centuries.

The nose was stuffed with resin and the mouth with sawdust.

The cheeks are so tightly stuffed that the lower part of the face (below the level of the eyebrows) has become almost circular. Although the introduction of foreign materials into the mouth had been in vogue ever since the time of Siphtah, this is the first mummy in which the cheeks are really filled out : in the late XIXth and XXth Dynasties only a small amount of packing material was introduced between the gums and lips; but from Notmit's time onward the cheeks were tightly packed (pl. LXX). This stuffing has elongated the upper lip (pl. LXX and LXXI), which is o m. 028 mill. long.

The nose is small, short and somewhat flattened, and in profile (pl. LXXI) is graceful in form. The brown wig and the smooth plump cheeks give Notmit a youthful appearance, which however is belied by the bald vertex and scanty fringe of grey hair, hidden under the wig.

The body has been considerably damaged by tomb-robbers, probably some of the modern dwellers in the Thebaid. There are gashes made by some sharp instrument in both cheeks (pl. LXX and LXXI), in the bridge of the nose, the forehead and the front of the chest. The left humerus is broken close to the shoulder; both wrists are broken; and the legs are badly injured.

The breasts are pendulous and flattened against the chest wall (pl. LXX). They are small, partly no doubt as the result of general emaciation, and possibly also from senile changes.

The body-cavity is stuffed with sawdust; but neither in the neighbourhood of the embalming-wound nor of the cleft in the thorax (pl. LXX) was I able to find any trace of viscera.

No attempt had been made to treat the pudenda in any way.

The hands were not placed in front of the pudenda, but vertically alongside the hips. This position is not to be explained by Notmit's sex, for in the XXIst Dynasty it became the custom once more to place the arms in this position in both men and women, as had been the practice at the commencement of the XVIIIth Dynasty.

Although the tomb-robbers inflicted so much damage on this mummy they did not strip it completely of all its adornments. On the right arm there was the impression (in the resinous carapace) of a band-bracelet that had been stolen in modern times : but I found in situ upon each wrist a bracelet of very small, cylindrical carnelian beads, set on a string consecutively in a single row. Each bead was a little more than one millimetre in diameter and in length.

On the right wrist there was also a string of large (about 4 millimetres in diameter), spherical lapis lazuli beads, with a carnelian lotus bud at each end. This string was sufficiently long to make one and a half turns around the wrist and to permit its ends to be intertwined upon the front.

Upon the left wrist there was a bracelet composed of cylindrical beads of solid gold and lapis lazuli, arranged alternately in linear series. Each bead was about 2, 1/2 millimetres in diameter and about 5 millimetres long.

On the sole of each foot there was a bandage bearing an inscription in hieroglyphics. That on the left foot simply read «High Priestess of Amon»; and that on the right foot contained a reference to «the first year of Pinotmou».

The bandage on the left foot was rolled up and placed longitudinally in the hollow of the sole.

In contact with the right side of the body was a bandage bearing the name «Notmit» in a cartouche.

Notmit's mummy, including the wig, is 1 m. 548 mill. in height.

The height of the upper margin of the symphysis pubis (from the heels) is o m. 720 mill. : height of nose above symphysis pubis, o m. 663 mill.; pubis to chin,

o m. 590 mill, and pubis to suprasternal notch, o m. 510 mill. Estimate of
length of femur, o m. 365 mill., and of tibia, o m. 304 mill.

Breadth of shoulders, o m. 320 mill.; interacromial breadth, estimated at o m.
270 mill.; bitrochanteric breadth, o m. 280 mill.; bi-iliac breadth, o m. 270 mill.;
interspinous (iliac) breadth, o m. 220 mill.

Estimate of length of humerus, o m. 250 mill., and of radius, o m. 221 mill.

Maximum length of hand (from radiocarpal joint), o m. 170 mill.

Cranial length, o m. 176 mill. : actual breadth cannot be measured; including the
wig, it is o m. 150 mill.; total facial height, o m. 127 mill.; upper facial height,
o m. 080 mill. : nasal height and breadth, o m. 055 mill. × o m. 036 mill.;
interorbital breadth, o m. 022 mill.; bizygomatic breadth, o m. 126 mill.; bigonial breadth, o m. 100 mill.; minimal frontal breadth, o m. 091 mill.; right orbit,
o m. 040 mill. × o m. 030 mill.; and left orbit, o m. 041 mill. × o m. 028 mill.

61088 and 61089. The Mummies of Queen Mâkerî and her baby, the princess Moutemhît (pl. LXXII, LXXIII and LXXIV).

The wrappings of the mummy of Queen Mâkerî were torn open (pl. LXXII) by
modern tomb-robbers (see *Les Momies royales,* p. 577). In June, 1909, I removed
certain of the torn bandages on the trunk and arms in order to elucidate certain
details of the embalmer's technique in this mummy, which is the earliest example
of the curious XXIst Dynasty practice of stuffing the body.

Within the coffin that contained this mummy was found a linen parcel o m. 41 cent.
long (pl. LXXIV), which, so the inscriptions inform us, is the baby princess
Moutemhît. M. Maspero tells us that «La reine Mâkerî, épouse du grand-prêtre et
roi Pinotmou Iᵉʳ, mourut en mettant au monde l'enfant qui fut enseveli avec
elle».

The mummy of Mâkerî, together with its wrappings, is 1 m. 522 mill. in height. The
wrappings on the top of the head are o m. 2 cent. thick and the hair adds to this
at least another centimetre. Judging by comparison with the mummy of Hent-Taui
(*vide infra*) at least one centimetre must be allowed for the thickness of the foot-
bandages. If we deduct these four centimetres this reduces the height of the body
to 1 m. 482 mill.

The body had been embalmed, packed and bandaged with extreme care and in a
most elaborate manner.

Various foreign substances had been introduced under the skin of every part of the
body and moulded into some semblance of the queen when alive; and then the
mummy was wrapped in linen of a fineness and a variety of texture unknown before
this dynasty. But tomb-robbers had ripped through the carapace of linen from
the forehead to the pelvis, so that the front of the body is hidden by a mass of
torn linen, intermingled with sawdust, which has escaped from the body-cavity
through its damaged walls (pl. LXXII). The hands were in front of the thighs; but
both are now badly damaged. The plunderers in the search for bracelets and other

jewels slit up the wrappings of the arms and broke the left forearm so that the hand was hanging attached to it merely by a thread of bandage.

A large quantity of mud was put into the mouth, stuffing out the cheeks so unduly as to lend an almost Eskimo-like aspect to the face (pl. LXXII). Stone eyes have been introduced under the eyelids.

The face was painted with a mixture of yellow ochre and gum; and the nostrils were plugged with red resin. Powdered resin was also sprinkled over the face; and a sheet of thin muslin was then applied to it. The muslin has now become quite adherent, the gum in the paint acting as the adhesive material.

The hair is dark brown, interspersed with a few grey hairs: it was parted in the middle and arranged in very loose plaits, or in some cases left in the form of mere wavy strands, which were brought round the sides of the face, covering the ears, to form a large mass under the chin. The ends of many of the plaits had blobs of solid material (resinous paste) attached to them. Two very loosely plaited wisps of hair were carefully arranged, one on each side of the forehead immediately in front of the main mass of the hair, so as to produce the appearence of a curled fringe.

Fixed to the main mass of hair near the parting, but behind the attachment of the fringe-plaits just mentioned, there is a fine string of plaited leather, which passes through the hair to the right side of the head as far as the neighbourhood of the ear, where its end has been torn off. No doubt the plunderers removed some amulet from this string. In contemporary mummies small gold amulets, sometimes a small square plate or a uraeus, were fixed to the hair in front of the forehead.

The lobules of the ears are pierced and greatly stretched.

The head was enclosed in a strong carapace of linen and resin, 11 millimetres thick, which was built up in the following manner. It was first wrapped in a sheet of muslin of exceeding fineness until a layer 3 millimetres thick was formed : to the surface of this a layer of resinous paste 4 millimetres thick was applied : to this was added a quantity of very fine linen until a layer 1 millimetre thick was formed, and finally another three millimetres of resinous paste was applied.

Somewhat similar treatment had been applied to the limbs, after they had been packed in the manner to be described below. The carapaces of the legs are still intact (pl. LXXII) : they are bound together below the knees, and across the ankles and feet, by broad bandages, smeared with resinous paste.

In the process of embalming the viscera were removed through an incision in the left flank; and, after the body had been preserved by long immersion in a preservative bath, the embalmer introduced into the neck a quantity of fat (possibly butter) mixed with soda, which is now a cheese like mass, and with this distended the skin so as to give it the fulness of the living neck in place of the emaciated caricature seen in mummies not treated in this fashion (compare pl. LXXVII and LXXVIII). This cheesy material was introduced into the neck by the embalmer inserting his hand into the wound in the left flank and passing it right up through the body cavity. It was not possible (without damaging the mummy) to determine how the thoracic opening of the neck was treated, but in the other mummies of the XXIst Dynasty I found linen plugs inserted so as to close the thoracic inlet.

The body cavity was packed with sawdust : but no trace of viscera, funerary genii or any other object are now present in this stuffing material. Perhaps the plunderers removed these things.

The coverings of the embalming-wound in the left flank have been removed, presumably by the tomb-robbers, for such objects were of very great value, as the account of the next mummy in this series will show (see pl. LXXVI, fig. 2).

The embalmers separated the skin from the underlying muscular tissues in the anterior margin of the embalming-wound; and into the space thus formed the operator placed his hand and forced it up under the skin on the front of the chest, afterwards packing the cavity underneath the skin with coarse linen. No attempt was made to pack the breasts, but the rest of the bust was moulded upon this foundation of cloth.

Mâkerî's breasts were enormously enlarged, probably because she was lactating. They were flattened against the chest wall and were pulled away from the front so that their lower extremities were alongside the inferior margin of the thorax in the mid-axillary line. The thorax thus packed was protected by a complicated series of coverings. In the process of unwrapping eight layers of very fine muslin were first removed, then a carapace of a resinous paste (2 millimetres thick), then, eleven layers of fine but exceedingly closely-woven linen, then a layer of resinous paste (1 millimetre thick), then another sheet of linen and another layer of resin (2 millimetres thick) and then were exposed those curious leather objects (Diagram 21) commonly referred to as «braces».

They consist in this case of a folded band of red leather, passed around the neck and crossed on the front of the chest, where the ends [one is now missing] were furnished with a piece of yellow parchment, framed by the leather; and an independent pair of parchment tablets of different shapes, also framed

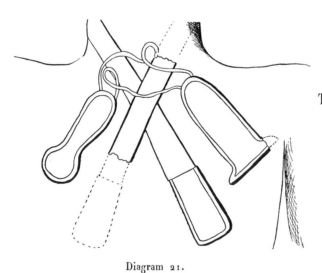

Diagram 21.

in red leather and fastened, the one to the other, by means of two narrow strips of red leather.

The parchment tablets are so thickly plastered with resinous material, which adheres firmly to their surfaces, that it is not possible to see the pictures or the inscriptions impressed upon the parchment.

A similar set of «braces» and leather tablets (with the embossed designs and inscriptions undamaged) was found on the «Leeds mummy», which belongs to the transition-period between the XXth and XXIst Dynasties (William Osburn, *An Account of an Egyptian Mummy, presented to the Museum of the Leeds Philosophical and Literary Society;* Leeds, 1828, Plate 2).

Resinous material was spread freely over these «braces» fixing them to the underlying coverings of the mummy, which consisted of the following : eight layers of moderately fine linen, covering a coating of resinous paste (2 millimetres thick), under which there was a sheet of finely and closely-woven linen, another sheet of similar texture stained red, then a thin layer of resinous paste and then two more sheets of fine (white) linen.

The skin of the abdomen was loose and somewhat puckered. Taken in conjunction with the large size of the breasts, these facts support M. Maspero's hypothesis that Mâkerî died in childbirth or soon after giving birth to the baby princess buried with her.

The tomb-robbers ripped up the whole of the right arm (pl. LXXII), and thereby enabled me to examine the details of the process of stuffing the arms. They also broke off the left hand and I was thus able to study the elaborate method adopted for packing the hands.

From an incision on each shoulder fine straw-like sawdust had been packed under the skin of the arm in sufficient quantity to fill it out to the size of the living arm. By means of a stick or some form of pushing instrument it had been forced down, not only as far as the elbow, but also beyond it to the wrist, both on the front as well as on the back of the forearm. In the case of the right arm the sawdust was pushed (from the shoulder) even on to the back of the hand, but on the left side it stops at the wrist, where a natural plug has been formed by a mass of tendons pushed down from the forearm. Below this plug a quantity of coarse linen has been introduced under the skin on the dorsum of the left hand (pl. LXXIII, fig. 2).

There are deep circular groves on the fingers, the impressions of string tied around the nails to fix them in position while the body was in the preservative bath. The need for fixing the nails during this stage of the embalming process was due to the fact that the epidermis peeled off during the soaking in the bath and unless special precautions were taken it carried the nails with it.

On each thumb (pl. LXXIII, fig. 1) there are three plain rings composed of metal wire 1 mill. 5 in diameter. The intermediate ring is silver, the other two gold.

The baby's mummy was not unwrapped (pl. LXXIV).

61090. The Mummy of Queen Honittaoui (pl. LXXV and LXXVI).

M. Maspero exposed the mummy to the extent shown in plate LXXV in the year 1886. The large hole in front of the thorax and abdomen was made by tomb-robbers in ancient times. It extends not only through the resin-impregnated carapace, but also through the wall of the body itself; for there is a large hole, 0 m. 18 cent. in diameter, in the epigastrium.

When I came to examine this mummy (for the purpose of writing this Catalogue) in June, 1909, I noticed in the broken edge of the carapace the end of a fine string wrapped in red linen. It was lying upon a sheet of exceptionally fine linen, which was in direct contact with the skin; and it passed around the abdomen immediately below the level of the umbilicus.

As my experience of a large series of mummies of this period had taught me that string was never used except for the purpose of fixing in position amulets or other important objects I decided to remove a little more of the broken carapace on the left side of the body to find out where the string led. I chose the left side because that was the usual site of the embalming incision, where any object placed upon the abdomen would most likely be located.

The string was traced to a large embossed gold plate (pl. LXXVI, fig. 2), covering the embalming-wound. Apart from being the most valuable and magnificent sample of these protective plates yet found, it is also unique in having, in addition to the customary eye-design, representations of the funerary genii (the children of Horus) and a nome standard (or support d'honneur) and a series of hieroglyphic inscriptions :

M. Daressy has supplied me with the following note concerning this plate :

«La plaque d'or qui couvrait l'incision dans le flanc gauche est la plus belle de celles trouvées jusqu'à ce jour. Large de 0 m. 108 mill., haute de 0 m. 075 mill., les bords sont renforcés par des bandes minces de 0 m. 001 mill. 5 de largeur, soudées pour donner au contour une épaisseur de 0 m. 001 mill. L'ornementation comprend des figures estampées en relief et gravées, et des inscriptions gravées. Au milieu on voit l'uza ou œil sacré posé [hieroglyph] sur le support d'honneur [hieroglyph]. Sur les côtés les quatre génies funéraires sont représentés debout, avec leur nom inscrit au-dessus d'eux. A droite c'est [hieroglyphs] «Mesta, dieu grand, seigneur de l'Occident», à tête humaine, et [hieroglyphs] «Hapi, dieu grand, ton fils qui t'aime», à tête de cynocéphale. A gauche [hieroglyphs] [hieroglyphs] «Duamutef, dieu grand, fils d'Osiris», à tête de chacal, et [hieroglyphs] [hieroglyphs] «Kebhsenuf, fils d'Osiris», hiéracocéphale. Sous le support, deux inscriptions verticales de trois lignes chacune donnent les titres de la défunte. A droite [hieroglyphs] «la fille royale de son flanc, fille de la grande épouse royale, mère royale, maîtresse des deux terres, l'adoratrice d'Hathor *Hent-taui*». A gauche [hieroglyphs] «la première prêtresse d'Amon-râ, roi des dieux, maîtresse des deux terres, l'adoratrice d'Hathor *Hent-taui*».

There was a small perforation in each corner of the gold plate (pl. LXXVI, fig. 2) to which a string was attached, which passed around the abdomen to the fixed to the corresponding hole on the opposite site of the plate.

The body was embalmed in accordance with the curious methods in vogue in the XXIst and XXIInd Dynasties, which I have already described in detail elsewhere. (*A contribution to the Study of Mummification in Egypt, with special Reference to the curious methods employed during the XXIst and XXIInd Dynasties*, Mémoires de l'Institut égyptien, 1905) and some of which have already been exemplified in this Catalogue in the case of Mâkerî's mummy.

As the greater part of this mummy (pl. LXXV) is still encased in a hard carapace of resin-impregnated linen, only those parts where this has been broken through are available for examination. These parts are the head, a small area of thorax and abdomen (vide supra) and the right foot, from which the toes and their wrappings have been broken away.

As in the mummies of Notmit and Mâkerî, and in fact all the mummies of royal and wealthy people of this and the following dynasty, the wrappings consist of linen of quite exceptional fineness. As in the case of Mâkerî, one of the innermost sheets is stained red.

The hands are placed in contact with the thighs, the left being further forward than the right. The hands are slightly flexed (pl. LXXV).

Upon the head there is a wig made of black string, representing hair parted in the middle and framing the face after the manner of the real hair in Mâkerî's mummy. It is composed of loosely-coiled spirals, each about o m. oo5 mill. in diameter and o m. 35o mill. long. The lower ends (from o m. o4 cent. to o m. 1o cent. in different cases) are tightly coiled to form rope-like strands, which are brought around under the chin, where they are clumped together in a thick mass (pl. LXXVI, fig. 1).

Both the cheeks and the right foot were stuffed with that curious cheese-like mixture of fat (? butter) and soda, such as I have described as the packing material employed for stuffing Mâkerî's neck. This material was frequently employed during the XXIst Dynasty for stuffing the mouth and neck; but this is the only mummy in which I have found it in the feet.

The body is that of a very plump, apparently young, woman, 1 m. 518 mill. in height (including the wig), with very large, full, pendant breasts.

An exceptionally large quantity of the cheese-like material was packed into the mouth; and with the deliquescence of the salts mixed with the fat, the stretched skin of the cheeks has burst open on each side, from the outer angle of the eye downwards to the chin (pl. LXXV and LXXVI). Thus her own skin has separated like a mask, which some writers have mistaken for an actual mask.

Honittaoui had small, well-proportioned features. Stone eyes, like those of Notmit's and Mâkerî's mummies, were employed in the case of her's also; but their exposure to the salts, liberated by the bursting of her cheeks, has exerted a disintegrative influence upon the stone.

The usual crescentic patch of black paint has been applied to the superciliary regions.

The face has been painted with yellow ochre and gum and the lips (and possibly the cheeks also) have been painted red.

The body-cavity is lightly packed with very fine, reddish, aromatic sawdust. In searching through as much of this material as could be reached through the wound in the epigastrium or from embalming-incision I found four teeth, seven pyramidal seeds (? pine), two wax genii, two fragments or intestine and 44 beads made of gold (? or electrum). As it was not possible (through the two restricted openings referred to) to explore the whole body cavity there may be many other objects still within this mummy.

The teeth consist of a well-worn canine and three molars, one unworn, one slightly worn and the third worn to about the same extent as the canine. From the circumstances under which these teeth were found they were placed in the body-cavity by the embalmers and probably belong to Honittaoui. If so, they indicate that she was a young adult.

The wax figures are mummy-shaped with heads of the jackal and the hawk respectively. The jackal was found in the epigastrium immediately behind the sternum — the position usually occupied by the stomach and the associated jackal-headed genius in XXIst Dynasty mummies. It is o m. 104 mill. long, including the erect ears. The hawk-headed figure was not in its usual position (in the abdomen), but high up on the right side of the thorax, in contact with the vertebral column. It is o m. 095 mill. long.

The beads found are of three varieties, (1) barrel-shaped beads made of circularly-corrugated beaten gold, each about o m. 01 cent. in length and o m. 005 mill. in diameter; (2) more slender beads shaped like maggots; and (3) spirally-coiled gold wire forming tubes, about o m. 012 mill. long, slightly wider at one end than the other.

The embalming-wound was in the high infracostal position, which was customary not only in the XXIst and XXIInd Dynasties, but also in the early XVIIIth.

In Honittaoui it is o m. 13 cent. long and gapes widely. Its lower part extended downward in front of the anterior superior spine of the ilium for a distance of o m. 04 cent.

A large plug of resinous paste, in which was embedded a good deal of coarse sawdust and some of the gold wire spirals (vide supra), was pushed into the embalming wound, forcing its edges apart for a distance of o m. 05 cent. and inverting them (toward the abdominal cavity) for o m. 03 cent.

On the outer surface of this resin plug there was a plate of wax. It was not accurately adjusted to the embalming wound, for, together with the gold plate applied to its outer surface, it had slipped backward to the extent of about o m. 04 cent.

When the viscera were removed from the body the pelvic cavity was cleared completely of all its contents and a plug of linen was applied to the perineum and secured in position by means of a thick string, which was passed through the rima pudendi and pelvis and out through the embalming incision, down to the perineum again.

This is the only example of this curious procedure that I have seen.

61091. **The Mummy of Taiouhrit** (pl. LXXVII and LXXVIII).

The mummy of Taiouhrit was exposed (still enclosed in its carapace of resin-impregnated linen) on June 29th, 1886 (*Les Momies royales,* p. 578); and on July 6th, 1909, I removed part of the carapace so as to expose the face.

M. Maspero makes the following statements in the *Guide du Visiteur* : «la chanteuse d'Amon-Râ, roi des dieux Taiouhrit. Le papyrus de cette femme, conservé à Leyde, nous apprend qu'elle était fille du père divin d'Amon, Khonsoumos, et de la chanteuse d'Amon Tantamanou ».

Including the carapace (on the head and feet) the mummy is 1 m. 606 mill. in height.

The carapace was built up like those already described in the mummies of Mâkerî and Honttaoui of fine linen and resinous paste. But the latter is freely mixed with sawdust in this mummy; and in places the fine muslin bandages are stuck together with masses of gum. As in the other mummies of this dynasty one of the innermost sheets of linen is dyed red.

In plate LXXVII the posterior part of the carapace is seen in situ. I left this part so as not to weaken the attachment of the head to the rest of the mummy.

The nostrils were covered with circular discs of wax; and on the sides of the nose large buttresses of wax were placed (pl. LXXVIII) to support and prevent distortion of the nose. There is a large wax plate in front of the right eye, but none in front of the left, where the usual artificial stone eye can be seen. The lips are widely separated and the space between them filled with a large projecting mass of wax (see plates LXXVII and LXXVIII).

The ears are covered with hair arranged in curls, probably a wig. Her own hair is freely intermingled with white, but there are very few white hairs in the part which seems to be the wig. One of the curls passes down on to the right eyebrow.

The cheeks are stuffed like those of the other three mummies just described.

The skin of the face, and especially that of the forehead, has been damaged extensively by insects (pl. LXXVIII).

In the XXIst and XXIInd Dynasties it was the custom to cover the embalming wound with an oblong plate, bearing the conventional eye design. It was made of gold, electrum or bronze; at other times of wax or a mixture of wax and other substances.

In the XVIIIth Dynasty the only plates that I have seen were fusiform or leaf-shaped and perfectly plain, i. e. had no design of any kind upon them.

I have not seen any plates from mummies of the XIXth or XXth Dynasty, so that I am unable to say when the fusiform, plain plate gave place to the oblong, engraved variety. On the mummy of Taiouhrit the embalmers, for some unknown reason, did not make use of the form of plate that I have found in more than forty mummies of her time, but a plain fusiform plate, 0 m. 150 mill. × 0 m. 052 mill. 57 such as the embalmers of the XVIIIth Dynasty employed.

61092. The High-Priest and General-in-chief Masahirti (pl. LXXIX).

M. Maspero removed the wrappings from this mummy on June 3oᵗʰ, 1886 (*Les Momies royales*, p. 571). It had been plundered in recent times by the Luxsor people.

M. Maspero described Masahirti as «grand prêtre d'Amon, général en chef, fils du roi Pinotmou Iᵉʳ et père de la reine Isimkhabiou».

The mummy is that of a large, heavily-built and corpulent man, 1 m. 696 in height, with a very short sparse white beard on the chin, submaxillary region and lower part of the masseteric area, but only a few sparsely-scattered hairs to represent moustaches. The hair of the scalp is also short and white; but it is now thickly smeared with resinous material.

The face and the whole body was painted with a thick layer of red-ochre, as was customary in the mummies of men in this dynasty. The body has been submitted to the packing-procedures customary at the time it was embalmed; but the cheeks, as usually happened (vide supra) were much too tightly stuffed (pl. LXXIX), so that they have an unnaturally puffed-out appearance.

The lobules of the ears have small perforations.

The arms and fingers are extended; but the hands are placed fairly near together in front of the pubes. By reason of the corpulency of the body the hands do not come low enough to cover the pudenda (pl. LXXIX).

The embalmers departed from the custom of their time in choosing the site for the embalming incision : for instead of making it high up above the level of the iliac spine, they reverted to the custom that prevailed in the late XVIIIᵗʰ and again in the early XXᵗʰ Dynasties and made it parallel to and alongside Poupart's ligament. In plate LXXIX it is hidden by the left hand. It is o m. 120 mill. long.

My study of the large series (44) of mummies of priests of Amon of the XXIˢᵗ Dynasty revealed occasional departures from the prevailing custom; but in all cases there was some obvious reason for it. By analogy with these anomalous cases it seems to me that in Masahirti's case his corpulence was the reason for choosing the anterior site for the embalming incision. In a subject of his bulk the attempt to eviscerate the body through the loins in the way customary at his time would have presented very great difficulties.

The skin is soft and flexible. It bears impressions on the front of the chest of the so-called «braces» and of a pectoral ornament.

On all the fingers and toes there are impressions made by string employed to fix the nails in position during the progress of the embalming operations. In addition the middle finger of the right hand bears a gold thimble, which covers its two distal segments.

61093. The Mummy of Queen Isimkhabiou (pl. LXXX).

The wrappings of this mummy were so complete and perfect in every way (pl. LXXX) that M. Maspero (*Les Momies royales*, p. 577) decided not to disturb it.

The outer shroud of the mummy is held in position by five circularly-arranged bandages, one longitudinal sagittal bandage and two lateral (marginal) bandages. In addition there are two oblique bandages simulating the so-called «braces» in arrangement.

Each bandage is composite, being formed of linen of two different colours, a deeper bandage (red) folded upon itself to form a ribbon o m. o56 mill. wide and a superficial one folded to form a narrower band, o m. o4o mill. wide.

Height of mummy, 1 m. 568 mill.

61094. The Mummy of the High-Priest of Amon Pinotmou II (pl. LXXXI).

This mummy was first exposed by M. Maspero in June 28th, 1886 (*Les Momies royales*, p. 571 and 572). In the *Guide du Visiteur* M. Maspero refers to Pinotmou II as «grand prêtre d'Amon, général en chef, fils d'Isimkhabiou et du grand prêtre Manakhpirrî».

The mummy was enclosed, like those of Mâkerî and Honttaoui described above, in beautifully fine muslin in large quantities, with several layers of resinous paste interspersed amongst it. The muslin is not only exquisitely fine, but also has coloured borders and fringes.

Upon the remains of the thoracic part of the carapace there are the remains of the two crossing strips of red-leather «braces» (pl. LXXXI) and also the impression of part of a pectoral ornament of the usual form. Each leather band of the «braces» is folded to form a structure o m. o2 cent. wide.

Unlike the mummy of Masahirti (vide supra), in which there was a curious departure from the custom of the times in the selection of the site for the embalming-wound, that of Pinotmou II exhibits the proper vertical incision, extending from the ribs to the left anterior superior spine of the ilium. It is o m. 148 mill. long and is widely gaping.

The face is a fine ovoid with a narrow aquiline nose. The embalmers had now learned not to over-pack the cheeks : hence the features of Pinotmou II have been preserved without the grotesque distortion seen in his immediate predecessors.

The face was sprinkled freely with powdered resin, much of which has «caked» and become adherent to the skin.

There is a fairly abundant, short white beard on the chin and underneath it but the upper lip was shaved (white hairs o m. oo2 mill. are visible).

The hands are placed vertically fully extended upon the lateral aspects of the thighs.

The arms are packed with mud.

Several parcels of viscera were placed in the body cavity.

Height of mummy (with wrappings), 1 m. 7o6 mill.

61095. The Mummy of Queen Nsikhonsou (pl. LXXXII, LXXXIII and LXXXIV).

This mummy was partially unwrapped by M. Maspero on June 27th, 1886 (*Les Momies royales*, p. 578 and 579), and I completed the process just twenty years later.

This is a typical example of the distinctive technique of embalming of the XXIst and XXIInd Dynasties; but its freedom from the gross distortions of face and members that marked the earlier attempts at packing is perhaps a distinguishing mark of XXIInd Dynasty work.

The neck is stuffed with the cheese-like material in the manner described in the case of Mâkerî's mummy (vide supra).

There is a vertical incision, o m. o3 cent. long, on the antero-lateral aspect of each shoulder (pl. LXXXII and LXXXIII), from which a small quantity of packing material was introduced under the skin of a localized area of the extreme upper and lateral part of the chest wall, and also into the arms as far as the wrists. The stuffing consists of sawdust; and the moulding of the arms has been skilfully done. The hands are not packed. The arms are placed vertically at the sides of the body; and the fully extended hands are placed alongside the lateral surface of the thighs (pl. LXXXII).

The legs are stuffed in the customary manner. The embalmer introduced his hand into the embalming wound in the left flank and forced the packing-material (in this case a mixture of mud, sawdust and the cheese-like material, to which I have already referred), into each leg. In plate LXXXII the skin on the inner side of the right thigh can be seen to be broken away, so that the packing material is revealed in situ.

The feet are stuffed; but I was unable to determine the spot where the packing material was introduced.

Flowers were wrapped around the great toe of each foot and a flower on a long stalk was placed upon the upper surface of the left foot, and another encircled the left ankle.

The breasts are large and pendulous : but no attempt was made to pack them and restore the form of the bust.

The pudenda were treated in the way that was customary in the XXIst and XXIInd Dynasties : the labia majora were pressed together so as to hide the rima.

The embalming wound is in the situation characteristic of this period : it is a vertical incision passing from the margin of the ribs to within o m. o35 mill. of the anterior superior spine of the left ilium. It is visible in plate LXXXII alongside the left elbow.

The embalming wound is o m. 125 mill. long and gapes to the extent of o m. o5o mill.

It was covered by a wax plate of the usual form but without the usual eye design. Onion scales were placed upon the surface of the plate.

The body cavity is packed with sawdust.

The skin of the abdomen is loose and pendulous; and the mammillae are large and prominent. These two signs make it certain that Nsikhonsou was parous.

Nsikhonsou is 1 m. 615 mill. in height. There is nothing to give any definite indication of her age; but she has no grey hairs.

The face is of a graceful, narrow, elliptical form and the light colour of the skin suggests that it must have been very fair originally.

The face is thickly encrusted with powdered resin, and large cakes of resinous material cover the eyes, nostrils and mouth. Underneath the resin shields artificial eyes of stone are found, but the material is badly disintegrated. The ears are pierced and the lobules drawn out into long strings (o m. 16 cent.) — see the left ear in plate LXXXIII.

The long, dark brown hair hangs down as far as the front of the chest (pl. LXXXIII and LXXXIV). There are a few small plaits, but most of the hair consists of simple wavy strands. Most of these have been collected into two large masses, each of which is held together by means of a bandage wound spirally around it. One of these masses is brought down on the side of the neck to the front of the chest.

The hair is thickly strewn with powdered red resin.

The following measurements were made. Those of the head and face are merely estimations, for the thick mass of hair and the encrustations of resin render precise measurements impossible.

Height of upper margin of symphysis pubis	o m.	83o mill.
Height of chin above pubes	o	61o
Height of nose above pubes	o	69o
Height of umbilicus above pubes	o	175
Breadth across shoulders	o	412
Interacromial breadth	o	366
Bitrochanteric breadth	o	295
Bi-iliac breadth	o	28o
Length of humerus (estimate only)	o	315
Length of radius (estimate only)	o	248
Length of femur (estimate only)	o	43o
Length of tibia (estimate only)	o	353
Length of hand, from radio-carpal joint	o	19o
Cranial length	o	185
Cranial breadth	o	137
Minimal frontal breadth	o	1oo
Total facial height	o	126
Upper facial height	o	o8o
Bizygomatic breadth	o	132
Right orbit	o m. o45 mill. × o	o33
Nasal length and breadth	o o52 × o	o32

The nose in narrow and aquiline, but not prominent : its profile passes in a straight line into the brow; and there is a sloping forehead, low and receding.

Foot, o m. 224 mill. long and o m. o65 mill. broad.

61096. The Mummy of Nsitanebashrou (pl. LXXXV, LXXXVI, LXXXVII and LXXXVIII).

This mummy was unwrapped by M. Maspero on June 30th, 1886 (*Les Momies royales*, p. 579 and 58o). The inscription on her coffin refers to her, according to M. Maspero, as «prêtresse d'Amon, fille de Nsikhonsou», and he adds «probablement de Pinotmou II» (*Guide du Visiteur*).

XXIst-XXIInd period. The face especially has been very successfully treated and the filling out of the cheeks and the artificial eyes of stone help in conveying a good idea of how this haughty, Bourbon-like lady must have appeared in the flesh (pl. LXXXVII and LXXXVIII).

She was about 1 m. 620 mill. in height. Only a moderate amount of packing was introduced under the skin of the limbs, which on the whole were well moulded.

This is perhaps the best example of embalming that has been preserved from the But the body cavity was very tightly stuffed with exceptionally fine sawdust, or rather powdered wood, which still has a strong pungent aromatic odour.

The embalming wound in the left flank extended vertically upward from the anterior superior spine of the ilium. It is only 0 m. 092 mill. long and less than 0 m. 040 mill. broad. Into it was stuffed a crumpled sheet of most exquisitely fine linen with a blue pattern on the edge and a fringe. On the surface of this muslin was placed a lump of reddish translucent resin (0 m. 087 mill. × 0 m. 033 mill. × 0 m. 019 mill.). There is a distinct impression upon the skin and this piece of resin of an oblong plate (0 m. 122 mill. × 0 m. 093 mill.).

On the outer surface of each shoulder, opposite the head of the humerus, there is a vertical incision (0 m. 03 cent. long on the left side and 0 m. 21 cent. on the right). Each is neatly stitched up with a running thread. Through these openings the arms were stuffed. A wound upon the front of the left shoulder (pl. LXXXVI), presumably the work of ancient plunderers, reveals sawdust and a plug of linen as the materials used.

Little attempt was made to model the anterior wall of the chest, and no packing material was introduced into the large pendulous breasts.

The legs were packed in the usual manner and the modelling of the limbs has been accomplished in a very successful manner. The common practice of making an incision between the great and second toes for the purpose of packing the foot was resorted to in this mummy.

Both the toe-nails and finger-nails have been neatly trimmed with a crescentic edge.

There are well-marked impressions upon the fingers and toes of the string which was tied around them to keep the nails in position during the embalming process.

The hands were placed in front of the thighs.

The right labium majus has been pushed inward to hide the rima pudendi.

The surface of the mummy seems to have been painted with the mixture of yellow ochre and gum, to which I have referred in the case of other mummies of women of this period.

The skin of the whole of the back, face, neck (pl. LXXXVIII), shoulders, abdomen, and thighs presents a series of roughnesses or maculae, but whether they are due to some pathological condition or merely the result of the process of embalming it is impossible to say.

There are brown patches of discoloration upon the face, possibly due to the resin or the deliquescence of salts used in embalming. The rest of the skin is of a light yellow colour, which is not wholly due to the yellow ochre applied to it.

The superciliary ridges have been painted brown in the usual way.

Height to symphysis pubis . . . . o m. 836 mill.

Height of nose above pubes . . . . o   635

Height of suprasternal notch above pubes . . . . o   501

Height of umbilicus above pubes . . . . o   160

Breadth of shoulders . . . . o   377

Biacromial breadth . . . . o   311

Bitrochanteric breadth . . . . o   282

Bi-iliac breadth . . . . o   289

Breadth between anterior iliac spines . . . . o   240

Length of humerus (estimate) . . . . o   299

Length of radius (estimate) . . . . o   225

Length of hand, from radio-carpal joint . . . . o   179

Length from mid-Poupart point to external condyle of femur . . o   431

Length of tibia (estimate) . . . . o   346

Length and breadth of foot . . . . o m. 213 mill. × o   061

Cranial length . . . . o   188

Cranial breadth cannot be measured but estimated at . . . . o   153

Cranial breadth, *including hair* . . . . o   160

Minimal frontal breadth . . . . o   104

Circumference (*including hair*) . . . . o   565

Total facial height . . . . o   129

Upper facial height . . . . o   085

Nasal height and breadth . . . . o m. 061 mill. × o   027 mill. 5

Bizygomatic breadth . . . . o   131

Bigonial breadth . . . . o   097

Interorbital breadth . . . . o   025

Bipalpebral breadth . . . . o   103

Left orbit . . . . o m. 048 mill. × o   039

Stone eyes made of white and black materials, are placed under cover of the semi-closed eyelids, and lend a realistically life-like appearance to the face (pl. LXXXVIII).

The nose is very narrow and high-bridged, and although the cartilaginous part is slightly fallen in, there was probably a distinct angle at the junction of the bony and carti-laginous supports of the nose. Both nostrils were packed with resin.

There is an unbroken line of brow and nose in profile.

The upper teeth project slightly, so that their almost unworn edges can be seen pro-jecting through the resin with which the rather full lips and the narrow cleft between them had been smeared.

The lobules of both ears are pierced but the holes have not been widely stretched.

Each ear measures o m. 062 mill. × o m. 032 mill.

The hair is brown (probably bleached somewhat by the embalming materials), and wavy, and arranged in short curls which hang downward, some of them reaching midway down the neck. The hair was not pulled down over the ears in the usual manner. The margins of the hair-bearing area of the scalp are thickly smeared with resinous material. Immediately above the right ear (pl. LXXXVII and LXXXVIII) there is a mass of the cheese-like mixture of fat and soda, to which I have referred above.

The packing and modelling of the neck has been unusually successful in this mummy.

61097. The Mummy of Zadptahefônkhou (pl. LXXXIX, XC, XCI, XCII and XCIII).

Some of the wrappings were removed from this mummy by M. Maspero on June 29th, 1886 (*Les Momies royales*, p. 572 and 573), and I removed the rest in September, 1906.

In the *Guide du Visiteur* M. Maspero refers to Zadptahefônkhou as «prêtre d'Amon, *fils royal de Ramsès*», and makes the following comments on the latter title : — «Le titre *fils royal de Ramsès* appartient à plusieurs personnages de la XXIe et de la XXIIe dynastie; il ne suppose pas qu'un Ramsès aurait régné vers cette époque. De même que la famille des Ramessides se perpétuait en des reines, qui transmettaient à leurs enfants des droits héréditaires, elle se perpétuait en des princes qui avaient quelques-uns des titres et des honneurs de la royauté; un Ramsès de cette famille n'avait pas besoin d'être roi pour que ses fils eussent le titre de *fils royaux*. Zadphtahefônkhou se rattachait à la famille de Pinotmou II par un lien qui nous est encore inconnu. Les bretelles que sa momie porte sont estampées au nom du grand prêtre d'Amon Ouapouti, fils du roi Sheshonq Ier.»

When M. Maspero removed some of the wrappings in 1886, some bandages were left in position on the arms, feet and part of the abdomen. I removed these on September 5th, 1906, and brought to light a large series of amulets and other objects (pl. XCIII).

On many of the fingers and toes (all the fingers of the left hand, except the index, Plate XCIII; the middle and ring fingers of the right hand; the fourth and fifth toes of the left foot and the second toe on the right) there were thin band-like rings of gold, varying from 0 m. 002 mill. to 0 m. 003 mill. in width. Impressions of rings on other fingers and toes were found on the skin, as well as on the wrappings. These rings were used, no doubt instead of string, to fix in position the thimble of epidemis which secured the nails.

On the left arm, just below the elbow there was fixed a string of carnelian amulets and a bunch of other amulets made of a variety of stones was tied alongside it (pl. XCIII).

The carnelian objects represented eyes (2), a uraeus, a serpent's head, a heart (*Ab*), a lotus bud, a barrel and an object of this shape. At the ends of the various strings in the bunch were a lapis lazuli bead : a scarab and an eye, made of mottled black and white stone; two lotus buds, a scarab and a *dad*, made of a light green stone; a cylindrical bead, a ram (*Amon*), an eye and a *dad*, made of lapis lazuli; a broken object made of black stone; and a boomerang with the figure of *Thoth* engraved on it.

An oblong bronze plate with the usual eye-design in raised lines upon it covers the greater part of the embalming wound (pl. XCIII). It measures 0 m. 104 mill. × 0 m. 085 mill. Twenty years before, M. Maspero had found upon the neck of this mummy figures of two serpents and a lotus flower wrapped in the folds; and upon the chest a «heart-scarab» and a silver figure of a hawk with expanded wings.

The mummy is 1 m. 695 mill. in height.

The height of the symphysis pubis is................... 0 m. 870 mill.
The height of the nose above the pubes................. 0   690
The height of the suprasternal notch above the pubes....... 0   522
The height of the umbilicus above the pubes............. 0   155

The embalming wound is vertical and ovoid (0 m. 125 mill. × 0 m. 090 mill.) : its lower extremity (pl. XCIII) is 0 m. 028 mill. above the level of the anterior superior spine of the left ilium (seen as a pale egg-shaped area in pl. XCIII).

The body cavity was packed with lichen (*Parmelia furfuracea,* Ah).

Occupying the left iliac fossa and hypogastrium there was a large parcel wrapped in a linen bandage. When the bandages were unrolled the parcel was found to consist of intestines along with a figure of the Ape-headed Hapi. Although this association agrees with that quoted in most works on Egyptian Archaeology (based upon Pettigrew's examination of *one* mummy of the XXIst Dynasty) my observations upon the large series of mummies of priests of Amon from Deïr el-Bahari (Mémoires de l'Institut égyptien, 1905) showed that Hapi was usually associated with the stomach, and that the intestines were usually guarded by the Hawk-headed son of Horus. [On this subject see the discussion on «*Heart and Reins*» in the *Journal of the Manchester Oriental Society,* vol. I, 1911].

The liver, wrapped in a linen bandage but without any funerary genius, was found in the epigastric region. Another parcel was found in the umbilical region and upon removing the linen bandage contained two organs which seem to be the kidneys, but no funerary genius.

It was impossible to explore the body cavity any further from the incision in the left flank.

The mouth is packed with sawdust. The neck has been carefully stuffed, but is not quite symmetrical (pl. XCII). Only a small area of the back, in the neighbourhood of the embalming wound, has been stuffed : there is no packing in the buttocks and the skin is pushed inwards and downwards (towards the perineum) — plate XC.

Only a small part of the legs and very little of the arms have been stuffed. A vertical incision (visible, though out of focus, in plate XCI), 0 m. 03 cent. long on the antero-lateral aspect of each shoulder (0 m. 03 cent. below the acromion process) in now sewn up with a running stitch. Through it a small quantity of linen bandage was packed under the skin in front of the shoulder and arm, but none was pushed in front of the thorax or into the axilla.

The usual incision for packing the foot was found between the great and second toes. The finger nails were long (0 m. 003 mill. of dirt-margin) and untended. Zadptahefonkhou seems to have been a fairly young man, for the four front teeth that are exposed are only slightly worn. They are clean and healthy. Moreover there is no trace of grey or any thinning in the hair of the head.

The face is broad and heavy-jawed, with a very prominent, high-bridged nose (the cartilaginous part now flattened by embalmer's bandages), prominent superciliary ridges and sloping forehead. The usual crescentic area of dark brown paste is found on the brow-ridges.

The usual kind of artificial stone eyes have been inserted under the half closed lids. They consist of pieces of white stone, into the front of each of which a circular patch of black stone was inserted to represent pupil and iris.

The hair of the head was left long and was thickly plastered with resin. It is of a reddish brown colour (possibly due to partial bleaching and staining with embalming materials). Much of it is curled into pendant wisps, each about o m. o15 mill. in diameter, which are so disposed that they cover the ears and part of the masseteric region; while a few stray curls hang down behind (pl. XCI).

The moustache and beard had not been shaven for some days before death, and this fact and the presence of much white powder (pl. XCII) and resin gives the face a very dirty and unkempt appearance. The moustache and beard (o m. oo5 mill. long) are of the same colour as the scalp hair.

The lobules of the ears seem to have been pierced, but they are thickly smeared with resinous material and hidden in great part by the hair.

The cranial cavity is partly occupied by powdered resin, which was introduced through the right nasal fossa.

The cranial length is about o m. 192 mill. but it is impossible to measure the breadth by reason of the matted, resin-impregnated hair : with the hair it measures o m. 150, but in reality it is probably not much more than o m. 130 mill.; for the cranium is of a long, narrow ovoid form.

Total facial height		o m. 120 mill.
Upper facial height		o	o75
Bizygomatic breadth		o	130
Minimal frontal breadth		o	100
Bigonial breadth		o	108
Interorbital breadth		o	022
External orbital breadth		o	096
Right orbit	o m. o43 mill. × o	o33
Nasal height and breadth	o m. o55 mill. × o	o33

Left orbit, each diameter a fraction of a millimetre less.

As in the mummies of the queens described above (Mâkerî, Honttaoui and Taiouhrit) one of the innermost wrappings of this mummy was a red-coloured shroud.

61098. The mummy of an unknown man «E» (pl. XCIV and XCV).

This body was unwrapped by Dr Fouquet on June 3oth, 1886 (*Les Momies royales*, p. 548-551).

M. Maspero makes the following statements in reference to this mummy. After describing the dreadful appearance of Saqnounri's mummy the account proceeds (Bulletin de l'Institut égyptien, 1886, p. 267 and 268) : «Une autre momie du même groupe est plus effrayante encore. Elle était enfermée dans une caisse blanche, sans inscription, et n'avait rien sur elle qui permît de constater son identité. Une peau de mouton l'enveloppait, puis un épais lacis de bandelettes, puis une couche de natron blanchâtre, chargé de graisse humaine, onctueux au toucher, fétide, légèrement caustique; un second maillot, un second lit de natron et le cadavre. Il n'avait pas été ouvert, et les viscères qu'on avait coutume d'extraire de la poitrine et du ventre sont encore en leur place. Les matières préservatrices n'avaient pas été injectées, on les avait répandues autour du corps avec une habileté qui trahit une longue expérience de ce genre de travail. On avait voulu éviter les longueurs ordinaires, les soixante-dix jours de l'embaumement réglementaire, et l'aspect du personnage suffit à montrer pourquoi on avait eu recours à ce procédé expéditif. Il avait été empoisonné : la contraction du ventre et de l'estomac, le mouvement désespéré par lequel la tête se rejette en arrière, l'expression d'angoisse et de douleur atroce qui est répandue sur la face, sont autant d'indices certains. Les bras et les jambes avaient été tordus par la souffrance : on les ramena, on les maintint par de fortes ligatures, et on s'en remit aux embaumeurs du soin de faire disparaître toute trace du crime. S'agit-il d'une simple intrigue de harem? L'homme avait vingt-trois ou vingt-quatre ans et sa jeunesse autorise pareille supposition. Est-ce plutôt un prétendant au trône qu'on aura supprimé discrètement? Le fils aîné d'Amenhotpou Ier mourut avant d'avoir régné; peut-être est-ce lui que nous avons retrouvé dans le cercueil sans nom. Nous savons que les conjurations étaient fréquentes en Égypte ; Ramsès III fit juger et exécuter un certain Pentoïrit, qui semble avoir été un de ses frères, et qui avait comploté de le détrôner. La forme du cercueil et la main-d'œuvre de l'emmaillotement m'empêchent de reconnaître dans notre personnage un prince de la XXe dynastie. C'est à la XVIIIe qu'il appartenait et les monuments nous révéleront peut-être un jour le secret de sa vie. On ne l'ignorait pas sans doute à Thèbes, près de mille ans après l'événement, sous le règne des grands prêtres d'Amon. Les inspecteurs de la nécropole continuaient à lui rendre les honneurs princiers et à se taire sur son nom et sur la cause de sa mort : aucun d'eux n'a osé tracer sur le cercueil ou sur le maillot le moindre de ces procès-verbaux qu'il écrivait si volontiers sur les autres morts. »

The body is that of an apparently young man, 1 m. 709 mill. in height. The arms are extended and the hands are placed near together, but without touching, in front of the pubes. No attempt was made, however, to compose the features or to put the head into the position usual in mummies.

The head is thrown back and set somewhat obliquely on the neck and the mouth is widely open.

The hair is plaited : the ears are pierced : the teeth are worn only very slightly.

There is no sign of any beard or moustache and the genitalia are absent.

There is cheese-like material amongst the hair (pl. XCV). The skin of the face is thrown into ridges like that of Anhapou's (vide supra).

There is no embalming incision.

This body has been treated in a manner that differs from all other known mummies of the time of the New Empire, to which presumably it belongs.

For this reason it is not possible to assign a date to it, although it is probable that it is early XVIIIth i. e. anterior to the time of Thoutmosis II.

There does not seem to me to be any evidence to support the hypothesis put forward by D[r] Fouquet (vide supra) that this man was poisoned. A corpse that was dead of any complaint might fall into just such an attitude as this body has assumed.

Without any clue whatsoever to indicate the period in which this individual lived or to suggest his identity it is idle to speculate on the history of his death.

61099 and 61100. Two mummies from the tomb of Thoutmosis III (pl. XCVI).

In the *Guide du Visiteur* M. Maspero summarizes the history of the finding of these two mummies. «En 1898, M. Loret, s'inspirant des rapports de quelques Arabes, reprit la piste, mais dans le Bab-el-Molouk lui-même. Les fouilles, menées avec une ténacité remarquable, furent couronnées de succès et aboutirent, le 12 février 1898, à la découverte de l'hypogée de Thoutmôsis III, violé dès la XXe dynastie et dont la momie avait été cachée dans le trou de Déîr-el-Baharî par les grands-prêtres d'Amon thébain. M. Loret y récolta divers objets curieux, entre autres des panthères et des statuettes en bois bituminé, et deux momies de femme.»

M. Loret inclined to the view that these mummies were the remains of some members of the family of Thoutmosis III; but M. Maspero was not convinced that there were any real reasons for this belief, and in September, 1905, he instructed me to remove the wrappings from one of the mummies (n° 61100), leaving the other (n° 61099) intact.

Plate XCVI, fig. 1, represents the appearance of n° 61100 in its coffin before it was unwrapped; and fig. 2 represents (on a somewhat larger scale) the back of the mummy to show the way in which the shroud and the various circular and longitudinal bandages were fixed at the back.

I removed the bandages from this mummy on September 10th, 1905, in the Cairo Museum. There was no sign of any writing to indicate the identity of the person whose mummy we were investigating; but the body (or, rather, skeleton) was that of a woman, 1 m. 542 mill. in height, which was embalmed and wrapped several centuries at least after the known royal mummies, as the manner of wrapping and the treatment of the body show.

The flesh and the innermost wrappings were entirely corroded by the preservative materials employed in embalming the body, so that the bones of the skeleton were found lying amidst a large quantity of black powder. But I had to remove 42 bandages or sheets of linen before reaching the charred wrappings.

The mode of wrapping the body was obviously inspired by that in vogue in the XXIst and XXIInd Dynasties, of which it represents a degenerate form.

The mummy belongs to the late dynastic or early Ptolemaic period and was certainly intrusive in the tomb of Thoutmosis III.

TABLE OF CONTENTS.

CORRIGENDA.

Page 5. For «coronoird» *read* «coronoid».

Pages 11 and 14. For «Fig.» *read* «Diagram».

Page 17. For «succesion» *read* «succession».

Plate I

Saqnounri's hands.

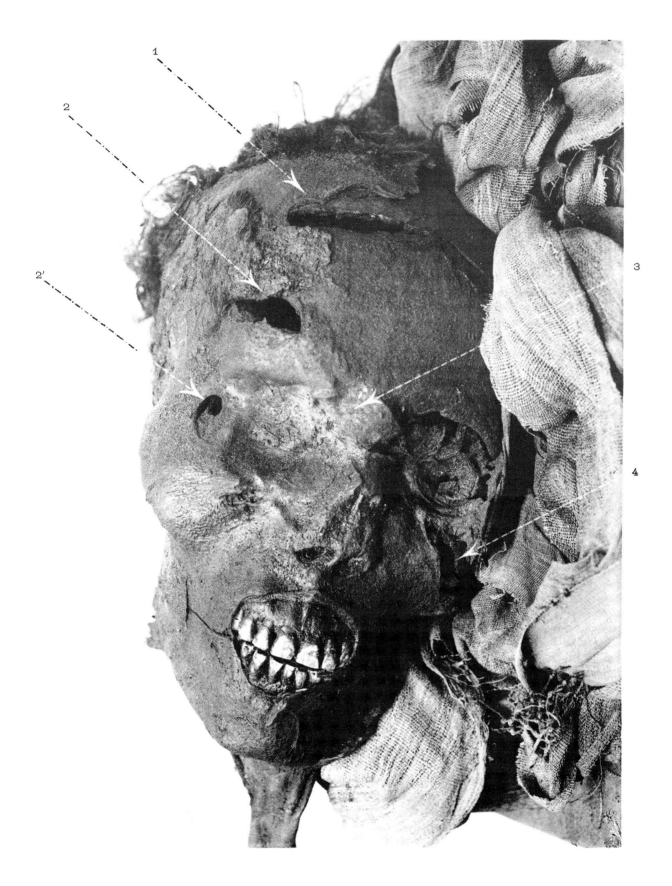

Saqnounri.

5

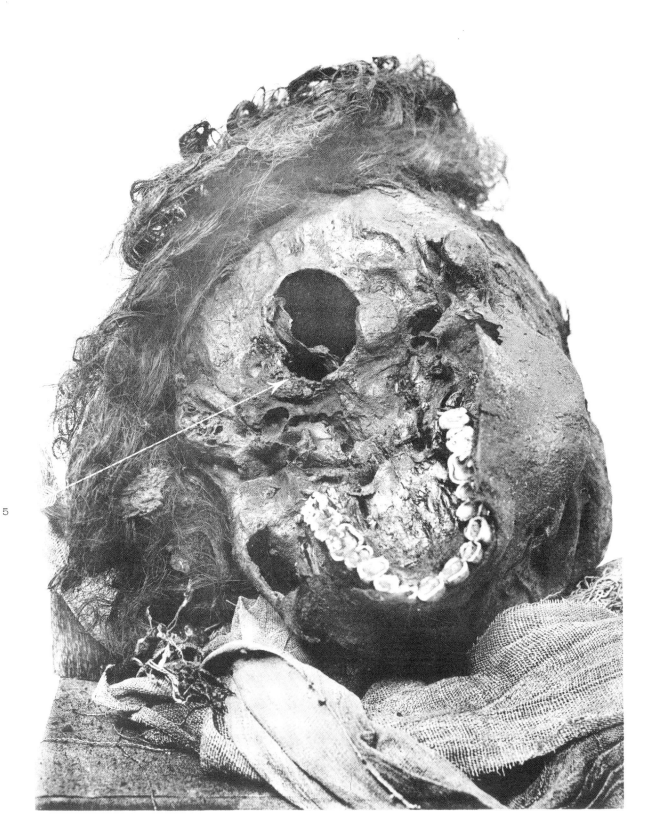

Saqnounri.

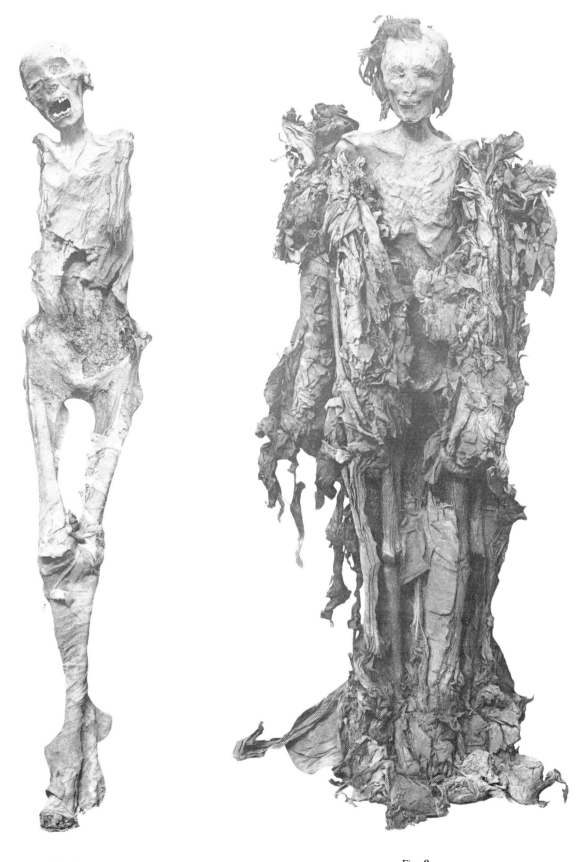

Fig. 1

An unknown woman " A "
perhaps Meritamon.

Fig. 2

Queen Anhâpou.

Queen Anhâpou.

Fig. 1

Fig. 2

The lady Raï.

Plate VII

Fig. 1

Fig. 2

Queen Nofritari.

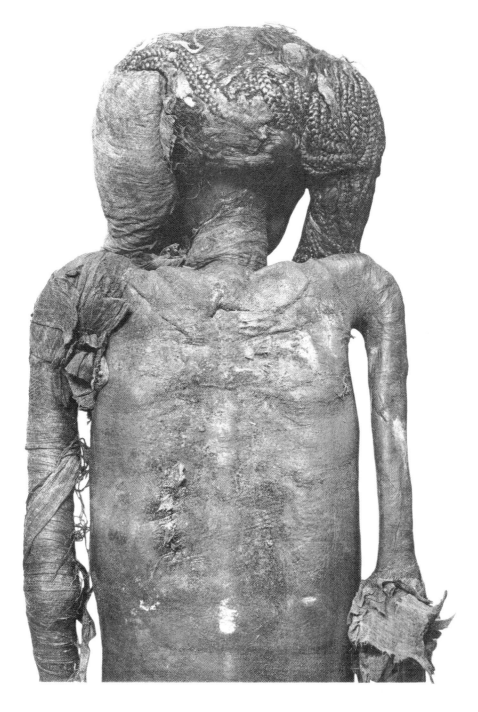

The lady Raî.

An unknown woman " B ".

Plate X

Fig. 2

Fig. 1

The woman " B "

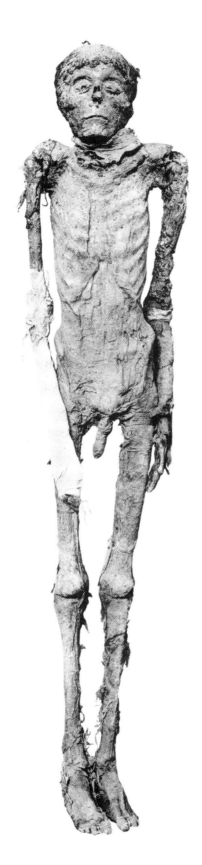

Ahmôsis I.

Ahmòsis I.

Plate XIII

Amenothes I.

Honttimihou.

Hont-m-pet.

Hont-m-pet.

Fig. 1
Hont-m-pet's wig, upper aspect.

Fig. 2
Hont-m-pet's wig, under aspect.

Queen Sitkamos.

Plate XIX

CATALOGUE DU MUSÉE DU CAIRE. — *ROYAL MUMMIES.*

Fig. 1

Coffin-lid of prince Sipaari.

Fig. 2

Coffin and mummy of prince Sipaari.

Fig. 3

Mummy of Sipaari after removal
of outer shroud.

Fig. 4

The remains of prince Sipaari.

Mummy supposed to be Thoutmosis I.

Thoutmosis I.

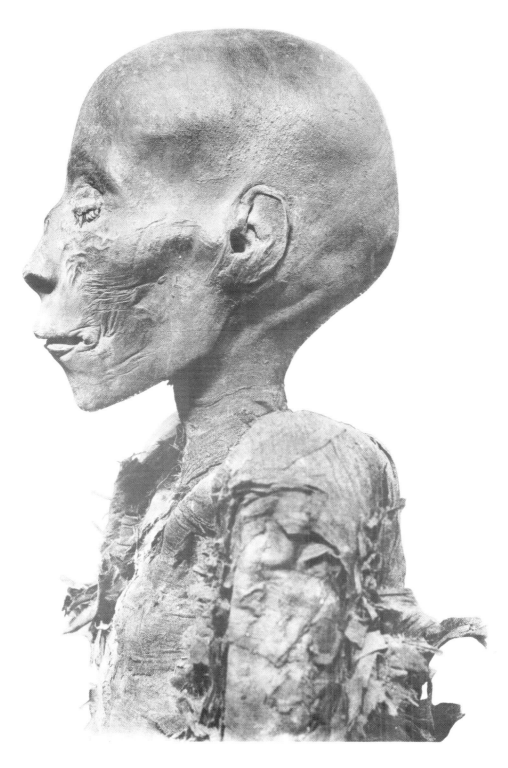

Thoutmosis I

Thoutmosis II.

Plate XXIV

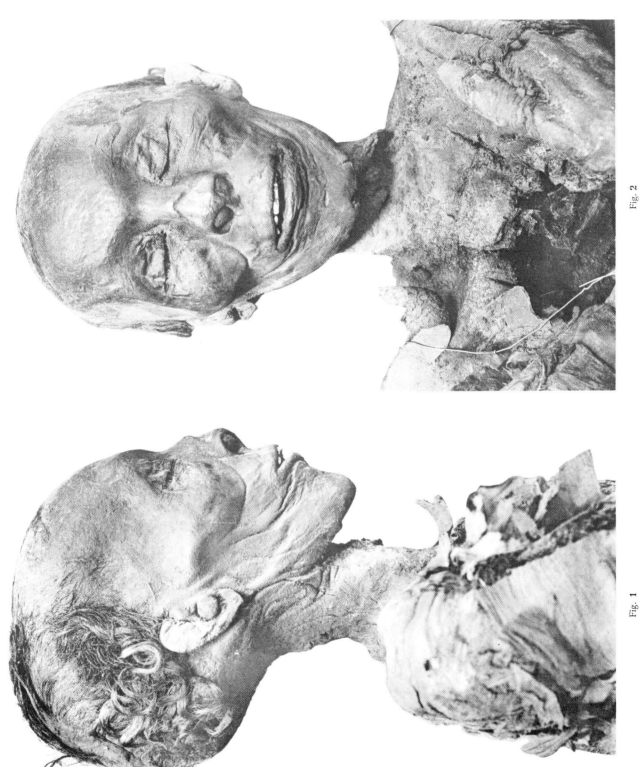

Fig. 2

Fig. 1

Thoutmosis II

An unknown man " C ".

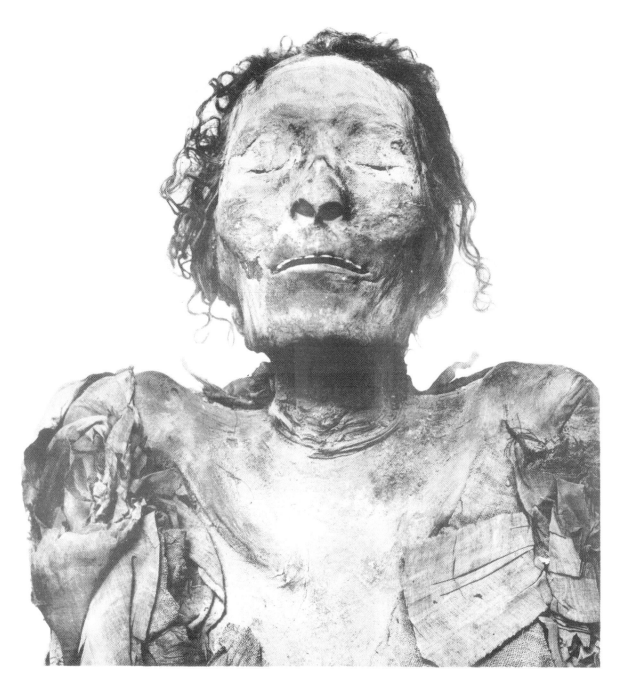

An unknown man "C".

An unknown man " C ".

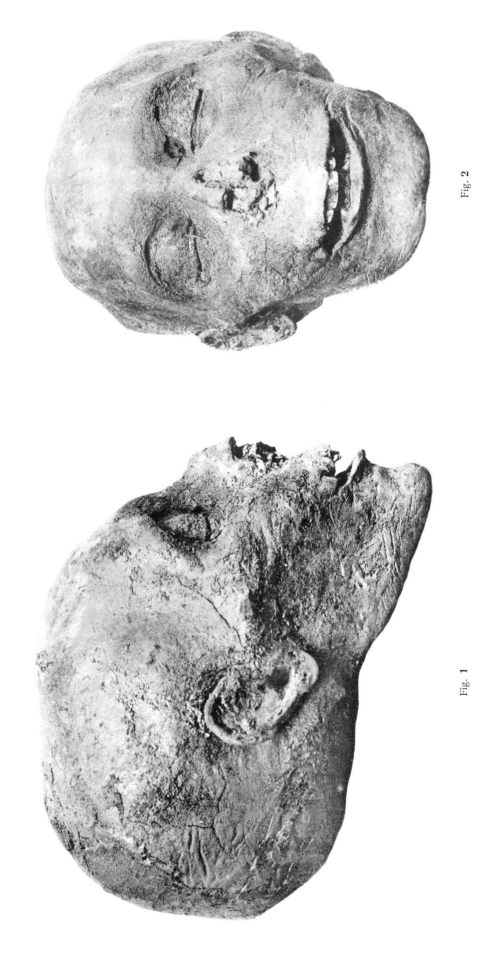

Fig. 2

Fig. 1

Thoutmosis III.

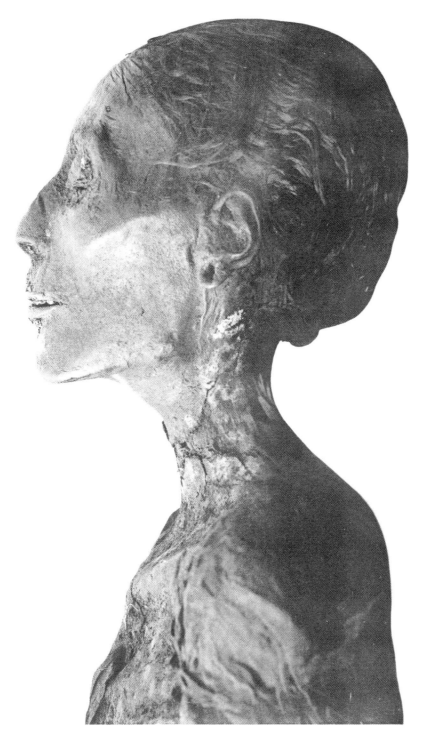

Thoutmosis IV.

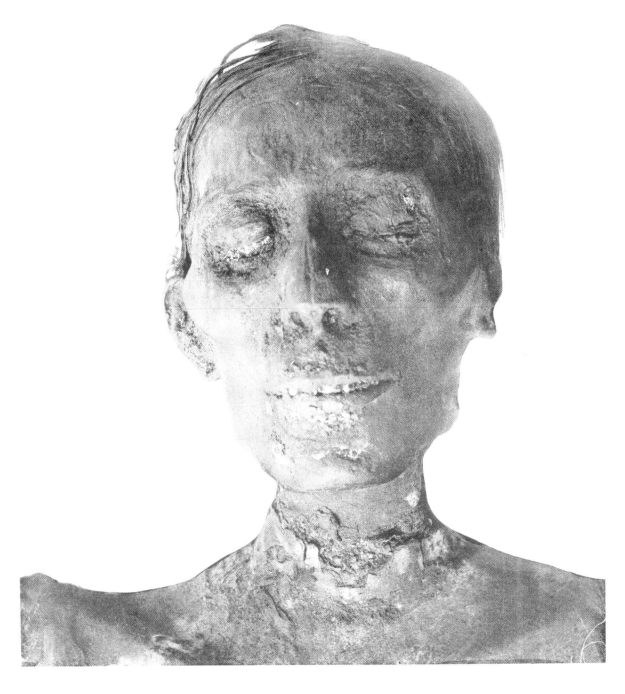

Thoutmosis IV.

Fig. 1

Fig. 2

Coffin containing Amenothes III.

The inscription.

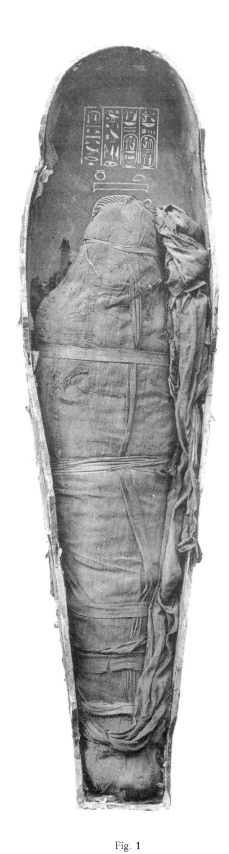

Fig. 1

Amenothes III.

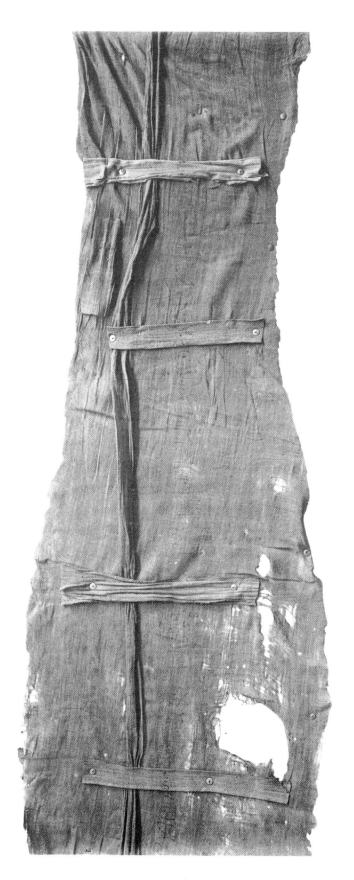

Fig. 2

The inscription on the shroud.

Plate XXXIII

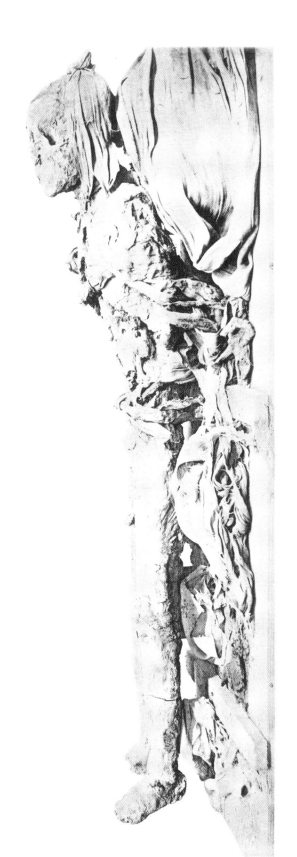

Amenothes III.

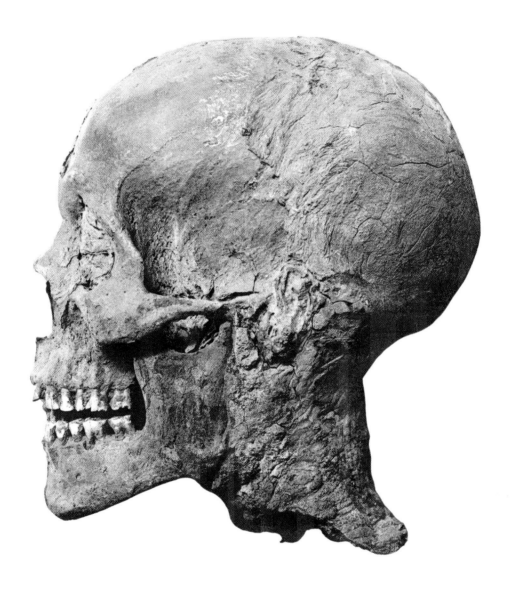

Amenothes III.

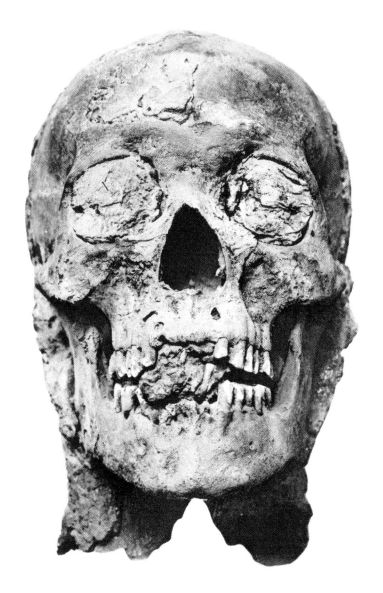

Amenothes III.

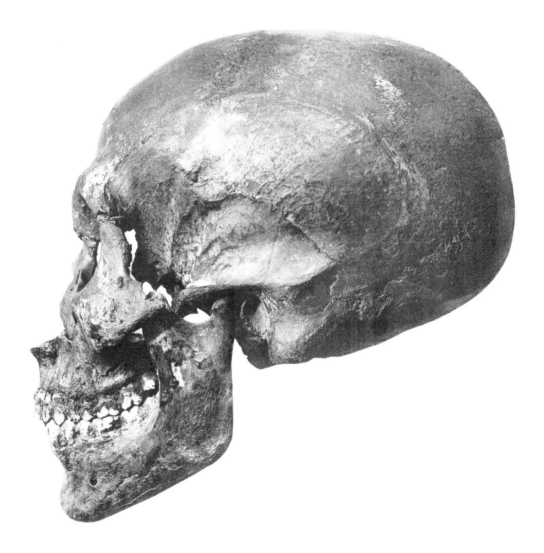

? Amenothes IV.

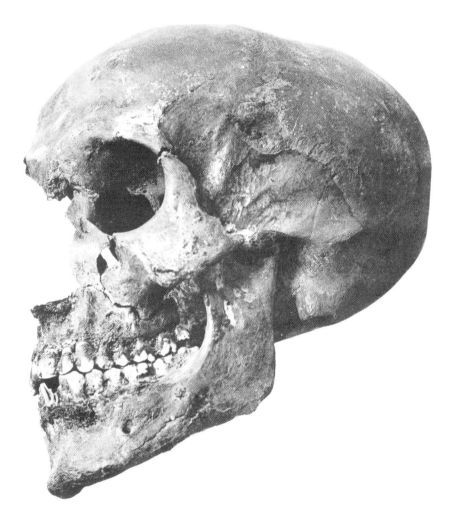

? Amenothes IV.

Seti I.

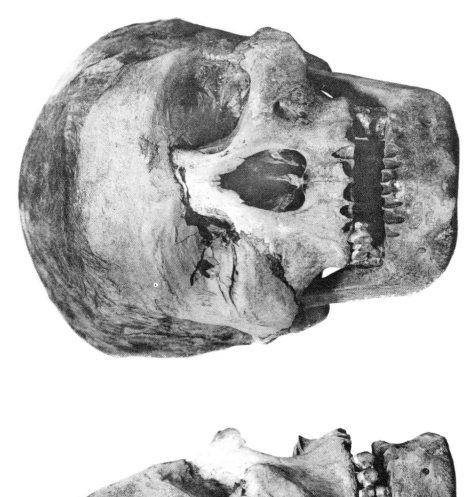

Fig. 1

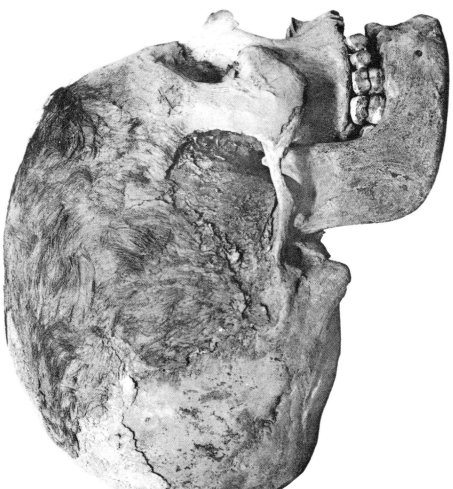

Fig. 2

Skull from baqt's coffin.

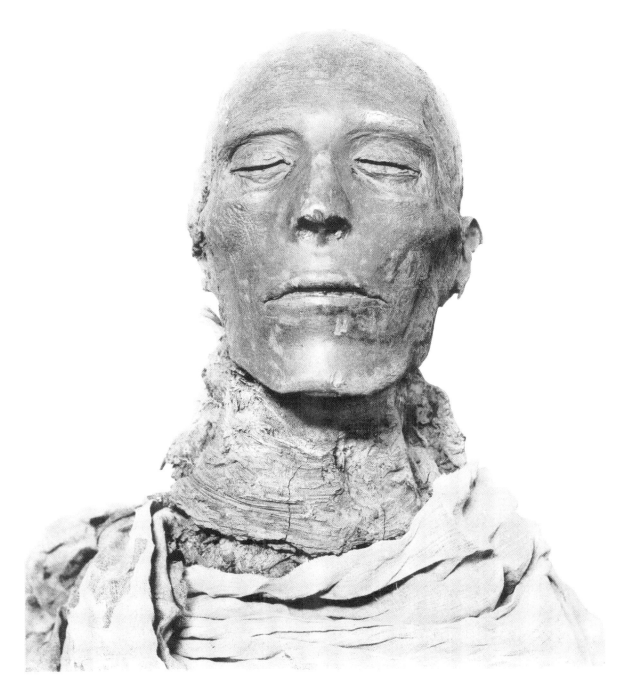

Seti I.

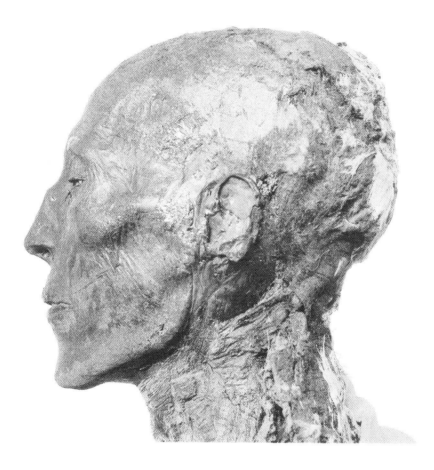

Seti I.

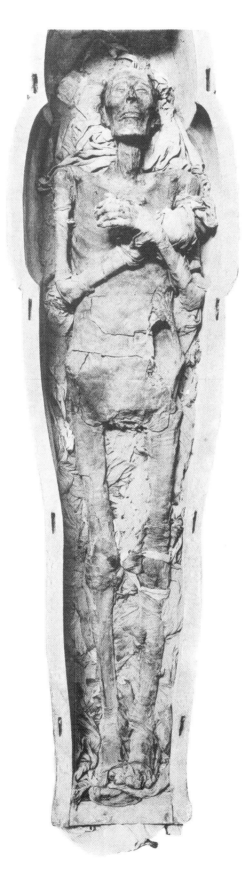

Ramses II.

Fig. 2

Ramses II.

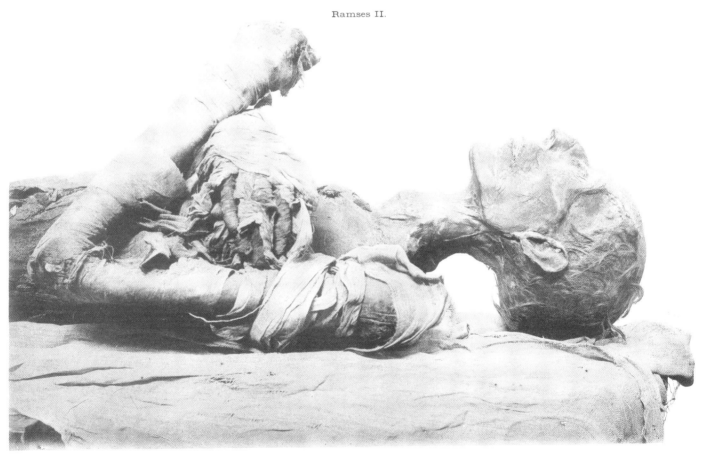

Fig. 1

Ramses II.

Plate XLIV

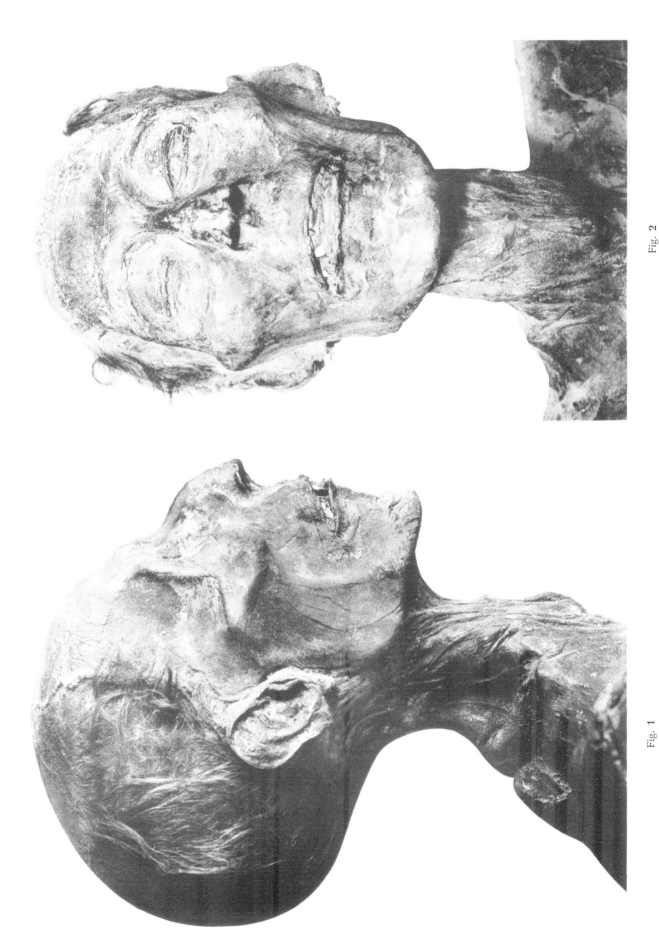

Fig. 2

Fig. 1

Ramses II.

Fig. 1
Menephtah.

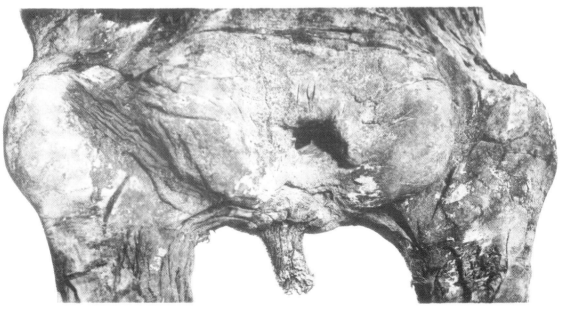

Fig. 2
Menephtah.

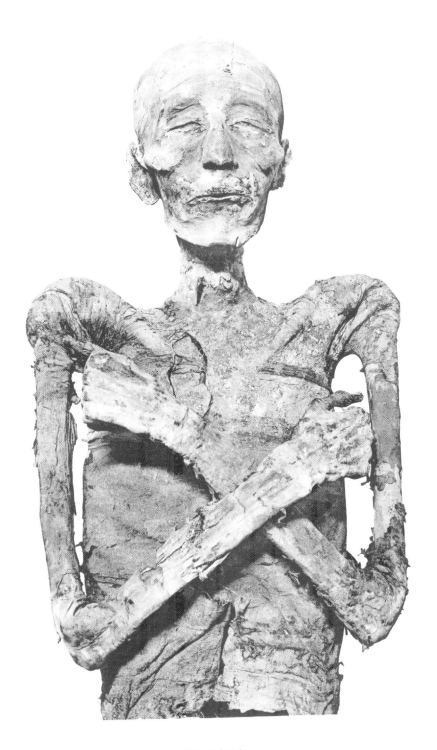

Menephtah.

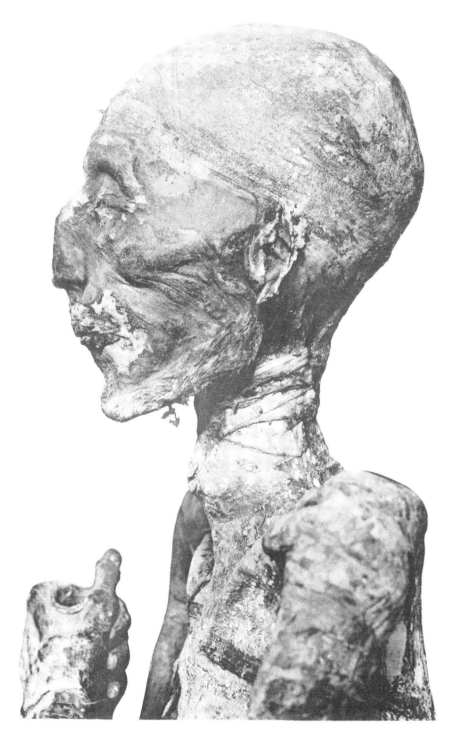

Menephtah.

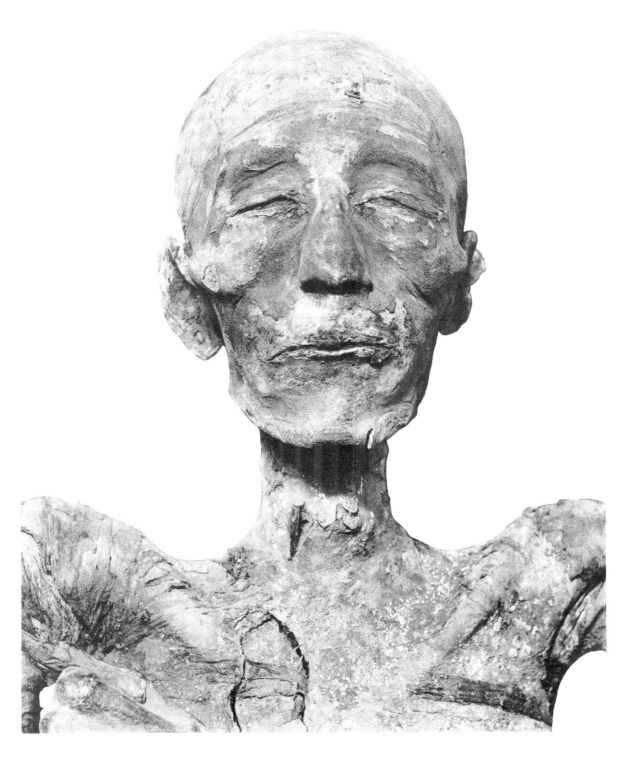

Menephtah.

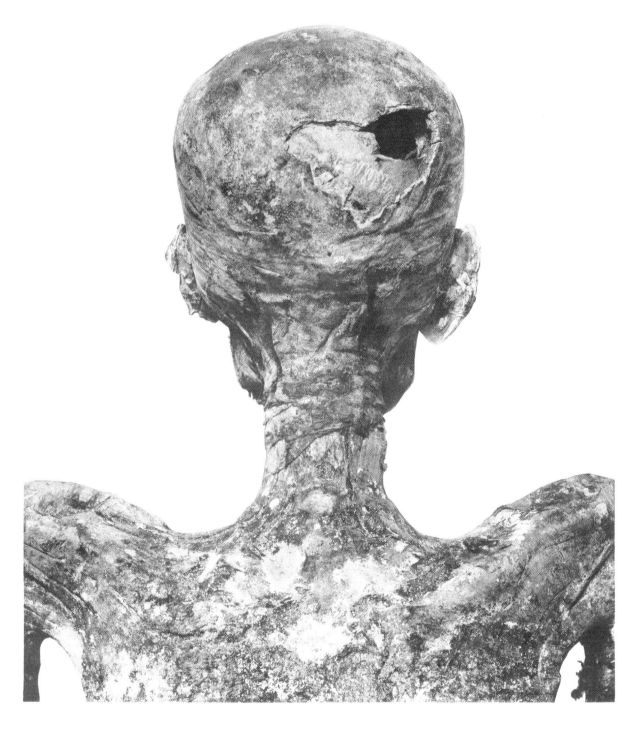

Menephtah.

Ramses III.

Ramses III.

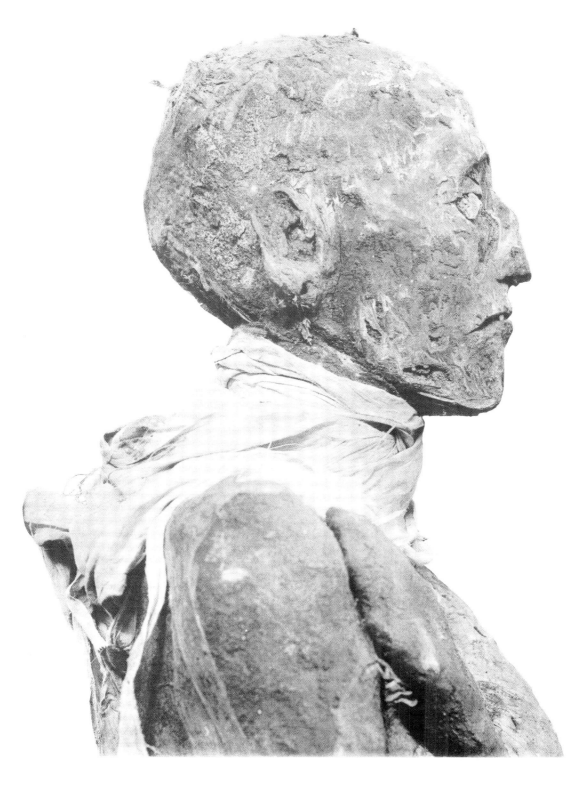

Ramses III.

Ramses IV.

Ramses IV.

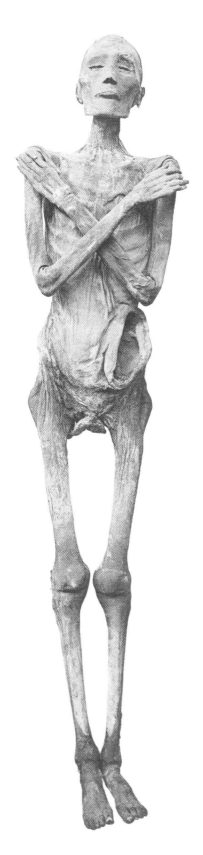

Ramses V.

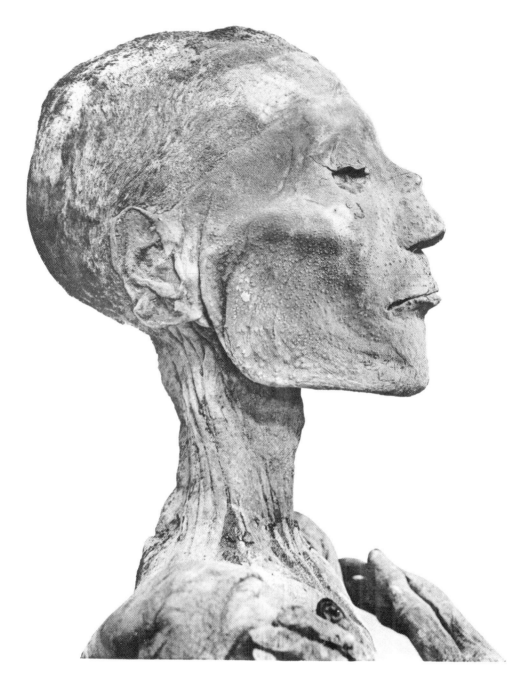

Ramses V.

Plate LVII

Ramses IV.

Ramses V.

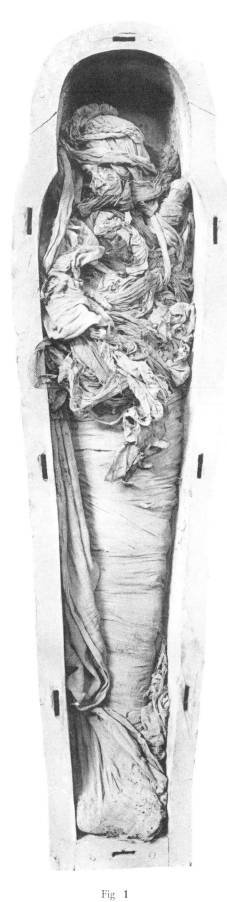

Fig 1

Fig. 2

Ramses VI.

Ramses VI.

Fig. 1   Fig. 2

Siphtah.

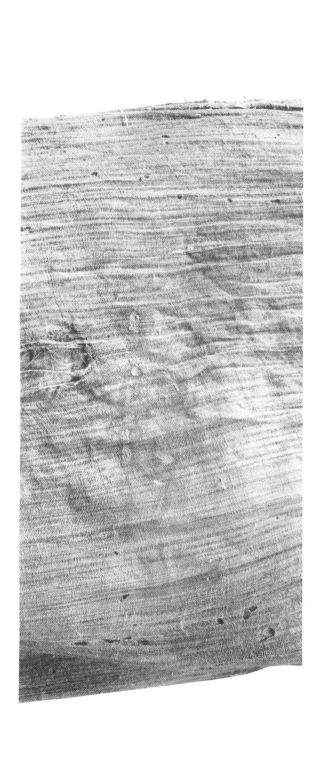

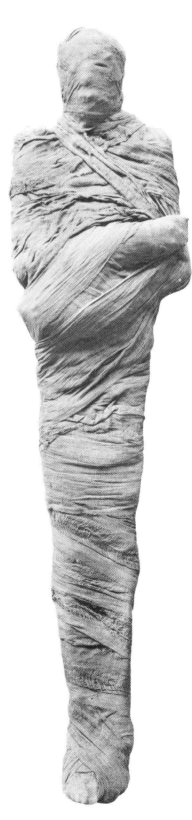

Fig. 1

Siphtah. Writing on shroud.

Fig. 2

Siphtah.

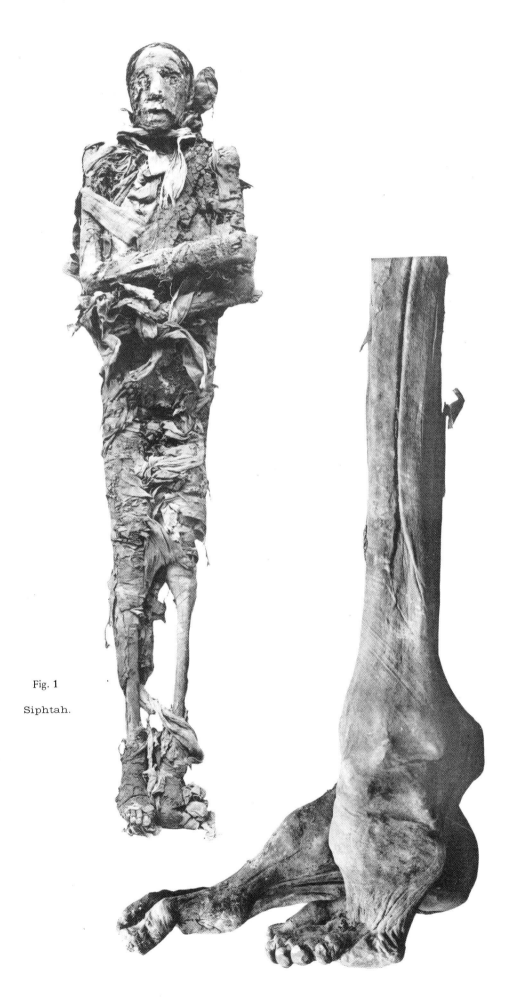

Fig. 1

Siphtah.

Fig. 2

Siphtah's feet-talipes of left foot.

Plate LXIII

Fig. 2

Siphtah.

Fig. 1

Siphtah. An inscribed piece of linen.

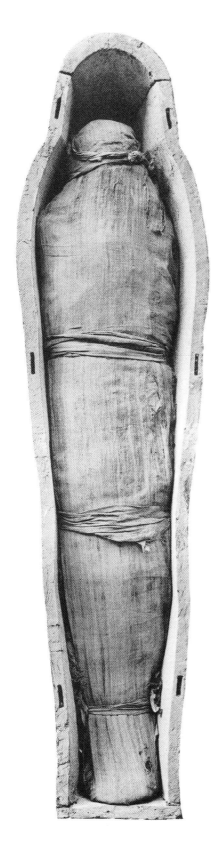

Fig. 1

Seti II.

Fig. 2

Seti II after removal of shroud — fine linen
shirts thrown around the mummy.

Seti II.

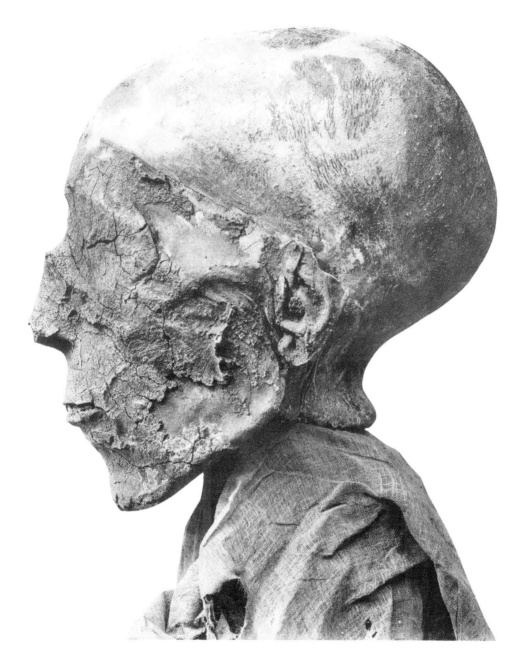

Seti II.

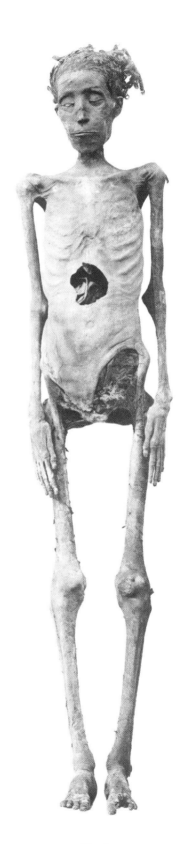

Fig. 1

Mummy of unknown woman " D "
in coffin of Setnakhiti.

Fig. 2

The unknown woman " D ".

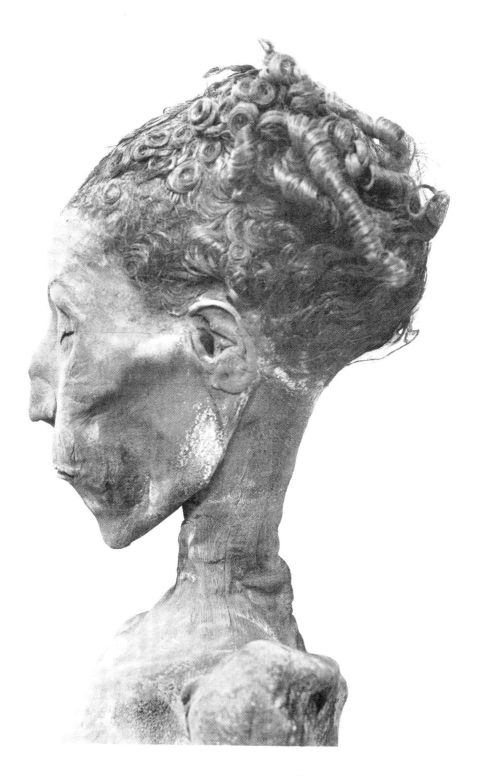

The unknown woman " D ".

Queen Notmit.

Queen Notmit.

Queen Notmit.

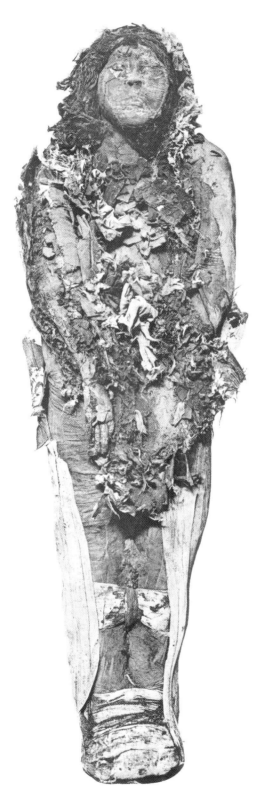

Queen Makeri.

Plate LXXIII

Fig. 1

Makeri's right hand with three rings on the thumb.

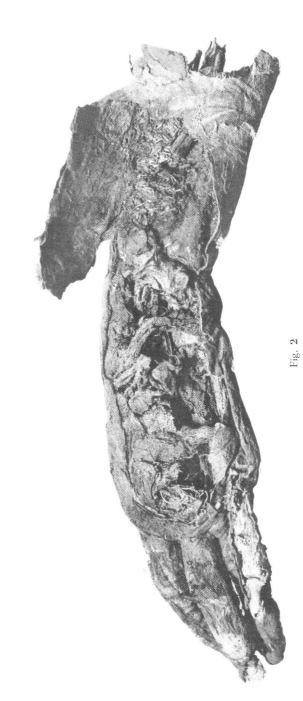

Fig. 2

Makeri's left hand opened to show linen packing under the skin and sawdust in the forearm.

Queen Makeri's baby princess Moutemhit.

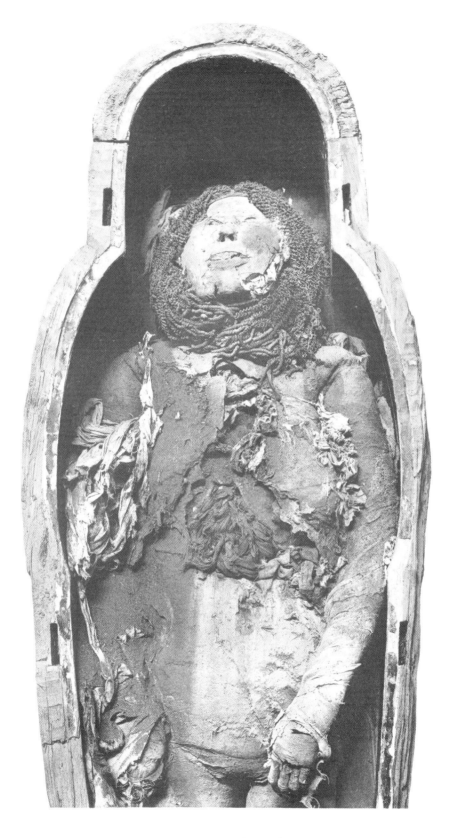

Queen Honittaoui.

Fig. 1
Queen Honittaoui.

Fig. 2
Honittaoui. — Gold plate covering the embalmer's incision.

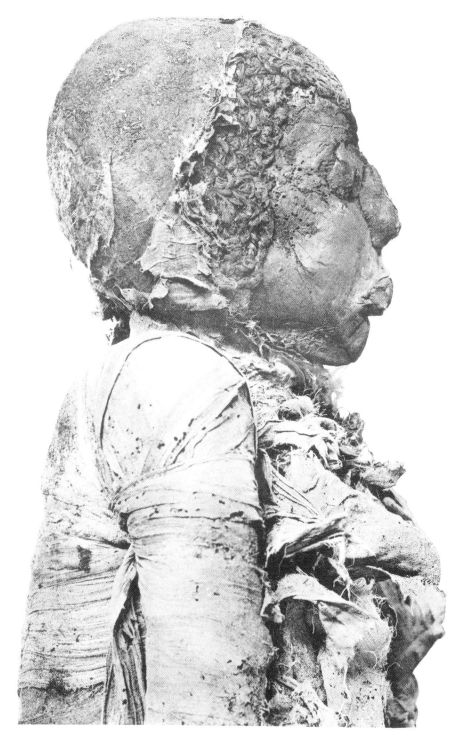

Queen Taiouhrit.

Queen Taiouhrit.

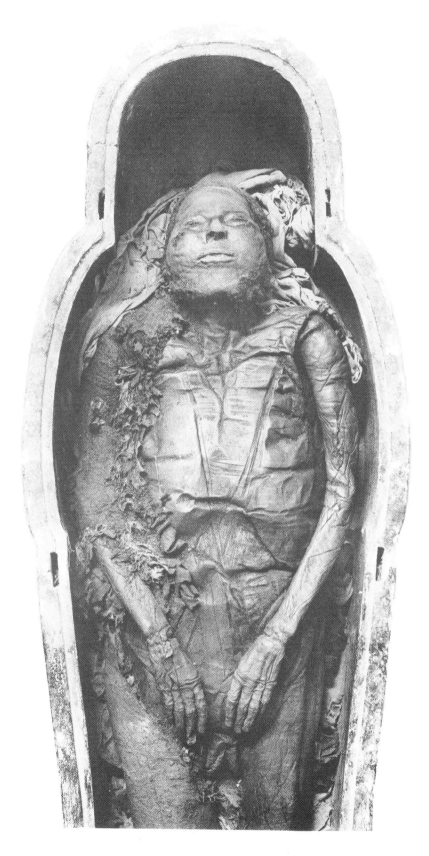

The high-priest and general-in-chief Masahirti.

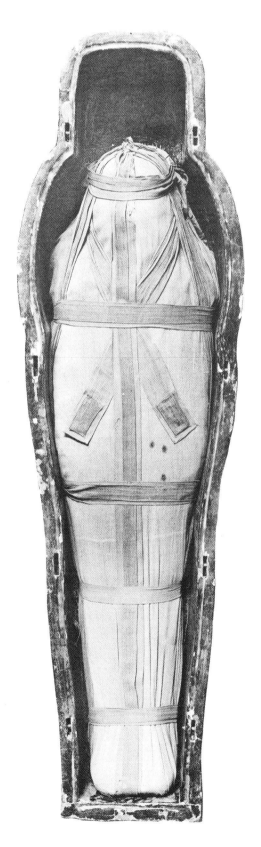

Queen Isimkhobiou.

The high-priest Pinotmou II

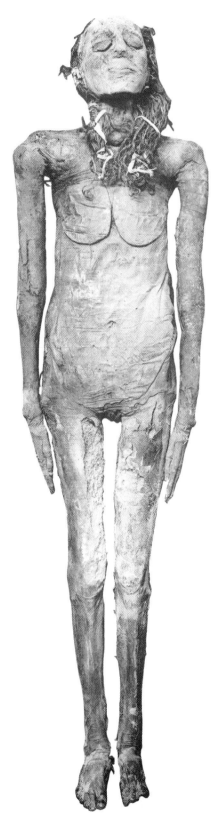

The priestess Nsikhonsou.

Nsikhonsou.

Nsikhonsou.

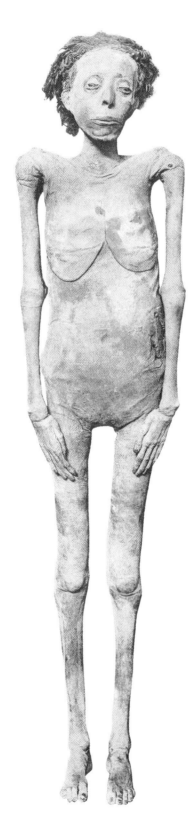

Princesse Nsitanebashrou.

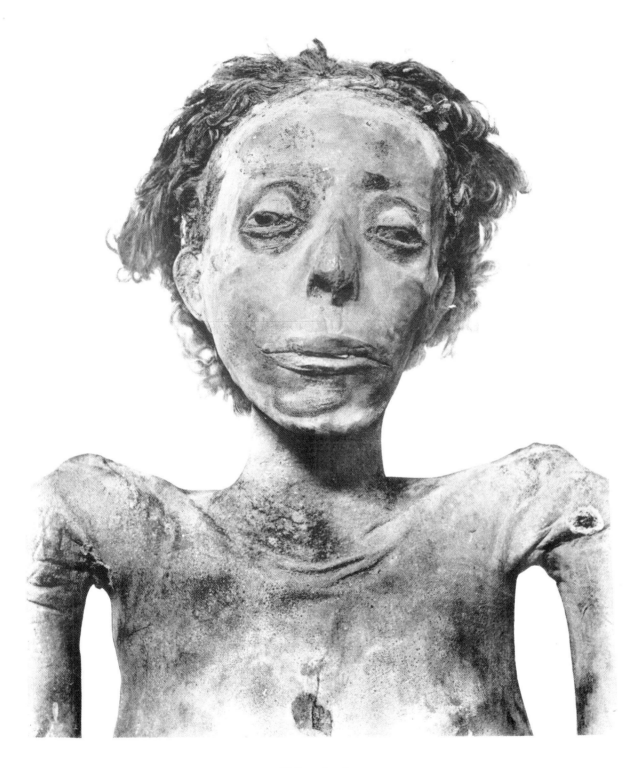

Nsitanebashrou.

Nsitanebashrou.

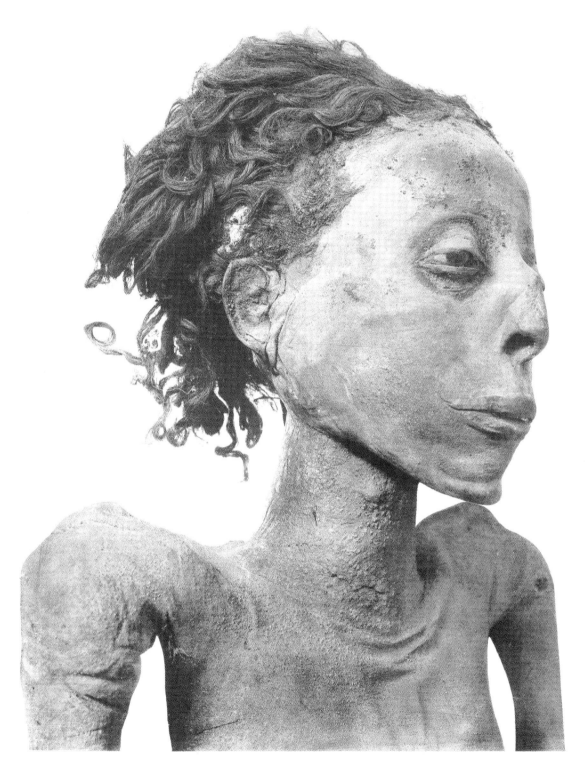

Nsitanebashrou.

Zadptahefônkhou.

Zadptahefonkhou.

Zadptahefonkhou.

Zadptahefonkhou.

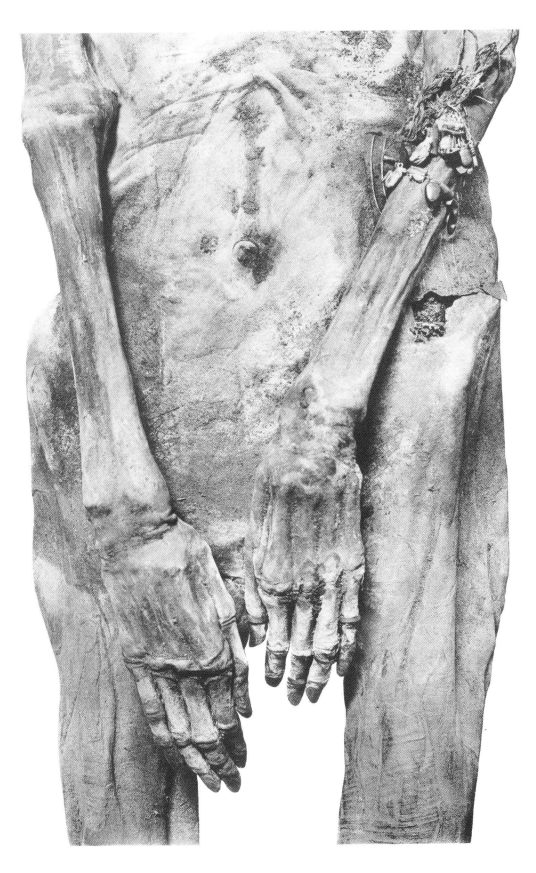

Zadptahefonkhou.

The body of an unknown man " E ".

The man " E ".

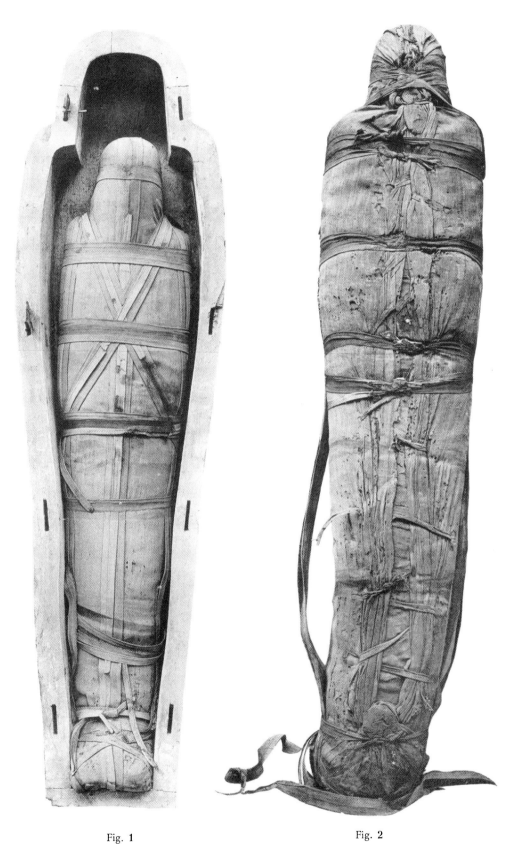

Fig. 1

Fig. 2

Tomb of Thoutmosis III.

Back view of mummy.

Plate XCVII

Catalogue du Musée du Caire. — *Royal Mummies.*

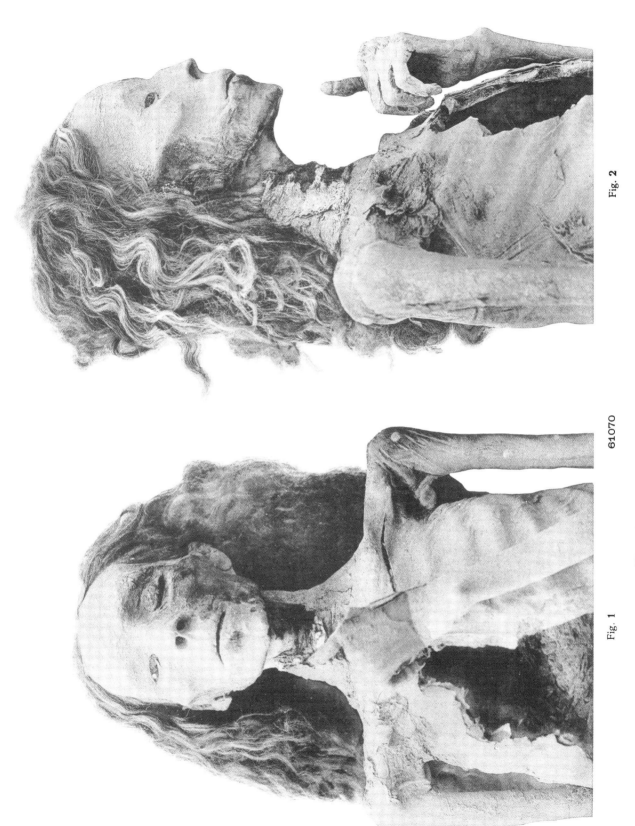

Fig. 1

61070

Fig. 2

The elder woman in the tomb of Amenothes II.

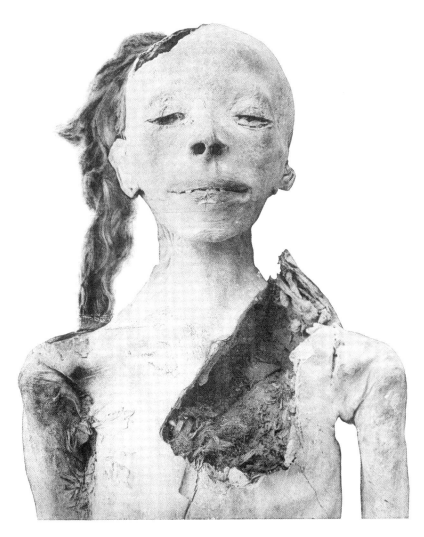

61071

? Prince Ouabkhousenou.

Plate XCIX

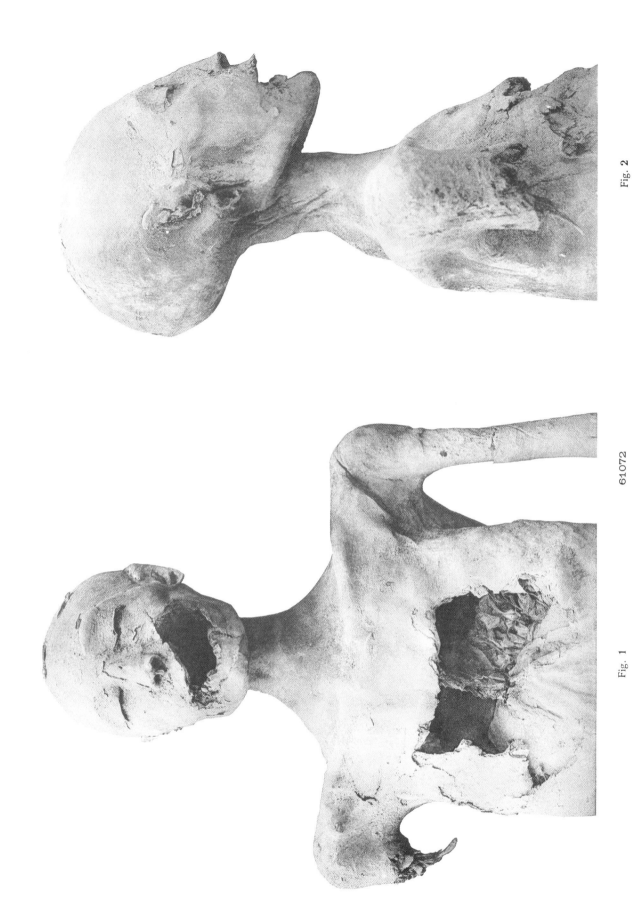

Fig. 1

61072

Fig. 2

The younger woman in the tomb of Amenothes II.

Writing on the Shroud of Amenothes III.
(Compare Plate XXXII.)

Continuation of Plate C.

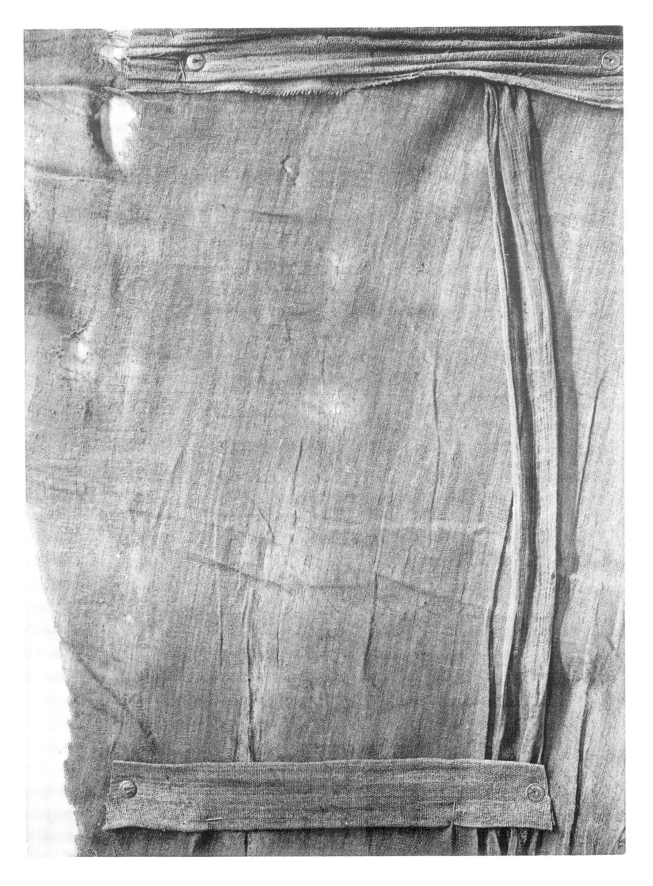

Continuation of Plate CI.

Continuation of Plate CII.